The Marriage
You've Always Wanted

The Marriage You've Always Wanted

Ron R. Lee
General Editor

Chariot VICTOR
PUBLISHING
A DIVISION OF COOK COMMUNICATIONS

Victor Books is an imprint of ChariotVictor Publishing,
a division of Cook Communications, Colorado Springs, Colorado 80918
Cook Communications, Paris, Ontario
Kingsway Publications, Eastbourne, England

Editor: Barbara Williams
Design: Bill Gray
Cover Photo: Helstrom Studios

Library of Congress Cataloging-in-Publication Data
The marriage you've always wanted / Ron R. Lee, general editor.
    p.   cm.
    Includes bibliographical references and index.
    ISBN 1-56476-674-8
    1. Marriage--Miscellanea. 2. Communication in marriage--
Miscellanea. 3. Marriage--Religious aspects--Miscellanea.
I. Lee, Ron R.
HQ734.M4134 1997
306.81--dc21
                          97-10337
                          CIP

1 2 3 4 5 6 7 8 9 10 Printing/Year 01 00 99 98 97

CONTENTS

CHAPTER THREE: CLOSER FRIENDSHIP

CHAPTER FOUR: SUCCESSFUL SEX

CHAPTER FIVE: VITAL FAITH

CHAPTER SIX: WORTHWHILE WORK

CHAPTER TEN: LESSONS OF LOSS

CHAPTER ELEVEN: TEAMING UP

ACKNOWLEDGMENTS

A book, like a strong marriage, is the result of a team effort. This volume benefited from the combined efforts of a likeminded, yet diverse, group.

I'd like to thank the individuals and couples who are interviewed on the following pages. They generously shared their time, their wisdom, and their life experience. Their willingness to pass on their hard-earned expertise will bear fruit in the marriages of those who read this book.

Second, I extend a hearty "thank-you" to the interviewers—a small band of journalists who asked the right questions and refused to settle for superficial answers.

Third, I am indebted to the staff of *Marriage Partnership* magazine: Annette LaPlaca, Louise Ferrebee, Barbara Calvert, and Joy McAuley. They played a significant role in pulling together the material from back issues of the magazine, updating it, adding discussion questions and indexes, and tying up all the loose ends to make this project a success.

Last, I am grateful for the efforts of ChariotVictor Publishing in making these interviews available to a new audience. Karl Schaller and Julie Smith, in particular, did a masterful job of guiding the manuscript through every stage of development—from initial concept to finished product.

Your labors will not go unrewarded.

Ron R. Lee, Editor
Marriage Partnership magazine

INTRODUCTION

Any time I pick up a book, the same question comes to mind: "Is this book really for me?" In case you're wondering the same thing, you can find the answer by taking this short quiz.

1. Are you:
   [ ] a man?
   [ ] a woman?
2. Are you:
   [ ] Married?
   [ ] Seriously considering marriage?
3. Are you:
   [ ] In a fulfilling love relationship?
   [ ] In a relationship that has grown a bit stale?
4. Are you:
   [ ] Seeking solutions to marital problems that just
       won't budge?
   [ ] About to give up hope?

If you checked any of the above answers, then this book was written with you in mind. Let's say you're a man, or a woman. It doesn't matter which one, because this book addresses marriage challenges from both perspectives. It even sorts out some troublesome issues along gender lines, so you can better understand why women and men approach marriage differently. And a plus for you guy readers is that this book doesn't make you out to be the heavies.

Let's say you're a married person, or perhaps you're simply considering marriage. Either way, things will go more smoothly with a little advance preparation. And it's never too late to learn, even if you're already married. The advice in this book applies across the board—from day one to your Golden Anniversary.

Let's say you're already enjoying a fulfilling love relationship, or maybe you're feeling stuck in a somewhat stale one. Good marriages remain strong only if they receive regular investments of time and energy. And stale ones can't improve without focused effort. This book gives you clear directions on how to proceed in either situation.

Let's say you're becoming desperate to find solutions, or that you're on the verge of losing hope. This book is for you too. The experts interviewed on the following pages face the hard issues of marriage head-on.

Nothing is candy coated. Nowhere will you find "five steps to marital bliss." Instead, this book offers abundant hope and real help in the form of workable suggestions for positive change. So no matter what you are struggling with—conflict, sex, parenting, work, money, stress, failure— you'll find honest answers, practical solutions, and encouragement in the interviews that follow.

But let's say you really don't like to read all that much. Don't let that discourage you. This book caters to the overly busy, the exceedingly stressed out, and even those who don't like books. It can be read in piece-meal fashion, if you need specific help with the marital challenge you're facing right now. Or you can think of it a little like *People* magazine. Read about your favorite marriage experts and see how they messed up in their own marriages, but figured out later how to turn things around. Or just leave it on the back of the commode and see what happens. A few spare moments of reading could make a big difference in your marriage. (On the other hand, if you really like books, read this one front-to-back to gain a comprehensive overview of marriage in all its many facets.)

Plus, there's a bonus. To help you take steps to address the challenges you are facing, each chapter ends with questions for you and your mate to discuss together. The questions also make this book a useful discussion guide for marriage classes and small-group Bible studies.

Here's wishing you a lifetime blessed with a growing, rewarding mar-riage. Happy reading!

Ron R. Lee, General Editor

Chapter One

BETTER BEGINNINGS

Expectations
H. Norman Wright

Family Influences
Kevin Leman

The Purpose of Marriage
Larry Crabb

Boundaries
Dennis and Lucy Guernsey

H. Norman Wright

Expectations

Why we think our spouse should act in certain ways; and why those expectations are usually wrong. How to rethink our expectations to make them match reality.

Interviewed by Lynda Rutledge Stephenson

*I*t's hard to overemphasize the importance of good beginnings. Whether it's learning to play a musical instrument or joining your life to another in marriage, getting the right start will enable you to avoid a lot of problems later on. That's why we're beginning this book with an interview about beginnings. And who better to ask than H. Norman Wright?

Wright is one of the best-known and most widely respected marriage experts in the Christian community. In thirty years of counseling, speaking, and writing, he has produced more than sixty books, including *Communication: Key to Your Marriage* (Regal), *Secrets of a Lasting Marriage* (Regal) and, with Gary Oliver, *Kids Have Feelings Too!* (Victor). In this interview, Wright shares ideas on how to get your expectations in line with reality—an essential first step toward a healthier marriage.

Why is it important to establish good habits as early as possible in marriage?

Most couples don't realize that the pattern they set in the initial years of their marriage is the pattern they will follow from then on. It's not that these patterns can't be changed; it's more that most couples just allow things to happen. We need to pay much more attention to the patterns we are establishing in our marriages.

In the Old Testament, a newly married man was freed from the rigors and responsibility of going to war during the first year of marriage. There is a lot of merit in that idea. Couples need to give time and thought to anticipating what might occur in the next few years in terms of their individual development, how their marriage is going to change, and what will happen when they have children. If they don't prepare for these in advance, they will later look back and ask, "What happened? Why are we where we are?"

Is this where marital expectations enter the picture?

Exactly. When people marry, they bring with them a hidden agenda of expectations. They've got this dream of what their marriage will be like, what their partner will be like, how he or she will act. Unfortunately, these expectations create the hidden, painful surprises that spring up later.

What are the most common expectations people have about marriage?

Most women have expectations about romance and intimacy. They look forward to spending time with their husband, having in-depth conversations, and getting a good share of his attention. But typically, the more they expect along these lines, the more they are disappointed.

Men tend to be more single-minded. After a man gets married, he feels he has "accomplished" that task and it's time to pour his energies into his work because that is the source of his identity.

Actually, these differences are part of our basic makeup. A woman's brain structure allows her to juggle a number of things at once, flipping from one side of the brain to the other. A man's brain, though, usually forces him to focus on one thing at a time. So what men normally bring to their romantic, intimate relationships is whatever is left after they have finished doing other things. Usually, this is at most a sexual response.

What happens then?

Just what you'd think: His wife is disappointed. If a man isn't geared toward intimacy and romance, and if his wife can't persuade him during the first few years of marriage that he's able to fulfill both the work area and the intimacy area of his life, she'll get discouraged. Then, to meet her own intimacy needs, she'll spend more time with her children.

You end up with the classic "parallel marriage"—the husband busy with work, the wife busy with the children. They are running on parallel tracks, and they don't connect with each other. The children become the glue that keeps them together. And when the children leave home, you have two empty people looking at each other and asking, "Why are we still married?"

What happens if they don't have children?

In those situations, the woman usually devotes herself to her work. And especially during the early years of marriage, she might be more vulnerable to a man other than her husband who gives her the attention she craves. In fact, that danger is present with or without children.

Intimacy—where two people share from the depths of their hearts—can occur at any stage of marriage. But often, if it isn't done in the early years, the wife will give up. And yet she still needs intimacy and will find it somewhere else.

Are you saying men don't want intimacy?

For the most part, our culture doesn't encourage men to deal with the intimate, emotional area of their lives. They're trained instead to deal with facts and bottom-line issues. Usually it takes men until somewhere in their mid-forties to tune into intimacy, because that's when their values and priorities begin to change. But it's best if they recognize their need for intimacy a lot sooner.

What can be done to help men identify their need for intimacy in marriage?

I'll speak for husbands, since I'm a man. We tend to neglect the important issues. We think marriage just happens, but that's not true. A strong marriage requires a tremendous amount of effort. So men need to realize that our identity is more than our work. Our identity is a gift that God has given us, and we can create balance between doing our best at work and still saving time and energy for the marriage relationship.

What are some steps to take to achieve what you're suggesting?

A good place for a husband to begin is to start focusing on significant conversation with his wife. Men need to listen to what their wives' expectations are. For example, most couples take for granted that they both find the same things romantic. But that's hardly ever true. So spouses need to tell each other what they find romantic. Some people like to hear things, such as music or the spoken words "I love you," to feel romantic. Others like to see things—love letters, romantic cards, or flowers.

A man might try to romance his wife by giving her a card that he finds romantic when she doesn't find it romantic at all. Yet when he starts being more auditory, saying "I love you. You really look wonderful tonight," she responds. It means learning the language that best communicates to your partner.

How can you learn your mate's individual language?

Listen carefully to the style of the phrases he or she uses, the types of words, the length of the sentences, whether your spouse is an "amplifier" or a "condenser." An amplifier is someone who makes a statement and then explains it; and a condenser is one who shortens everything to the minimum number of words.

If you begin to understand your spouse's language, then you can talk in a way that will connect with your mate. Most often, one spouse is quite verbal and the other one isn't, so they are continually missing each other when they talk. The less verbal partners don't want to bring up certain issues because they're afraid it will lead to an hour-long conversation on a ten-minute topic. That often happens, in fact, because the verbal partners are so starved for communication that when their mates do open up, they jump in with both feet.

And then the onslaught of words causes the quiet spouse to shut up?

Exactly! The verbal partner (usually the wife) doesn't know it, but she's putting a lid on her nonverbal spouse. But there is a way to handle this difference. I've seen beautiful things happen when the wife goes to her husband and says, "Honey, I want to talk to you for ten minutes, and even if I'm in the middle of a sentence, I promise I'll stop talking after ten minutes. Would you try it with me?"

At first, her husband might be wary, but he'll probably go along with it. And after a few of those experiences, when his wife actually ends the conversation after ten minutes, he might say, "Hey, I can talk for another ten minutes, let's follow through with this discussion." The husband needs to know that if he opens up, he's not going to lose control of the situation.

You said earlier that romance and intimacy are major expectations in a woman's mind. What is a major expectation for a husband?

Most men are looking for someone to admire and support them. Many men look at marriage and home as a refuge, a place to unwind and relax. And men, typically, don't find talking to be relaxing. Since most wives place a high value on talking, you can see how these expectations conflict.

The solution involves seeking a balance in meeting each other's needs for the day. Just giving each other space doesn't work. Marriage is a servanthood relationship where each person's needs should be met, and each mate needs to give to the other.

It can be as simple as asking your spouse the question, "What is the best way to greet you at the end of the day?" Our expectations clash because we assume the person we love—our spouse—ought to know everything about us. But no one is a mind reader.

What about expectations as a dual-career couple?

It gets back to communication. One thing they should do at the end of the day, maybe two or three evenings a week, is agree that they won't talk about work. "How was work today?" is a natural question to ask, but there is a whole arena of other issues to deal with. Every couple, no matter how long they've been married, should agree not to talk about work or children on certain nights of the week.

Wouldn't those couples spend a lot of time quietly staring at each other?

Maybe, but that's okay. It would force them to share what they've read or heard, to look into new areas of interest together. There's a basic principle in a good marriage: When something is important to one person it becomes important to the other as well. Let's say a woman really enjoys decorating her house. Her husband may not be interested in wallpaper, but he'll get interested in it to show his love for his wife.

He'll be interested in wallpaper?

I'm not saying he'll get terribly excited about it. I'm saying he will make a basic commitment to explore it with his wife. I'll give you a personal example. I'm a diehard fisherman, and it's a hobby my wife, Joyce, used to have very little interest in. But when I was willing to be less intense about it, it became a lot more palatable to her. Now Joyce has opened up new vistas for me. She talked me into buying a raft, so now when we go fishing, I also notice the vegetation, the flowers, and the river—with her. We take our camera along and take wildlife pictures.

If you don't iron out your conflicting expectations of marriage and of one another, there's a vicious circle you can fall into. It has to do with who has the power. Most people are fearful of being dominated and controlled by others. That fear will cause a person to filter his spouse's behavior, requests, and actions as an attempt to control him. So that person reacts in a negative way: "I'm not going to do that." Such partners may not even know why they feel the way they do.

For example, a wife will make a simple request, something her husband might even enjoy doing. But since his wife suggested it and it wasn't his idea, he'll dismiss it. Often our fears get in the way of hearing the good and affirming things our partner may be saying to us.

How can couples cope with their conflicting expectations?

I have two ideas, both of which involve making lists to help us keep our expectations realistic. One "listing exercise" involves each partner making a list of his or her own strengths. Then they discuss what they each have to contribute to the marriage. Both should understand their partner's strengths, and defer to their partner in areas in which he or she is more capable.

The other listing exercise addresses marital expectations. Both the husband and the wife should list the expectations they have for their partner. They should write their expectations down—being as specific as possible—then share them with each other. This will give each spouse the opportunity to say, "This seems reasonable; I think that would work" or "I'm not sure I can live up to this expectation" or "What kind of alternative can we work through?" Being that honest can prevent a lot of pain later on.

Actually, this exercise should be done every five years. As you grow as an individual, the things that are important to you change, your attitudes change, your values change, and your needs even change. Revising your lists every few years enables you to keep pace with the ways each of you is changing.

Marriage brings together two unique people, with their own opinions and priorities and different ways of doing things. The beauty of marriage is that it's a relationship that uses your differences to complement each other. When your expectations are realistic, you can learn to delight in each other's strengths. And that will ultimately strengthen your relationship.

Kevin Leman

Family Influences

Sometimes it's not until you get married that you realize how much your childhood influences affect how you react to others. Here's one way to make your partnership operate more smoothly.

Interviewed by LaVonne Neff

When you get married you learn a number of new things about yourself. And one of these revelations is how much your childhood experiences with your siblings affect the way you relate to others as an adult.

Counseling psychologist Kevin Leman is cohost of the "Parent Talk" radio program, a popular speaker, and the author of seventeen books, including *Bringing Up Kids without Tearing Them Down* (Focus on the Family), *Winning the Rat Race without Becoming a Rat* (Thomas Nelson), and *The Birth Order Book* (Dell). We asked him how birth order affects the way a person acts toward—and reacts to—his or her mate.

What is it about a person's birth order that makes such a difference in his or her personality?

Birth order shapes our personalities because it affects how we learn to see life within our own families. Research has been done for a number of years on the personality characteristics of firstborn children, only children, middle children, and babies of the family. It's really interesting what you can tell about people based on their birth order.

For example, firstborn children come into the world, look up, and see parents. They don't see other children. Parents look down and see one child, not three or four of them. So the parents spend a lot of time with that child.

Middle children are squeezed. They endure wearing clothes and playing with toys that are hand-me-downs. In a lot of ways, they get a bum rap.

Babies in the family never want for attention. They aren't powerful, so they develop expertise in charming and manipulating those around them.

Who first thought of the significance of birth order?

Swiss psychologist Alfred Adler is credited as the first to recognize the importance of one's family position in regard to personality development. In 1958 he wrote about "the rivalries and competitive strivings of children who have not felt themselves an equal part of their whole family." Since then a number of other psychologists have studied the effects of birth order. Walter Toman studied the effect of birth order on marital relationships. He found, for example, that the best man for a woman to marry is the youngest male in a family with older sisters, and the best wife is the baby of a family with older brothers. Why? Because both are going to be very sensitive to the opposite sex.

How did you become interested in writing about birth order and its effect on marriage?

It was because of Oscar Christensen, a refreshingly normal counseling professor at the University of Arizona. He believes birth order affects a person's entire life. I liked that idea, because my family was a perfect example of it.

My oldest sister, the firstborn, never got anything less than an A in graduate school, and she still irons the davenport in her spare time. My brother was the rough-and-tumble middle child, but he was also the firstborn male who went on to get a Ph.D. in psychology. Then there was me, the baby of the family, who graduated near the bottom of my high school class. But I was good at entertaining people, from doing birdcalls to crawling out of history class on my hands and knees. As I looked at birth order, I said, "That's us!" Then, as I watched my own children unfold, I saw evidence of it all over again.

You've said you can identify a person's birth order at twenty paces. What does a firstborn look like?

The firstborn child will be the best reader in the family, get the highest SAT scores, and prepare for the most prestigious profession. Accountants, engineers, dentists, airplane pilots, and magazine editors tend to be firstborn children. In any area where people go out and distinguish themselves, firstborns are going to be very well represented.

Firstborns grow up to be list makers. In fact, sometimes they make lists of lists. They are structured in their thinking: A comes before B, which comes before C. They tend to be goal-oriented, conscientious, and reliable. If you want a job done, hire a firstborn.

They also tend to be perfectionistic. I've tried to bring this to people's attention, because perfectionism is a type of slow suicide. There's a lot in the news about teen suicide. The greatest percentage of people who kill themselves are firstborns and only children, and they are the children least likely to feel they measure up.

What about a second born?

You can predict what the second child in the family is going to be: He or she will become the exact opposite of whatever the firstborn becomes. The first two children in the family will be as different as night and day. This is especially true if there are fewer than five years between them and if they are of the same sex. The closer they are in age and gender, the more they will compete. Lots of times they will compete in different areas because it's safer to do so.

The second child in a two-child family probably will develop the characteristics of the baby. Although if one is a male and the other a female, you could end up with two firstborns who are both perfectionistic, conscientious, and reliable—but with interests that lie in completely different areas.

Is it really so bad to be a middle child?

It isn't easy. The middle child is probably best characterized by the family photo album. Notice the 12 pictures of the middle child contrasted with the 3,507 pictures of the firstborn. But it's not all bad. Research indicates that middle children are the best adjusted of all.

For instance, they are the most monogamous. I say with tongue in cheek, "If in doubt, marry a middle child." They make good marriage partners because they know how to negotiate and compromise—it's a way of life for them.

Do youngest children tend to be spoiled?

They're often self-centered. They tend to be good attention-getters at a very young age. Often they are written off because they're the littlest, so they develop a fierce sense of competition—an "I'll show you" attitude.

If there's a late bloomer in the family, chances are it's the youngest child. To her family, little Snookie is still going to be Snookie at age forty. Many youngest children tell me it's hard for them to adjust because nobody ever gives them credit for growing up.

Babies tend to be natural sales people, in part because they are outgoing. They never met a stranger.

What about only children?

They're just like firstborns, only more so.

Of all the possible combinations, which is the best one for a happy marriage?

It sounds strange to talk about matching people according to their birth order. But generally, you're better off marrying outside your birth order because there is more natural balance there. Whoever first said "opposites attract" should be given a medal. It's certainly true in families. The firstborn and the baby are natural friends.

What's the most difficult combination in marriage?

The most disastrous relationships that walk through the door of my office are spouses who are both firstborns. Now that's not to say that two firstborns can't have a strong marriage. But the classic problem marriage is two firstborns. Both of them are perfectionistic and they are both list makers. They go crazy if their checkbook isn't exactly right.

What have you learned about other matched pairs—two babies or two middles?

With two babies, each waits for the other to take the lead. Both want to be the center of attention. Neither one wants to get too serious. The Beach Boys sang a song years ago that characterizes that kind of marriage, "Fun, Fun, Fun." That's how it is when two babies marry each other.

Two middles avoid confrontation. You put two avoiders in a marriage, and before long you have no communication.

How do you counsel couples whose personalities are too closely matched?

Firstborns need to have the courage to be imperfect. They want all their ducks in a row, but God can use crummy, imperfect people. Remember, Jesus' disciples were far from perfect people.

Babies need to realize the real pluses in life come from helping other people. I tell them to take on some family projects that are unselfish, or to do something for someone else in the church or neighborhood.

Middles would walk a mile to avoid confrontation. They're like balloons that are inflated to the breaking point. They need to let out some air before they pop—to communicate their feelings, even if they have to write them down.

What problems result when you marry outside your birth order?

My wife, Sande, is a firstborn and I'm a baby. When we first got married I remember thinking, "Lord, thank You for giving me this wonderful woman to take care of me—to pick up my socks, to fix the food I like." When a firstborn is married to a baby, you can have a neurotic relationship. The firstborn is naturally a good caregiver, and the baby is naturally a taker. Fortunately, my wife gently but firmly made me grow up.

You have said that firstborns can be controlling, wanting those around them to "live by the rules." What should a person do if he or she is married to a controller?

A good piece of advice is never to ask the controller "why"—it immediately puts that person on the defensive. Instead, when the controller makes a demand that doesn't seem right, say, "Oh, tell me more about that," or "That's interesting." A statement such as that is more open-ended and less threatening.

There is a time, though, when you need to simply pull the rug out from underneath an overly controlling spouse. You refuse to be his or her slave, and you make some demands of your own. A person's degree of self-worth will often determine whether she or he stands up to a controlling mate.

Larry Crabb

The Purpose of Marriage

Why Christians, as servants of God, really don't have any "rights." Why expecting your mate to meet your needs will almost always result in frustration, anger, and resentment. And what to do about it.

Interviewed by Gregg Lewis

*L*arry Crabb holds a doctorate in clinical psychology from the University of Illinois. He is a counselor, teacher, author, speaker, and recognized marriage expert. But he freely admits that he doesn't know everything. When it comes to marriage, it's important for all of us to recognize that we still have a lot to learn.

Crabb is the author of fifteen books, including *The Marriage Builder*, *Men and Women: Enjoying the Difference*, and, with Dan Allender, *Hope When You're Hurting* (all published by Zondervan). In addition to his heavy writing and seminar schedule, Crabb serves as distinguished scholar in residence at Colorado Christian University. But perhaps the most impressive thing about him is the candid way in which he talks about his own thirty-one-year marriage to his wife, Rachael. Here's what Crabb recommends for couples seeking to develop a biblical approach to marriage.

You write and speak extensively about marriage, and you've done marriage counseling for years. What effect does your reputation as a marriage expert have on your own marriage experience?

Sometimes it makes me feel like a phony. I love to intellectually systematize and organize things. But in my own marriage I find that half of my packaged theories just don't work. I have to admit I don't have it all figured out. That's why, when I write and speak, I try to tell stories from my own experience that don't have a clear resolution. I have to admit, "I don't know what to do about this. I've read my book and it was no help."

However, my work does allow me to observe a lot of marriages, and I see the kind of damage that bad relating does to the human soul. I see how spouses suffer when X, Y, or Z happens. I sometimes realize, "Hey, I've been doing that to my wife," and I'm motivated to be a better husband. While the details of other marriages may differ, the core issues of my clients' marriages are the same issues I face in my own marriage.

What are some of the drawbacks that come with the territory of "professional marriage expert"?

There's a tendency to slip out of my husband mode and into my "professional" mode at home. A few weeks ago Rachael and I went through a difficult time. When I asked, "What would you like me to do differently?" she said, "I wish you wouldn't evaluate everything so much!" Instead of accepting little tensions as a normal part of a relationship, I try to understand what's going on inside each of us. And I drive Rachael crazy by analyzing everything.

What lessons have you been learning about your marriage?

Just recently, Rachael and I hit a low point when we realized there were things that were keeping us from connecting with each other in the way we'd like to. We didn't feel the deep sense of joy and union we had felt before.

We talked about how some issues I had been going through had caused Rachael to feel as if I were distant. We'd go out for dinner together, or with friends, and I'd follow the conversation; but I'd really be concentrating on my personal concerns.

She felt I wasn't really there with her, or for her. She was right, but I didn't know what to do about it. I knew I could fake it; but when I tried, she picked up on it in a second.

I went for a drive to do some thinking, and it hit me: The one thing I wasn't doing was expending my energy to reach out to Rachael, to devote myself to her well-being and try to meet her need for my support and involvement in her life.

When I thought about that I felt anger welling up. I felt like saying, "But I'm dealing with more important problems right now—my problems." Then I saw my selfishness and my need for repentance. And I said to myself, "Instead of thinking about the things I feel I can't do, what are the things I *can* do for my wife?" I drove home with a deep sense of hope and joy. And since then we've been having a great time.

You raise the issues of selfishness and self-centeredness. Those are major themes in some of your books.

The temptation to focus on ourselves instead of others might very well be the most serious challenge we face in any relationship. Certainly in my own marriage, my deepest problem has been an immature, demanding, basically self-centered spirit.

For example, I got home from an exhausting trip last night about 9 o'clock. When I walked through the door Rachael had a thousand things she wanted to tell me. I found myself annoyed, thinking, "Well, a few things happened to me today too. And I wouldn't mind you asking a question about that." I didn't say it, but I felt it.

That's my immature, demanding nature that says, "If someone loves me, she should really be sensitive to me." Instead, I should recognize that God has already shown His love and sensitivity toward me, and that should free me up to be sensitive to my wife. Whatever sensitivity others show toward me is a plus (and my wife is unusually sensitive and supportive)—but it's not something I should demand.

I think any system of ethics would say it was appropriate for me, who had worked hard all day while Rachael spent the day skiing, to expect her to give me a hug and ask me how I was doing. But I have to realize it's wrong for me to demand that. It's not wrong to desire it, or to ask for it. It's not even wrong to be upset if I don't get it. But it's wrong to require it. Learning to call that attitude wrong is half the battle.

You're making a distinction between desiring something and requiring it.

Yes. If I make it my "goal" to get my wife to respond in a certain way, that's sinful. Of course I want to be noticed when I'm hurting. But to think that I deserve it and that someone else ought to give it to me, that's where my sinfulness starts showing.

How do you break out of that?

You start by calling it wrong. I have to be able to say, "Right now I'm failing my wife—I'm a redeemed, but still sometimes cruddy, guy." Yet God is smiling at me and I can celebrate His forgiveness. And the strength that comes in realizing I don't deserve His mercy softens my heart.

The loving actions grow out of that realization—not that it's always easy. There is a teeth-gritting effort sometimes. But even in those times when it's a hard, deliberate choice, my response can feel real as opposed to forced. It's right to love our mates the way God wants us to—even when we don't really feel like it.

You have written that the most central meaning in the universe is found in relationship. What do you mean by that?

I'll give you an example. Several years ago, the codependency movement became popular, in part, because it dealt with a basic core phenomenon that the church too often failed to address: That beneath every other problem is some kind of relational dysfunction.

That's why people involved in codependency recovery groups felt they were being helped in such a meaningful way—because it touched something deep within them. In contrast, too often in church we're content to try to deal with superficial issues or external behavior and fail to deal with the deeper, personal concerns.

How can the church, and individual Christians, deal with the deeper issues?

We've all been hurt by life, and many of us have been deeply hurt by our mates. But the most crucial advice I have is this: No matter how wounded you've been, you must see yourself in a way that the most important thing in your life is forgiveness. I know a lot of people would rather have healing. But until God becomes more important as redeemer than enabler, we haven't grasped the Gospel.

We all need help in developing a better self-image and in seeing ourselves as someone God loves. But the core assumption of the codependency movement is that people need to come to the point of realizing they are worthy of love. The idea that we need to focus on the wounds of life as the central thing that needs attention, versus the sin of life as the core thing that needs forgiveness, is wrong.

God can be our enabler, our soother, and our friend. But the beginning of the Gospel is a message of judgment and forgiveness. That's the foundation on which we need to build our lives and our marriages. We need a theology of suffering—not just recovery.

Dennis and Lucy Guernsey

Boundaries

How to set appropriate boundaries that define a new marriage. How to relate to in-laws. And how to create a new family "culture" that fits your marriage.

Interviewed by Scott W. Bolinder

Educators and counselors Dennis and Lucy Guernsey have devoted their lives to the study of marriage. For years they have taught others the best way to begin a marriage, and how to keep a relationship healthy for a lifetime.

At the time of his death in 1996, Dennis was a professor and chair of the Family Psychology Department at Seattle Pacific University. Lucy is dean of student development and campus life at the same Seattle, Washington, university. They are authors of several books, including *Real Life Marriage* and *Birthmarks* (both published by Word).

In their thirty-six years of marriage, the Guernseys lived and observed marriage from both sides—as husband and wife, and also as father- and mother-in-law. We asked them to describe the best way to get a marriage started off right.

You have written about the importance of couples facing the reality of their marriages, rather than holding on to an idealized image of marriage. When did you first face that dilemma in your own marriage?

Dennis : After we'd been married a few years, I realized Lucy wanted something from me that was quite different from the kind of relationship I was used to. I had expected that we'd have a fairly passive, congenial relationship—similar to the way I had related to my mother.

But that wasn't what Lucy had in mind at all. She wanted more intense, highly interactive sharing. She was mad most of the time, and she was bugging me. But I couldn't figure out what the problem was. My romantic, idealized view of marriage was upset by the reality that Lucy and I were having serious difficulties.

So what did you do?

Dennis: We had to figure out a way to communicate and understand each other's needs, because the only other option was to continue a miserable existence. We knew we wouldn't divorce. In fact, many times in our relationship we have gone back to a basic commitment to each other and to Christ that has sustained us.

Lucy: Before we were married, we talked for hours and hours about our commitment to Christ and the choice we would be making for a lifelong relationship. So when we started having difficulties in 1962, it never seriously occurred to me that I could quit our marriage. We had made a covenant with each other and to God. And even though we were angry, frustrated and mystified by our relationship, we knew we would have to make it work.

Dennis: These days, divorce—quitting a marriage—seems like an option. But for us it was not.

What would help young couples strengthen their commitment— the kind of commitment that helped you two through difficult times?

Dennis: We encourage couples to clearly understand the concept of a covenant. It's different from a contract, which presupposes a tradeoff: If you give something you're bound to get something in return. But a contract can be voided if one side doesn't satisfy the terms of the agreement. In contrast, a covenant is not based on performance, but on commitment—which means permanence and acceptance no matter what.

The marriage vows ought to say something like this: "I take you, Lucy, to be my wedded wife until death do us part, knowing full well that in the process you will fail me as I will fail you. Knowing full well that you will be unfaithful to me, at least in thought, and I unfaithful to you. Knowing that there will be times when you will be bitterly disappointed with me as I will be with you. But even in the face of all that, I commit myself to you."

Lucy: Couples need to realize that beginnings are difficult. I love the way Chaim Potok describes this in his novel *In the Beginning*. The first sentence reads ". . . all beginnings are hard." Potok elaborates through his main character, David, who describes how one evening when he was nine years old, he burst into tears because a passage of a Bible commentary had proved too difficult for him to understand.

David's mentor in his studies would welcome him warmly to his apartment and speak in a gentle voice: "Be patient, David, beginnings are hard; you cannot swallow all the world at one time."

Dennis and I resonate with this because it seems so true for marriage. So often we think of a marriage ceremony as the culmination of a courtship process. On the contrary, it is only a beginning that you have made for yourself.

Dennis: We recommend that couples take their marriage seriously, but they also need to keep their sense of humor. We see so many young couples who are incredibly intense. They don't realize that with some things, the harder you push, the worse it can get.

I'm always impressed with the world-class distance runners who know how to pace themselves for races so they can push when they need to. If they run at 100 percent all the time, they end up with no reserves. Marriage is similar to that. Pacing, along with learning to relax and having fun along the way, are key to making a commitment work.

It seems odd that having fun doesn't come more naturally. Why are so many couples so intense?

Lucy: Choices can bring stress. Couples now have more freedom to choose when they're going to have children. That gives them a lot of opportunity for experimenting with careers, travel, and their relationship. But their expectations are great, and that often clouds the opportunities and leads to disillusionment.

Sex is a perfect example. It's difficult to have a delightful sexual experience without being able to have fun, to laugh and relax. Yet our culture has elevated performance expectations so high that couples commonly approach sex as a task to be mastered with the same prowess as other successful experiences. Not surprisingly, the results are often disappointing. A little less seriousness and a bit more playfulness can make a big difference.

Dennis: One of the main distractions that prevents couples from developing a habit of having fun and relaxing is the commitment to careers. In some cases, the husband is committed to a fast-track career path and his wife is more interested in establishing their home, even if she has a job. In more cases, both husband and wife are in the midst of escalating, demanding careers, and at the same time are committed to establishing a healthy home and a thriving marriage. Such high stakes tend to breed intense relationships.

Lucy: Many people grew up in families that don't communicate well, so they have few models for how to relate in a relaxed, enjoyable way.

Dennis: I find it a strange paradox that the same people who found it difficult to provide good models on how to relate effectively are the ones who want to tell us how to live our lives. I'm speaking, of course, about in-laws.

Why are in-law relationships such a delicate area for couples, and what can be done to ease the awkwardness?

Dennis: That's an important question for me, because I'm an in-law myself.

Lucy: Being a mother-in-law has been one of the more significant challenges for me. Dennis and I are learning how we can best let go and still stay connected with our daughter and her family. But we are mostly impressed by how maturely Sheryl and her husband, Jaime, have interacted with us. They don't make us guess how we should relate to them.

Dennis: Not every decision they have made has been easy to accept, we should add. I remember the big flap in both families when they decided to each keep their own surname. When they first told us about their decision, Lucy looked at them and said, "Where do I put you in my address book?"

Even in jokingly pointing out the interesting dilemmas created by their choice, Lucy was acknowledging our understanding that they expected us to learn to live with their decision. In this matter, as in most, Sheryl and Jaime communicated with us lovingly, but firmly.

One of the first tests of in-law relations often occurs around holiday traditions. How has that worked for you with Sheryl and Jaime?

Dennis: They made their first foray into hosting a major holiday event one Thanksgiving shortly after they were married. They hosted our entire side of the family. They also took the occasion to make a statement about how they operate. One of their rules was that if you cooked part of the meal, you didn't have to help with the dishes afterward. For our extended family, that statement about the sharing of roles was radical.

Lucy: The positive thing was that Sheryl and Jaime took the initiative and let us know they wanted to participate in the larger family system. They even risked rejection by doing things a bit differently from what the older generations were used to.

A family in the next generation can belong to the larger extended family and still develop their own agendas and their own lives. Newlyweds need to take the risk of getting involved in the larger family, letting them know who you are as a couple, and what's important to you even though it may create some tension and require some negotiation.

What other things did your daughter and son-in-law do to get off to a good start in their early years?

Dennis: We've noticed how constructively they handle the area of giving and receiving criticism. Sheryl and Jaime are both committed to keeping short accounts with each other. If something is bothering one of them, they deal with it right away. Even if they're visiting at our house, they'll simply excuse themselves and go off somewhere for their negotiations. Lucy and I would be more prone to tuck it away and maybe dredge it up later, if at all.

Lucy: They also do a good job of differentiating between different types of criticism. If they decide it's something significant to work through, they keep at it until they agree on a solution. Then they use that solution as a precedent for future discussions. They keep trying to build their habits and understanding on principles already in place. Dennis and I have never been that sophisticated in our negotiations.

What advice do you have on keeping a marriage healthy and on the right track over the years?

Lucy: We are convinced that couples need mentors, no matter how long you've been married. The care and counsel of an older couple is a tremendous benefit to any couple. We all need other couples for support and instruction.

Dennis: You need mature friends—other than your parents—who can relate to you as collegial adults. Seek out a couple who have been through it and are willing to give you their experiences and their knowledge, so you'll do as well or better than they did. Recruit someone who functions in a way you respect.

Rookies need veterans, and at most stages of marriage we are both. So we envision couples having mentors and, at the same time, being mentors to others. Can you imagine the power this dynamic would have for the church in terms of cultivating healthy marriages? We would have a much deeper understanding of God's grace and its importance for married life in all its stages.

SOMETHING TO TALK ABOUT

1. At the beginning of this chapter, Norm Wright discusses the expectations everyone has of what marriage will be like. When we were first married, what surprised us the most about each other?
2. What aspects of our life together failed to match the dreams we each had about marriage?
3. In an earlier interview, Kevin Leman describes how birth order affects the way people approach life. What are our respective birth-order positions? Are we a match of similar types, or of opposites?

4. In what ways do our birth-order types complement one another? What conflicts in our relationship could be linked to birth order?

5. Larry Crabb points out the ways self-centered behavior damages the marriage relationship. Can we identify a current problem in our marriage that is linked to self-centered behavior? If so, can we forgive each other and, with God's help, commit ourselves to start putting one another first?

6. At the end of this chapter, Dennis and Lucy Guernsey discuss ways to establish a new "couple identity" and set appropriate boundaries. What aspects of our in-law relationships have been the most troublesome? How can we do a better job of handling those relationships?

7. The Guernseys also stress the importance of having fun as a couple. In what areas has our life together become too intense? How can we incorporate more fun and playfulness into our relationship on a regular basis?

Chapter Two

CLEAR COMMUNICATION

Being Heard
Jim and Sally Conway

Love's Languages
Gary Chapman

Gender Differences
Lee Ezell

Jim and Sally Conway

Being Heard

Why doesn't your mate communicate like you do? Why do men and women differ so widely in the way they make decisions? Here's what effective communication can do to bridge the gender gap in your marriage.

Interviewed by Ron R. Lee

*M*oney, sex, work, parenting. It's not hard to identify the causes of most marital disagreements. The challenge is finding workable solutions.

Jim and Sally Conway are familiar with the problems couples face. In his forties, Jim came close to leaving his pastorate, as well as Sally and their children, due to a mid-life crisis. And when their daughter Becki had a leg amputated because of cancer, Jim entered a period of despair and questioning God. More recently, Sally has been battling cancer, and Jim has learned to be her nurse.

But in the midst of pain and confusion, one thing holds true—the need for good communication. When couples learn to express themselves clearly and honestly—and listen to one another carefully and caringly—it becomes much easier to find solutions.

The Conways are cofounders of Mid-Life Dimensions, a counseling ministry that helps couples in crisis. They are also the authors of a number of books, including *Traits of a Lasting Marriage* (InterVarsity) and *When a Mate Wants Out* (Zondervan). Here are some of the things they've learned about the importance of good communication, and how couples can face their problems head-on—together.

In your nearly four decades of working with married couples, is there one complaint you hear more than all others?

Sally: Yes. We hear women say they wish they could get their husbands to talk more. Frequently, however, the husbands have tried to communicate but their wives didn't listen. Or perhaps they just weren't able to receive and accept their husbands' message. As a result, the men have given up trying. After a few years, this leads to bad patterns of communication.

What complaint do you hear most often from husbands?

Jim: Men feel that their wives talk too much. Many husbands think their wives aren't quiet long enough to let them speak. Sometimes the wife is thinking she and her husband have lived together for so long that she already knows what he's going to say. So he starts to say something...

Sally: And she jumps in and finishes the statement for him.

Jim: Men speak more slowly, generally, than women. And the woman interprets that slow speech pattern as the man saying, "I'm not interested in you." She jumps in and fills the gap, but it breaks the communication.

What other differences have you observed between husbands and wives?

Sally: One big difference is the way they arrive at decisions. Women tend to think out loud: They talk through their thinking process. The way a woman approaches personal growth and change is a back-and-forth thing. Sometimes she will voice conflicting messages while she works through a decision. That's her relational way of processing growth.

Meanwhile, the husband hears his wife say one thing, and in the next breath she says something that has a little different slant on it. That's confusing to him because he typically doesn't say anything until his mind is made up. If you understand the difference, you can learn to appreciate each other and let each other be the way you are.

Jim: In general, men make decisions—especially regarding their own personal growth—very privately. To the outside observer, there seems to be a long period of nothing happening, followed by a sudden change. But the change is actually happening all along. It's just that the husband doesn't express his decision to start doing things differently until he has finalized it in his mind.

What are the consequences of this difference in the way men and women communicate?

Jim: One of the most tragic ways we see this difference showing up is at the time when one of the spouses realizes the marriage is in trouble. If the woman senses the trouble, she'll verbalize that feeling over a number of months, maybe even years. She'll tell her husband, "I feel lonely," or "We don't ever do anything together anymore," or "Let's go on a vacation."

But if the husband is the one who senses that all is not right, he very often won't say anything. Then one day he'll come home and announce, "I'm moving out." He had been silent while he was processing all the dissatisfaction he was feeling. And by the time he expresses his feelings, he's already made a decision to leave.

Sally: If each spouse would work harder at communicating in ways his or her mate can understand, many marital break-ups could be avoided. For instance, husbands could work harder at verbalizing their feelings of unhappiness much earlier.

But at the same time, wives need to learn to listen. If a husband is unhappy with the way the marriage is going, he has probably been giving off signals that he is unhappy. But it's possible that his wife didn't tune in to the messages he was giving off. Whenever her husband does say something, she needs to allow him to go ahead and talk some more if he wants to. Listening, after all, is an essential component of the communication process.

But if many of the signals men give off are nonverbal, how can a woman learn to "hear" those silent signals?

Jim: For starters, a woman can be careful to pick up on the few signals her husband gives that are verbal. But she has to realize that communication between a woman and a man is very different from what happens when two women talk. When two women get together, they do a lot of explaining and restating and refocusing until the other person clearly understands what is being said.

But a man may come home and say something vague, such as, "I don't know. I guess my job is really tough." After making that short statement, he may drop it. His wife assumes that it must not be a big problem since he didn't say more than two sentences.

But she needs to understand that her husband has become as vulnerable as he can at that moment. She needs to pick up on the little phrase that he did say about his job being hard right now. He's feeling a great loss about the way his work is going, but he's not expressing it fully. Women need to listen to the small phrases—sometimes only one or two words—that their husbands are saying. For a man, this is sharing a whole wealth of feeling that lies behind the words.

But if his wife follows his short statement by saying, "Yeah, I had a tough day too," and then talks about her struggles, she has completely missed her husband's signal. Maybe a week later, the husband will drop another brief comment about his job. If his wife doesn't pick up on it the second time, he'll begin to think she just isn't listening.

This type of thing can go on for years, and all of a sudden some younger woman at the office will say to this man, "How in the world do you put up with all the pressure around here?" And he starts thinking, "Well finally, here is somebody who is interested in listening to me!" He didn't plan to get involved with another woman, but all of a sudden he's being drawn away from his wife. And he's not being drawn away by love; he's being drawn away by care.

Are there other ways couples are failing to connect emotionally in their marriages?

Jim: There are many, but one of the most common is that men in mid-life often feel mothered by their wives, rather than "girlfriended." By mid-life a man usually has shifted his focus away from professional achievement and career advancement, and instead begins to concentrate more on his marriage. But in the meantime his wife has become a mother to their children, and in a sense he has become just one of the children. He feels that he is being mothered, but what he really wants is to have his wife act like a girlfriend.

What would it mean for a wife to become her husband's girlfriend?

Jim: For one thing, having a girlfriend means spontaneity and a sense of freedom from responsibility. It might mean having a younger outlook on life, or a younger approach to the marriage relationship. The mid-life man might want to reach back to some of the imagery of when he was first dating his wife.

Sally: When Jim was in his mid-life crisis, I began to think in terms of how a younger woman would act around him. I decided to look at him with the eyes of a twenty-two-year-old and tell him what I saw in him and how I felt about him. I wanted to affirm him more and act more flirtatious.

At the time I was a teacher, and I was using very practical clothes. I started dressing with a little more youthful look, and I changed my hairstyle. But more than anything it was an attitude. I tried to be more lighthearted; I tried to find ways to get away with Jim when he wanted to get away, instead of saying, "I just can't. There's too much work to do."

Jim: It's that sense of couple-ness that is part of being a girlfriend to your husband. In a mother/son relationship there isn't any couple-ness. But in a girlfriend/boyfriend relationship there is a couple-ness that develops and grows. It's that "desire" for each other that couples are looking for.

When they first marry, a couple starts out quite happy. But according to statistics, they hit their lowest level of marital satisfaction by age thirty-five. And it stays low until about age fifty, when it starts to rise again.

Sally: The couples who are going to have long-term, happy marriages are the ones who make sure they have togetherness time on a regular basis. If their careers and parenting responsibilities make that difficult, then they need to schedule a breakfast appointment at a restaurant so they can get caught up with each other's lives. They make it fun, a secret time to be away; and also a time to learn about each other.

If your marriage has become stale, there's no better time than now to start doing romantic things—as well as the connecting things—that will make your relationship more satisfying. It's important that you do this, because you're going to go through several crises together. Things will happen with your children that will either be disappointments or tragedies. Your parents are aging, and it's likely that at least one of them will die sooner than you expected them to. And there's always the mid-life re-evaluation, which can be traumatic. You'd better have your marriage relationship working so you can make it through these times.

Jim, how old were you when you hit your mid-life crisis?

Jim: I was forty-five, but it usually happens sooner. The national average is forty-two-and-a-half, but we see them starting anywhere from age thirty-five to sixty. In my case, Sally and I had enjoyed twenty-five years of marriage, but I was ready to chuck it all. I was ready to leave God, my family, my home, my career, and just take off. Instead of seeing our marriage as a source of nourishment, I was viewing it as just another one of my responsibilities.

The good thing is that Sally didn't want to chuck it.

What did you and Sally do to turn things around?

Jim: It started to turn around when Sally became aware that I really was ready to run. She began listening to me in a way that she had never listened before. I found that I had a friend who would really listen to me. Before, I felt I was in more of a "business relationship" with Sally. But at that point, she began to deliberately, consciously tune in even when it wasn't comfortable for her to do so.

For example, I generally would not start talking until late at night. In the past Sally would have said, "It's late. We can talk about it tomorrow." That would make me feel like I wasn't connecting with her. But with her new approach, she was consciously working at it. Since our relationship was beginning to nourish me, it helped me to see our marriage not as just another obligation.

Sally: After days of silence, anger, and depression, Jim told me enough of what he was feeling that I knew I had to do something drastic. Some men don't ever give their wife a clue; and so the wife has to learn it some other way. But I knew something had to change, and I was willing to do whatever it took.

Jim: We began to realize that our marriage was connected to everything else we were doing—my career, everything. We were on a teeter-totter. Marriage isn't a separate thing; your career affects it. My aging affected it (I was getting more pooped out). And a very close friend of mine died right then, which was a terrible jolt.

All these things affected this teeter-totter we were on. So as I worked on some of these other areas of my life, it began to help our marriage. Sometimes it isn't the marriage per se that is wrong, but career dissatisfaction, or stress related to the aging process, or some other life stress.

For example, the self-identities of most men and career-oriented women are about 75 percent wrapped up in what they do for a living. So if what they do is in turmoil, then 75 percent of them is churned up. That carries over into marriage. Sometimes people run off to marriage counseling when their marriage has only a few little things that need to be tuned up. But it may be that major tuning needs to be done in the career area or some other area of their life. On this teeter-totter, if you can shift some of the weight from one end, then you're going to see things being more stabilized all across the board.

Sally: Jim needed to learn to take some leisure time. He was working too many hours at the church, and he had a heavy counseling load. I was teaching school so I didn't have weekdays free. He usually tried to take Monday off, and he didn't want to do something out of town if I couldn't go along.

About that time God provided a sailboat for us. Jim would go sailing for part of Monday and come back a different person. I took some personal leave days, and we'd go away for a day. Sometimes we'd go camping or take other mini-breaks. Learning to take a little time out each day to care for yourself and get restored was very key to getting through this.

Jim, you talked about Sally helping you survive your mid-life crisis. Now Sally is battling cancer, and you've been caring for her. What have the two of you learned through this ordeal?

Jim: When I was down, Sally carried me. Now, when she's going through breast cancer, I'm carrying her. Marriage is made up of that kind of thing. One person is up and the other one needs to be carried. It shifts back and forth throughout the marriage.

Sally: Jim's devotion to my recovery has been a model to everyone. Not only was he with me through the biopsy and the surgery and the immediate days after; but when I began chemotherapy and really lost my power, my dignity, and my hair, he stood by me emotionally and physically. He had to take over my ministry duties and my household duties. He served me as if he had been hired to wait on my every need.

I had an infection begin in my incision that had to be drained and dressed every day. My dear Jim would bend over me with his tender eyes, which were by that time getting a little dark-circled. He cared for that infection every day for nearly ten months.

Jim: In times like that, you just hang on to each other.

Sally: Jim went above and beyond the call of duty in helping me, and by being an encouragement to me. He let me be a miserable mess and helped me get through it.

Have there been other times when one of you has had to carry the other, because of some challenge to your marriage or your faith?

Sally: Yes. When our daughter Becki developed cancer in 1978, Jim believed God would answer his prayers to heal her. When that didn't happen, Jim became very angry at God.

Jim: I was just starting to come out of my mid-life crisis when Becki lost her leg to cancer, and I went down to the pit again. I was so convinced God was going to heal her. And when that didn't happen I was devastated. I was going to leave the ministry.

Sally: After the doctor told us he would have to amputate Becki's leg, Jim told me, "We're going to have to be very strong from now on because God isn't going to care for us."

Sally, what was going through your mind when Jim said he could no longer trust God?

Sally: I felt it was temporary, because I knew God wasn't going to let him go. But my more immediate concern was to make sure that I aided Becki in her recovery. Fortunately, Jim had two men who let him pour out his grief. They let him ventilate for hours on end over a period of two or three days. God did bring him through it, although there are still questions that trouble him even today.

Jim: It ultimately came to a point where I had to say, "I'm either going to trust myself, or I am going to trust God blindly." I realized if I trusted myself there would be nothing but despair, because I could not control life. So the only viable option was to trust God, but that doesn't mean that I don't still feel the pain of Becki's loss very deeply.

What advice would you give to couples who are about to lose hope?

Sally: It's not easy, but couples need to work through their problems and not become convinced that things are hopeless. There are ways of getting help—by reading books or seeing a competent counselor, enriching their outside friendships and really making the marriage something they both enjoy—so that they really do feel like each other's friends again.

Jim: Couples need to realize they're not trapped at the level they're at right now. Every marriage can be better than it is today. It can get better by talking to each other and working on little areas of correction and improvement. One little improvement ripples out into every area to improve the whole relationship.

Gary Chapman

Love's Languages

Why spouses don't express love the same way; and why we don't "accept" love the same way. How to approach love from a new direction—and make a big difference in your marriage.

Interviewed by Ron R. Lee

*I*n the previous interview, Jim and Sally Conway described differences in the ways men and women speak and listen. In this interview, Gary Chapman takes it a step further. He says people have different ways of expressing and receiving love—and it has nothing to do with gender. It's based more on what comes naturally—and what "feels like" love to you.

The problem is, doing what comes naturally to you probably doesn't communicate love to your mate—since most people marry their opposites. That's why we need to understand, and use, the appropriate "love language." Chapman has narrowed them down to five—and you're sure to see yourself, and your spouse, in there somewhere.

A pastor, counselor, and seminar leader, Chapman is the author of several books, including *Toward a Growing Marriage* (Moody) and *The Five Love Languages* (Northfield). He says if you or your spouse have been feeling unloved, it might be because you've been speaking the wrong language. The good news is there's a simple home remedy that works wonders.

People generally get married because they can't bear the thought of not spending the rest of their lives together. If couples start out with so much passion, why does loving each other become such a challenge later on?

Part of it is that when these strong emotions begin to die down, couples mistakenly think they don't love each other as much as they used to. They confuse emotions with love.

But isn't love a pretty emotional thing?

Sure, but love isn't dependent on emotions. Love is what you do and say, not what you feel.

Still, it *seems* like you have a problem if you no longer feel the same amount of love you used to. So what do you recommend?

We all need to do a better job of communicating love, which is a challenge since people usually marry their opposites. I've spoken to large groups of couples all around the country, and I've counseled hundreds of others. And in all the couples I've talked to, I have seldom run across a husband and wife who used and understood the same language of love.

What makes people so different in the way they express love?

I don't know if it's something we learn in childhood or a trait we're born with. But we all have a primary love language that shows up early in life. Think about your children. By the time they are five or six, you can begin to see how they express love. If your son is coming up and saying, "Oh, Mommy, let's sit down and read a book," then he's asking for quality time. Or if your daughter is always hugging you, her language is physical touch. It really doesn't matter how or when we develop a love language, the important thing is to identify what works for the people you love, and then to start doing it.

Why aren't more of us doing what works?

Most people express love in the way that comes most naturally to them, and we assume our mate recognizes those actions as expressions of love. But if our mate speaks a different language, most of the things we're doing just won't communicate. You end up with both spouses expressing love and wondering why the other one doesn't acknowledge it. At the same time, they're both wondering why their mate isn't doing any loving things for them. Both spouses fail to recognize their partner's love because they speak different languages.

What are the languages of love?

Based on case studies of the couples I have counseled over the years, certain themes are repeated. And those themes indicate that people give and receive love in five ways: sharing quality time; physical touch; expressing words of affirmation; giving and receiving gifts; and performing acts of service.

Can you give an example of each of these languages?

Let's start with words of affirmation. It simply means making statements—either spoken or written—that show you value your spouse. Statements such as, "You look nice today." "I love you." "Thanks for taking the garbage out." These are statements that focus on something your spouse has done or something he or she is.

The second language, giving and receiving gifts, is pretty self-explanatory. You know the old saying "It's the thought that counts." But it's not the thought left in your head that counts, it's the gift that came out of the thought that counts. It doesn't have to be expensive; it can be anything that shows your spouse you had him or her in mind when you selected the gift.

What are some examples of the other languages?

The third, acts of service, involves doing anything you know your spouse would like you to do. It could be cooking a meal, washing the dishes, vacuuming floors, or putting gas in the car.

The fourth is quality time, which means giving your spouse your undivided attention. It could be sitting on the couch together, talking; or going out to eat together; or taking a walk.

The last one, physical touch, includes things like hugs, backrubs, holding hands, and kissing. Some men jump to the conclusion that their love language is physical touch, because they have such a strong sex drive. But I'm referring to nonsexual touch, like resting your hand on your spouse's leg while you're driving.

If a lot of guys wrongly assume their language is physical touch, does that mean it's not all that easy to identify your own love language?

If you give it some thought, you can pin it down. First, ask yourself how you tend to express love. You may do all five from time to time. But if you think about it, you'll find one that is predominant.

The second clue is to ask yourself, "What do I gripe about the most?" If you tend to complain, "We don't ever spend any time together," then your love language probably is quality time.

The third question is: "What do I request most often from my husband or wife?" If you often say, "Honey, remember to bring me something back from your business trip," you like to receive gifts. If you put these three clues together, you'll determine your love language.

Now to the hard part. How can we identify our spouse's love language?

You use the same three-step process. You ask, "How does my spouse express love to me most often?" Then, "What does my spouse request from me the most?" And finally, "What does my spouse complain about?" The answers will tell you your mate's language.

If both spouses have been feeling unloved, how does your approach help them get back on track?

It depends on why they are feeling distant. If there has been infidelity, physical abuse, alcoholism, or drug abuse, you need to do a lot more than just learn a new way to express love. Those problems call for professional counseling. But if your problems are less serious, learning to speak your mate's language will create a climate that makes it easier to work on other issues. Expressing love is not the whole solution, but it's a critical part of any solution.

If you've been feeling unloved, what would motivate you to learn a foreign language just so you can love someone you feel isn't bothering to love you?

Motivation is important, but I never said this was easy. People have all kinds of reasons for not wanting to do this. They say it seems artificial or that "it's just not me." But those are excuses. There are a lot of things we don't like to do; and there are plenty of things that don't come naturally. But we learn to do them anyway.

One man told me he had been married seventeen years and had never known how to show his wife he loved her. Then he realized her language was receiving gifts, which was a start. But he didn't have the foggiest idea how to buy the right gifts. So he asked his sister to go with him to help him pick out some things for his wife. This guy realized he needed to learn a new behavior, so he went out and found the help he needed.

What do you suggest for people who have trouble putting their feelings into words?

When people tell me, "I didn't grow up in a home where we did that sort of thing. I'm just not a verbal person," I often respond, "So what?" I know it's difficult, but you can learn to do it. Whenever you hear someone pay a compliment, for example, write it down. Or as you read books or magazine articles, pick out expressions of love and start making a list. Then stand in front of a mirror and read your list out loud. After a while, it will begin to feel more comfortable.

Then, of course, you start saying these things to your wife or husband. Once you do it a few times it becomes much easier.

I can hear people saying, "Gary Chapman is one to talk. He's a marriage expert. This stuff comes easily to him!"

The truth is, some of these things don't come easily to me. My wife, Karolyn, and I had terrible struggles the first few years of our marriage. It's terrible to be married for three or four years and lose all your feelings of love for one another.

How did you rekindle your love?

I started studying the life of Jesus, and I saw how much of a servant He was to His followers. That's when the concept of a husband being a servant-leader began to dawn on me. And when I realized my primary role was to serve Karolyn, I started noticing other things. I could see that when I failed to help her around the house, the climate wasn't very good at home. But whenever I did some little thing to help her, it made a positive impression. I didn't have all the theories worked out back then, but I realized that my wife's love language was acts of service. After months of feeling totally unloved, she finally sensed that I did love her after all.

I'll be honest. I don't like running the vacuum. My mother made me do it when I was a boy, and I never have liked it. But I vacuum the floors about once a week now, and there's only one reason why: I love Karolyn and I want her to know it. Every time I vacuum the floor, my wife realizes, "He cares. He's helping me."

Vacuuming the floors is one thing, but what if your mate's language is meaningful time? In order for you to deliver on that one, you're going to have to give something up.

You've hit on a key truth about love: It's costly. But if you're not willing to give something up, you're saying the things that currently take up your time are more important than your marriage. It's a matter of seeing marriage as a priority, and then deciding what you can give up. Actually, we make those decisions all the time. If we want to go to a ball game, we give up the other things we could be doing with that time.

This stuff can feel pretty overwhelming. Is it okay to start off with something easy and then gradually work up to the bigger stuff?

Sure. Even a small step will begin to change the emotional climate of a relationship. I encourage couples to start with a specific assignment that is relatively easy: Each spouse determines one way he or she can express love during the coming week. Let's say a woman's language is acts of service. She could ask her husband: "How about taking out the garbage without being reminded?" He'd say, "Okay. How often would you like me to do it?" And she'd say, "How about every two days?" He would then set that as his goal for the week.

He starts taking out the garbage, and every time his wife sees the emptied waste basket she feels a little tingle inside. "Hey, he's really taking this seriously." She begins to feel better immediately.

What does she do for her husband?

Let's say his language is physical touch, and she's just not very expressive in that way. He would ask her to do something nonthreatening. "How about when you enter or leave a room, you touch me on the shoulder as you walk by?" And she'd say, "I can do that." As the week goes by, every time she touches his shoulder, inside he feels, "She's really trying. This is wonderful." He begins to have positive feelings toward her after months of emotional distance.

Does this approach work in situations where couples are so distant they've lost all positive feelings toward each other?

Under those circumstances, if a couple acted on their emotions it would only lead to further withdrawal and isolation. That's why it's important to understand that love is not an emotion. Love is, first of all, a thought and then a behavior. It is the thought that says, "I choose to look out for my spouse's best interests." And it follows that thought with effective action.

You can express love without having warm feelings toward your spouse. In fact, if you go ahead and start speaking the right love language, there's a high probability that it will stimulate positive feelings in your mate's heart. And if he or she reciprocates by expressing love in your language, your emotions will begin to respond. That gives you a lot of encouragement to keep going.

Let's say a woman's husband has been emotionally distant, and she starts expressing love in his language thinking it will turn him around. Isn't that being self-centered?

If that were her only motive, it would be self-centered. But there's nothing wrong with wanting to be loved. God made us creatures who desire to feel loved. And doing something in order to get love back doesn't have to be your primary motive.

It helps to remember that God took the initiative to love us while we were still rejecting Him. I don't believe God was being selfish by extending His love to us hoping that we would respond to Him. God cares about us unconditionally, and He challenges us to practice that same kind of love. That means I'll love my spouse even if he or she doesn't choose to love me in return.

If that's the outcome, how do you get through to an unresponsive mate?

Sometimes it takes awhile. I can't guarantee that if you love your spouse, that he or she will reciprocate. But I can say that emotional love is a desperate need for all of us. So if you'll speak your mate's primary language over the long haul, there's a high probability he or she will respond.

Most people want an intimate relationship. They want to have feelings of closeness. They want to have a sense that, as a couple, they are one. They just don't know how to get it. That's why I spend so much time helping people learn their mate's love language. It's one way you can both get what you need and want in marriage.

Lee Ezell

Gender Differences

Males and females are different by divine design, but those differences often create more confusion than harmony. Here's a way to understand, appreciate, and value the differences inherent in being husband and wife.

Interviewed by Louise A. Ferrebee

Some things that couples find confusing, such as conflicting preferences or competing goals, are based on individual differences that are unrelated to being male or female. But other gaps between spouses are clearly gender based.

After nearly three decades of the women's movement, some things have become more equal. For instance, career opportunities for women are nearly identical to the ones traditionally open to men. But equality and sameness are two very different things. Thankfully, females and males are still far from being identical.

Speaker Lee Ezell, author of six books on improving relationships, including *Iron Jane* (Vine), says the fallout from the feminist movement is men and women who are more confused now than they were before. Rather than strive to erase gender differences, she suggests we accept each other and work harder at understanding our differences. In this interview, she shows us a portion of the trail she has been blazing through the gender jungle.

In spite of the women's movement, negative stereotypes of both sexes remain widespread. My husband and I can't help but laugh at the stupid things Tim Allen does on his "Home Improvement" TV show. It's really funny, but I feel a little guilty about laughing at him.

Stereotypes do make for good comedy. But the real reason we're seeing such negative views toward men, in particular, goes a lot deeper. There are a lot of disappointed women who swallowed the feminist line of "look like a lady, act like a man, and work like a dog." And it hasn't brought them much satisfaction. As I deal with the secular media, I'm finding many of these women are in positions of power or influence.

Are you saying that angry women are setting the agendas for how the media portray the sexes?

You bet. Women with a string of justifications that would singe your hair as to why men are jerks. One unmarried woman told me: "Men are like parking spots. All the good ones are taken." I've heard other women say, "Men can't be faithful," and then tell about a father who walked out or a husband who left. But these women aren't limited to the entertainment industry. I've found my share of angry women in churches—they're just better at covering up their emotions.

So we all feed into this "him-versus-her" mentality?

Sure. Just yesterday in one of my workshops I humorously pointed out some of the common gender stereotypes. I wasn't bashing men, I was just using the stereotypes to explain "male meshing." Basically, male meshing calls for women (and men) to understand and accept our God-given differences. I don't believe that in making us different, God intended to strangle or frustrate us.

For example, I'm convinced my husband doesn't see the stuff sitting on the stairs—stuff that needs to be carried upstairs by the next person who makes a trip. It doesn't occur to him because he simply doesn't track like I do. I have to say, "Honey, when you go up, check the stairs." Rather than see his behavior as rejection or a refusal to help, I need to lovingly accept the differences between us.

So you have rejected the "we're all the same" message?

Right. Men and women are not identical. We tried the equality stuff for over twenty years and realized it's no good. Look at what it has produced—broken relationships, broken trust. We're finally saying, "Hold it. Men and women are different!" Let's work with our differences rather than fight about them or deny them. We can either use these differences as a dividing line that creates a big split, or we can be challenged to live together peacefully.

The Bible says iron sharpens iron—butter doesn't sharpen iron. A man must be strong in who he is and a woman must be strong in who she is, like two pieces of iron. Sure, they'll rub together and it won't always be pleasant. But it will be beneficial. Working through their differences is what makes couples strong.

Some time ago, I was sitting in a board meeting and I disagreed with something that was said. Well, I mouthed off and the room became real quiet. The chairman said, "My, you're a strong woman." I said, "Thank you." I'm ready to go toe-to-toe, not in the "pushy-broad" sense, but as a steel magnolia. I'll voice my opinion and be strong in where I stand as a woman.

Sounds like such a simple solution to a complex problem.

It is and it isn't. To mesh we need to fight fair; and that means refusing to surrender or deny our differences. We need to understand what it is to be a man or a woman.

Take showing love, for instance. To a woman, love means intimacy—long talks and walks. For a guy, expressing love means being a better provider—working longer hours or taking on a second job, if needed, so he can meet his wife's needs.

Well, I can tell you, if my husband is away from home working longer and longer hours, that doesn't spell love to me. But I need to see the situation from his perspective; I need to understand the differences and the tensions they cause. It's so easy, though, to resort to saying, "Forget it, he's a jerk. He'll never understand." Or, "She's too emotional. All she does is cry."

Or wishing he'd just change.

Right, because men and women will never be "changed" to be more like the other sex. God created two distinct sexes whose differences go back to the Garden of Eden. Because of what happened in Eden, a man will always have work as his number-one priority and women—well, think about it. The first thing Eve saw when she was created was another person. Relationships are her life.

So you're saying relationships drive women and work drives men?

Yes, but our world can't be all relationships and intimacy or all providing and independence. It has to be both.

It was with the realization of just how opposite the sexes are that I wrote the book *What Men Understand About Women*. It didn't take long to write—it was totally blank inside.

Totally blank?

Really. Because men and women are such opposite creatures, they are completely clueless about one another. My husband wrote the foreword to the book and said, "Look, guys, this book is true. If you accept it as truth, then interview the woman in your life. Fill every page of this book."

Men and women owe it to one another to speak the truth in love and then listen very carefully. Familiarity breeds contentment. And familiarity comes with asking questions—simple, specific questions.

If an important anniversary is coming up, a man needs to ask his wife what she would like as a gift. Unless he asks, he probably won't realize that what she really wants is a certain piece of jewelry, for instance. Or if a woman notices that her husband seems overloaded, she needs to ask him specifically how she can help out—not just assume she knows.

Are you saying women aren't the great communicators they think they are?

Women make assumptions. We think, "I've lived with this guy long enough, he should know what I want and need. He'd have to be some kind of idiot to still not get it." But women need to ask themselves, "Have I said, in the kind of nuts-and-bolts language a man understands, exactly what I need and expect?"

So a woman has to be strong in knowing what she needs, and

then make sure she lets her husband know.

Yes. And it's never too late to start. I was talking with a woman in her sixties who had heard author Gary Smalley's comment that when it comes to sex, men are like microwaves and women are like crockpots. She told me that after thirty-eight years of marriage she finally realized that if she ever wanted satisfying sex she'd have to tell her husband what she needed. All those years this woman had been hoping that somehow her husband could read her mind and change his approach to sex. And of course, it was never going to happen.

You've talked a lot about what wives need to do. But doesn't a husband have the same responsibility to help his wife understand his needs?

Certainly. For instance, when a man comes home in the evening, he needs to communicate to his wife, "Honey, give me a few minutes here. I'm not ready for all the problems of the day yet." Men don't immediately move from their work mode to their family-relationship mode. A major difference between men and women is that men are focused, compartmentalized thinkers. Take television viewing as an example. When my husband watches TV, he watches TV. Me—I'm doing the laundry, talking on the phone, writing letters, and watching TV all at the same time.

A woman doesn't organize her life into compartments. Her life is one big relationship. That's why a woman doesn't understand that when a man comes home from work he really hasn't come home yet. He has just sent his body home in time for dinner.

So if my husband doesn't seem to be listening, maybe it's because I chose the wrong time to try to talk.

If he is focused on something specific, then wait and talk later. When you do have his attention, most likely he'll give it to you totally. It's natural for men to approach the world in the role of focused problem-solvers. Think about a man going shopping. He has a clear objective. He wants to get in, bag the sucker, then get back to the car. The same thing is true in the area of sex and so many other areas of life.

But women are wired differently. They want emotional support, not just answers. When I was traveling some time ago, I ended up in a crummy hotel. And on top of that, I had to miss the wedding of a friend's son. I called my husband and described my frustration. To my comment about the crummy hotel, he said, "Find a new one." To my regrets about missing the wedding, he said, "Don't worry. He invited 800 people. No one will miss you." And on it went.

I had called him wanting emotional support, not solutions. And once I told him that, he no longer felt he needed to be Mr. Fix-It.

It sounds like being a peacemaker takes a lifetime of work.
It's not easy. Peace between the sexes must be a peace through strength—strength that comes from understanding and then communicating what it means to be a man or to be a woman. It means turning your swords into plowshares and making the decision that despite your differences, the relationship is worth it.

SOMETHING TO TALK ABOUT

1. At the beginning of this chapter, Jim and Sally Conway describe the different ways men and women typically express themselves. In what ways do we communicate like a "typical" male and female?
2. How are we different in the ways we make decisions?
3. How could each of us become a better listener?
4. Gary Chapman lists five ways people give and receive love. Of those five ways—physical touch, quality time, giving gifts, acts of service, and words of affirmation—how would we classify each other?
5. When it comes to expressing love, how has "doing what comes naturally" to each of us worked well? In what instances has it backfired?
6. What is one specific way we can each show love to the other this week?
7. At the end of this chapter, Lee Ezell refers to some common gender-related stereotypes. How have such assumptions about men and women influenced the way we perceive each other?

8. Do we agree with Ezell that men are driven more by career goals, and women by a desire for greater intimacy? If so, how has that affected our marriage?

9. Does a "him vs. her" sense of competition ever crop up in our relationship? When?

Chapter Three

C L O S E R
F R I E N D S H I P

Making Friends
Charles Swindoll

Being Friends
Jerry and Mary White

Charles Swindoll

Making Friends

Why it's so hard to find close friends. Why couple-to-couple friendships should be a high priority. Why spouses also need their own same-sex friends. And how to find and cultivate friendship.

Interviewed by Ron R. Lee

Some of the best marriages begin as friendships that develop into a love relationship and result in lifelong commitment. But many couples find that after they get married, friendships don't develop as readily as they did before.

In this interview, bestselling author and respected Bible teacher Charles Swindoll offers advice and encouragement on the challenge of developing and maintaining close friends. In forty-two years of marriage, he and his wife, Cynthia, have found ways to find and cultivate meaningful outside friendships. Swindoll is the speaker on the "Insight for Living" radio program, and also serves as president of Dallas Theological Seminary in Dallas, Texas. He is the author of more than forty books, including *The Grace Awakening* (Word), *The Strong Family* (Zondervan), and *Simple Faith* (Word).

Here is his advice on making friends after you're married.

We've heard many couples say they found it easier to make friends and maintain their friendships *before* they were married. Why is it so difficult, once we get married, to develop couple-to-

couple friendships? And why is it such a challenge to find friends
who can help us with accountability and spiritual growth?

I can think of three reasons. First, most people are not vulnerable by
nature. And before you can have intimacy—either with your spouse or
with outside friends—you need vulnerability. The problem is that as we
grow up, we learn to cover up what's going on inside us. It's easy to develop a fear that if someone comes to know me as I really am, he or she
won't like me nearly as much as I think they like me now.

The second reason is that many of us have never known the benefits
of intimacy. And since we haven't experienced the good results that can
come from it, we haven't developed a willingness to take some risks. We
have this fear of being found out and losing our friend completely: "What
if I tell them my secret and they turn on me?"

The third reason is related to the second: It's a hard fact of life that
some people can't be trusted. There aren't many people who really can
keep a confidence. So we're hesitant to tell our secrets to anyone. This is
sad, because there can't be intimacy without the sharing of secrets.

**Does this fear of vulnerability filter down into the marriage rela-
tionship itself?**

We see it all the time. Too many couples live lonely lives together, as
one fails to share secrets with the other. And this can lead to a lot more
than just loneliness. When one spouse tries to share secrets and the other
won't, then the one who is trying will usually find someone else to talk to.
And that often leads to an affair with someone who is willing to listen and
to share.

If husbands and wives could realize the value of sharing their secrets
with one another, and the benefits of being vulnerable, they would enjoy
their marriages a lot more. And they would avoid a lot of problems.

**Let's say a husband and wife do have a vulnerable, intimate rela-
tionship with each other, and they want to develop a close friendship
with another couple. Considering all the demands on their time,
how can a couple overcome the barriers and make new friends?**

Well first off, you're right: We're all busy. When Cynthia and I have a
little bit of free time, for example, we'd much rather do something alone,
to be frank about it. On the other hand, it's well worth your time when

you can find a couple who is trustworthy and of the "same soul" as you and your spouse. Paul said of Timothy, "He is like-souled; he is of equal soul." It doesn't mean all four of you have to like Italian food or all the same sports. But it means all four of you see life together. You have a lot of things in common so there is a natural flow in your friendship.

We were with a couple the other night and I said to Cynthia, "Isn't it easy to be with them?" That's what I mean. Some people are just easy to be with. They are trustworthy, congruent. All you need then is time and a place—your backyard or their living room or a booth at the coffee shop.

Other than having good times together, what are some additional benefits of this type of couple-to-couple friendship?

There is one very important benefit that drives couples together and holds them together: There is wisdom to be gained from another set of minds and people who come from differing backgrounds—friends who have another frame of reference. Let's say this other couple was raised on a farm, and you weren't. Or one of them grew up in a broken home, and you didn't. They have learned and grown through the things they have experienced, and you can benefit from their contrasting backgrounds. And, in the same way, your experiences can help them.

All marriages hit a hard spot and you wonder, "Is this the end? Are we at the point of no return?" Spending time with another couple creates more distance between you and the point of losing hope. You think, "We've had some tough times, but not like they've had. They went through a bankruptcy and they made it."

You just naturally want to be with people like that, and when all those givens are in place, you're free to be vulnerable with them.

I like your idea of finding a "like-souled" couple to spend time with. But how do you go about finding such a couple?

As Shakespeare would say, "Ah, there's the rub..." People aren't running around wearing a sign that says: "We're a like-souled couple. Be our friend!"

But first things first. Couples who really want to have this type of friendship with another couple will be praying about it—and I'm not throwing this in because it sounds pious. If you have just moved to a new area, for example, you might ask God to help you find somebody in your neighborhood. When our daughter and her husband moved to Solvang, California, they met a couple in a nearby town. And it wasn't long before they got involved in several social gatherings.

Another strategy is simply to keep your eyes and ears open. One of our sons has been involved in a men's accountability group. Some of the men in the group were friends of his before he got married. They've been meeting together for more than a decade, and they've really grown with each other. In the process, our son and his wife have gotten to know two or three couples they get together with socially.

You should look around at your Sunday School class or at adult fellow-ships. When I was pastor of First Evangelical Free Church, we encour-aged our adult fellowships not to be preaching services. Instead, we kept them smaller so people could get to know one another. When you're in that kind of setting, you begin to notice one or two other couples who show an interest in the same things you enjoy, or who have a sense of humor that's like yours. Or maybe you find out they have children the same ages as yours.

Once you identify those couples, what do you do?

You could invite them over for dinner or a game night, and as you get to know them you'll see if God starts to link heart with heart. You'll find out if you like the same things. It may be music or movies. It may be a hobby that you do in your spare time or the way you raise your kids. Or it could be that you've all gone through some of the same battles. Basically, you find out whether you think alike.

If you find a good number of similarities, you start looking for ways to link up. Maybe you start sitting next to them during adult fellowships, and after church you go to lunch together. If things keep going well, you can approach them directly. Just tell them, "We like the way you think, and frankly we need you as friends. Would you like to get together once a week or so?"

Is it more important to develop a "like-souled" friendship on a couple-to-couple basis, or for a husband to seek out a male friend and a wife to seek out a woman to be friends with?

That depends. In a few instances, it might be more important to develop individual friendships. Let's say a woman is going through a depression but she doesn't need professional counseling, she just needs a good friend to talk to. And let's say her husband is fulfilled in his work—he's got friends at the office that he loves to be with. But she's home all day with young children. She really needs a close friend right now.

Or, to look at it the other way, a husband may be out of work and his wife has a good job. Maybe he desperately needs a friend who can help him get through this tough time. Individual friendships may be a greater need right then than a couple-to-couple friendship.

But unless there's a dire need for one spouse to develop an individual friendship, couples really need to seek out the nurturing that other couples can provide. And often, individual friendships will grow out of couple-to-couple friendships. But let me add here, it doesn't work for the man to develop a friendship with the woman in the other couple, or vice-versa. I've seen those friendships lead to a very unfortunate set of incidents, including the break-up of a marriage.

Let's say two couples have been getting together to talk about spiritual growth and mutual accountability. In the past, you have written about the need to help others grow without forcing them into your own personal mold. How should a couple-to-couple accountability relationship operate?

You're talking about a relationship where the friends have the grace to allow one another to be the person God created them to be. Four things characterize that type of friendship.

First, there is caring without controlling. For example, Cynthia and I would never whip out a clipboard to check up on why our friends missed church last Sunday. If we did call them, it wouldn't be because we thought they should have been in church. Instead, we'd call because we care about them and are wondering if someone in the family is sick or facing some battle. That's what it means to care for someone without trying to control them.

Second, there is friendship without manipulation. This is a little broader than what I just described. You develop a relationship with another couple because you want to be their friends, and there is no hidden agenda. You don't become their friends and then try to sell them insurance or a long-distance service.

Third, spending time together is an invitation, not an obligation. True friends understand that they're always free to say "no." If Cynthia and I invite another couple over for a cookout, it's just an invitation. They aren't obligated to come. And if they can't make it, we don't expect them to give us nine reasons why. Furthermore, we don't expect to receive an invitation from them in a few weeks.

Finally, you can avoid legalism if you allow one another to be painfully honest. This gets back to the need for vulnerability. You can tell your friends, "You know, I loved the Lord a lot more last year than I do this year." And your friends aren't thinking, "We had a feeling he didn't really love Christ like we do!" You don't have that happening among couples who really care about each other. Instead, a friend will respond, "I've had that happen in my life. Three years ago I went through a long dry spell in my spiritual life."

But isn't there a balance between totally empathizing with a friend's struggles and challenging him or her to face up to issues that need to be addressed?

Yes, in most cases you need to do a little of both. If you're a true friend, you won't take a totally hands-off approach when someone shares their pain with you. You don't watch a friend playing in traffic and merely tell him: "Well, enjoy getting hit by that truck. I'll come visit you in the hospital." Instead, you care enough to confront the person when that is what's needed. But you never do it in an attacking manner.

Let's say Couple A feel that their friends, Couple B, need to be exhorted concerning a violation of a clear biblical teaching. How can they do that without coming across as legalistic or self-righteous?

Couple A need to be sure they're not getting bent out of shape just because Couple B went out and violated some personal conviction of theirs. It has to be behavior that runs counter to a clear biblical absolute. We don't exhort another couple simply because they violated our personal preferences on some matter.

Let's say it was a lot worse than an instance of violating someone's personal preference.

If Couple B did violate a clear biblical teaching, Couple A should use the art of conversation to broach the subject. They could say something like, "We care about you and we love you too much to just ignore what's happening. Maybe you have a blind spot in this area." Then they could share one of their own blind spots. That shows they realize we're all human.

When I recommend using the art of conversation, I mean conversation that is free from intense Bible quoting and dogmatic preaching. It helps tear down the defenses when you use more of a personal approach. Speak in a soft tone, and speak with compassion and true understanding. Admit your own imperfections and the difficulties in your own life. Then proceed with a short parable or word picture to set the stage for what you want to say: "When I was unaware of my own blind spot, and a friend pointed a few things out to me, I was grateful because he cared enough to tell me."

State your concerns briefly, specifically, and without relying on hearsay. And assure the couple that this conversation will be kept completely confidential. You should communicate a simple message: "Danger is on the way! Perilous things could occur." Just like a young child who is walking into the street, we wouldn't say, "God bless you, Sweetheart! We've raised you as best we can for five years." No, you'd grab the child and pull him back and then show him you love him. While he's crying over your immediate jolt, you're holding him close. A reading of Galatians 6:1-2 will help prepare anyone who feels led to help another person—or a couple—who is in a perilous situation.

A young child wandering into the street is a great illustration of imminent danger. But how does it apply to a situation in which one couple is warning another couple of the impending peril of their behavior?

Just as you would comfort a child, go ahead and hug the other couple. It will help affirm that you are in this with them through the long haul. Maybe words like, "Even if you don't change, we're not going to stop loving you. We still want to spend time with you. If there's ever a time you want to talk about it again, let's talk."

Then leave the results up to God. You don't have to tell them twice, and you don't have to follow up with a phone call next week.

I'll use my own marriage as an example. Cynthia doesn't have to yell to get my attention. On the contrary. If she talks seriously, very quietly, and with tears, I'm sunk—she's got me. Because that's when I realize I've hurt her.

Just recently something like this happened. I had done something, inadvertently, that hurt her deeply. She sat at the table and cried her heart out. She spoke in almost inaudible tones so that I had to listen real closely to hear what she was saying. And I assure you, it was the "reproof of the month" for me.

I told Cynthia in all genuineness of my sorrow, and I said, "I will not do that again. You have my word on it. And if I slip and do this again, I want you to tell me right away that I'm doing it." Her reproof was conveyed very effectively, and it was done out of affection and caring. It really got my attention!

We've talked a lot about situations that had successful outcomes. What about the times when couples seek friendships with other couples and it just doesn't work out?

We need to realize that even after giving it our best shot, sometimes a couple-to-couple friendship just isn't going anywhere. Or it might work for a year or two and then circumstances change and the relationship dissolves.

You might grow out of one kind of relationship and find that you need to grow into another. Or in the process of growing you might discover that you and the other couple aren't moving in the same direction anymore.

Once you establish a low-key accountability relationship with another couple, you shouldn't feel that you have to keep it up 365 days a year for the next decade to be pleasing to God. The benefits of friendship are great. And those benefits are never wasted, even when the friendship doesn't last the rest of your life.

Jerry and Mary White

Being Friends

How to be each other's friend. How to identify and guard against the hidden dangers of outside friendships.

Interviewed by Charette Barta

*I*n the preceding interview, Charles Swindoll emphasized the importance of couples developing close outside friendships. But for most of us, friendship remains somewhat of a mystery. Jerry and Mary White were good friends in college before they were married. Today, after thirty-eight years as husband and wife, the warmth and mutual respect that mark the best friendships are evident in their relationship.

Jerry is president and chief executive officer of The Navigators, a disciple-making ministry with more than 3,600 staff members working in 102 countries. Before joining the Navigators staff in 1973, he was an associate professor of astronautics at the U.S. Air Force Academy and worked as a mission controller at Cape Kennedy during the height of the space program. Mary, who earned a degree in English literature while raising their four children, has co-authored a number of books with Jerry, including *Friends and Friendship* (NavPress).

We asked the Whites to explain how couples can draw closer to one another as friends, and how to reach out in friendship to others.

What prompted you to write a book together on the topic of friendship?

Jerry: After one of our moves, we wondered who would keep in touch with us. We also wondered who we would keep in touch with. As we thought about friendships, we realized that people have a lot of acquaintances. But to a large extent, these acquaintances weren't friends because they wanted to be—they just needed to function together on a committee or in a group at church. That's when we started investigating the basis of real friendship.

What did you discover?

Mary: We found a common need for openness, vulnerability, and being a real person—a willingness to share "life to life," holding nothing back, even through conflict. We had to learn that in our marriage.

Was it difficult?

Mary: Oh, yes! It took a long time before we discovered the real person behind our idea of the other person. The thing that helped most was time together to develop trust. We knew each other almost two years before we were married, but much of our time was spent with other people. That was good preparation for missionary service, but not for discovering each other.

Do you think couples get so busy in shared ministry to others that it becomes a shield against really getting to know each other?

Mary: It does if there's an unwillingness to be open. But at the same time, if there's not a willingness to be open, anything can be used as a shield: children, time, work. To be open, we have to be willing to show our weaknesses. Jerry and I have tried to be sensitive to that. We tell each other, "If you see anything in my life that needs to be corrected, do it."

What is a healthy and loving way to correct your spouse?

Mary: Timing is important. Don't do it in the heat of the moment. Also, if it's just one incident, let it go. But if you see a pattern of unhealthy behavior emerging over a period of time, then you should lovingly speak to your spouse.

How important has friendship been in your marriage?

Jerry: It's important to develop a close friendship before marriage. One of the greatest hindrances to marriage and friendship in the first ten years is that the initial relationship was developed on the wrong basis. For most couples it grows too quickly into a physical—not necessarily immoral—

relationship carried on through hormones rather than intellect and mutual interests.

How does the friendship that you share enhance your marriage?

Mary: We are very committed to our marriage, and we verbalize that commitment often. We're also committed to continuing to develop our friendship, to devoting time to understand how the other is thinking and feeling. There is a trust and mutual commitment that undergird that kind of friendship, but it takes time and conscious planning.

Jerry: The commitment was there the first years of our marriage, but the building of the friendship wasn't. For at least ten years our activity cycle was so intense it simply didn't give us time to be with each other. When you have a number of small children and not much money, it's hard to get time alone. But that can become an excuse for not spending time together.

How can couples with no time to spare tend to friendships? It can be a real frustration.

Mary: If you have children, include them in your activities. And when you have people over, keep things simple. There's nothing wrong with ordering pizza. Think of a special occasion you remember from ten years ago. Do you remember what you ate? Probably not.

Jerry and I wanted to expose our kids to as many godly people as possible, so we always had missionaries and others in our home. You have to have a mind-set that you're not going to have perfection. We used to have "slumber parties" with our friends—we'd play games together, and the kids would sleep in sleeping bags on the floor. Once we had a supper of scrambled eggs and bacon, and the next morning we had cereal. You really get to know your friends that way!

What do the two of you do for fun?

Mary: We like to get away for weekends. We both like to read, and we read aloud to each other from our personal reading—especially funny stories. We both participate in sports, such as cross-country skiing. Every friendship needs humor and fun.

Do men and women have different approaches to friendship?

Mary: I have a need and personal preference for fewer and deeper relationships while Jerry can maintain more. I think it's a matter of temperament.

Jerry: I'm willing to live with more relationships that have less depth. Generally, it is more common for the woman to have more friendships than the man. Men, particularly when they grow older, tend to have fewer but not necessarily deeper relationships.

What are the primary benefits of couple-to-couple friendships?

Jerry: Married couples need to be accountable to someone. Proverbs 27:6 says, "Faithful are the wounds of a friend," and in verse 17 it says, "Iron sharpeneth iron; so a man sharpeneth the countenance of his friend" (KJV). You need people who will look out for you and call you to account when your life doesn't match your mouth.

Mary: That kind of friendship takes time to develop. And because people are so mobile, many times they just don't make the effort for that to happen.

What are the dangers associated with that type of accountability?

Jerry: If you open up to a friend and have that person betray your confidence, the result often is that you become even more closed around others.

Can friendships threaten a marriage?

Jerry: This usually happens when spouses start to live very separate existences, when one partner is going off and enjoying a lot of growth and the other is left behind.

Mary: Or there are those outside friendships that become so strong that the one who is left out feels no real access to the life of his or her mate. The time involved, the intellectual stimulation, the spiritual communication goes to someone other than the spouse.

How do you feel about friendships with the opposite sex—say, when you're serving together on a committee?

Mary: There needs to be a strong guard kept up that it's friendship only. It takes a godly spirit to keep it pure.

Jerry: When problems in the marriage are not solved, they will often be expressed in those relationships where men and women want someone to listen to them and understand them. And when they find someone outside the marriage who does listen and understand, it always raises a danger flag.

What are some other threats to friendship?

Mary: We shouldn't be exclusive in our friendships with our partners. A marriage is strengthened when you have other strong, supportive friendships in your lives. I'm concerned about a tendency I have seen to turning inward toward one's own marriage relationship and family.

Why has this developed?

Mary: One reason might be the pressure of our pace today. Another might be the tremendous emphasis on the family in Christian literature, broadcasting, and even in the churches. Certainly the family is our most important commitment, but it can be enriched by other relationships.

When we were ministering with cadets at the Air Force Academy, we had young children. We often discussed whether this ministry was drawing attention away from our children—depriving them—and giving it to others. Yet one of our children's biggest complaints when we left the academy was that we no longer had these young men in our home.

How can couples who want to build a closer friendship with each other and with others go about it?

Mary: You start by making sure both of you are committed to the friendship. And praying together is important. Couples should consider what kinds of interests they could pursue together. Another idea would be to set specific times to talk, and then be faithful to using that time for each other. If necessary, simplify your lifestyle to give time to one another.

A key element is understanding, allowing people to be who they are. It may be as simple as one being a night person and the other a morning person. It's important to allow the person to live within the framework of his or her own personality.

As you try to understand better, study your partner to see what his or her needs are. I learned this from a friend who said, "Study your kids." For years I would sit with pencil and paper, look at their needs and their strengths, and think, "How can I help in these areas?" Gradually, this study drifted over to my relationship with Jerry.

Do you have non-Christian friends?

Mary: We do have some non-Christians we spend time with. We're excited about them as friends—not just as potential believers. We find that evangelism in friendship takes longer as we get older; it takes longer to build the trust. One couple we knew took fifteen years before they received Christ. It takes time for the Holy Spirit to work.

How can we best model Christ to non-Christian friends?

Mary: Be yourself. I have a gifted relative who has taught me a lot, even though our lives have taken different paths. With her, I'm very natural about my relationship with the Lord. I had a blood pressure problem, and I casually told her I was praying about it. Then the doctors found the reason and were able to correct it. It's important not to make non-Christians feel that you're making a project out of them. They resent that, and rightly so.

SOMETHING TO TALK ABOUT

1. Charles Swindoll points out that true friendship requires vulnerability. How good are we at being vulnerable with each other, and also with our friends?
2. A couple's friendship needs change over time. What do we need most in our friendships at this stage of life?
3. What types of friendships are we currently lacking (man to man, woman to woman, couple to couple)?
4. What couple do we feel the most comfortable being around? What can we do within the next two weeks to begin developing a deeper friendship with them?
5. Mary and Jerry White stress the importance of being friends with your spouse. On a scale of one to ten, how would each of us rate the friendship aspect of our marriage?
6. When have we been successful at "correcting" each other? What did we do that worked well?
7. Has a friend ever made either of us feel threatened? If so, why did we feel that way?

8. Would either of us characterize any of our outside friendships as unhealthy? If so, in what way? What should we do to correct the problem?

Chapter Four

SUCCESSFUL SEX

Unfulfilling Sex
Dr. Clifford and Joyce Penner

Inadequate Sex
Mary Ann Mayo

Appropriate Sex
Stanton L. Jones

Dr. Clifford and Joyce Penner

Unfulfilling Sex

Expectations of marital sex. Messages about sex learned in childhood. The aftereffects of premarital sexual involvement.

Interviewed by Gregg Lewis

When a man and woman get married, they come into it with anticipations and expectations of their sexual relationship. The particulars vary, but, according to sexual therapists Clifford and Joyce Penner, all couples expect that marital sex will be, in a word, "great."

Unfortunately, many couples are disappointed. Whether they entered marriage as virgins or with prior experience, they find that marital sex doesn't seem to be as much fun as they had expected. A number of factors—including premarital sexual experiences, unrealistic expectations, and the messages a person received as a child—can combine to work against sexual fulfillment.

We asked the Penners, co-authors of seven books, including *The Gift of Sex* and *Restoring the Pleasure* (both published by Word) and *52 Ways to Have Fun, Fantastic Sex* (Thomas Nelson), to explain what couples can do to prevent or correct feelings of disappointment.

Among all the factors that affect a couple's sexual adjustment, what have you found to be the biggest hindrances in the early years of marriage?

Joyce: Two of the most frequent are inaccurate expectations and a lack of knowledge. Too many couples enter marriage with expectations based not on reality, but on the media's portrayal of romantic relationships. They have false expectations as to what the male role is, what the female role is. What they should get out of their sexual relationship and what they won't. What needs their sex life will and won't meet.

A lack of knowledge fits right in with these false expectations. Lack of knowledge as to how their bodies function and how to talk about it. Not knowing what's going on physically and emotionally in a sexual experience. What's normal and what isn't.

People come to marriage with many shoulds and shouldn'ts, and with myths about the sexual relationship. Plus, they don't understand there's a transition from the feelings you experience when you desire someone and can't have them, because you're not yet married, to the feelings you experience when you can have each other sexually all the time. It doesn't mean sexual attraction has lessened. But it can feel less powerful because you don't have all the excitement, adrenalin, and energy that goes with desiring something you can't have.

It seems odd that couples would still suffer from so much ignorance of sexual matters, given the many books, tapes, and other resources that are available. Also, aren't couples in general more sexually involved before marriage than they were a few generations ago?

Cliff: Yes. Nevertheless, the transition from premarital sexual contact—whatever the level of involvement might have been—to marital sex can be difficult. If a husband and wife were very involved before marriage, and that involvement contradicted their moral standards, they will probably have a sense of risk or guilt connected with sexual activity. Because there isn't risk or guilt in marriage, there's a letdown. The feelings of excitement that came with risk and guilt became an expected, essential part of the sexual experience.

Joyce: They associate those feelings of the adrenalin rush with being in love. But without the risk and guilt, they think, "Oh no! I must have made a mistake. I'm no longer in love." They have to be taught that the change in feelings is not a loss of love, but can actually lead to greater love and intimacy.

Then, because they've learned to connect intense sexual feelings with a feeling of risk or guilt, these people may be easily drawn into a new relationship with someone outside their marriage. If that begins to happen, the adrenalin excitement returns and it "confirms" that they married the wrong person and have now found their "real" love. Yet those feelings have nothing to do with love, intimacy, or a fulfilling sexual relationship. They have to do with the intense, adrenalin-fueled risk and guilt they have paired with sex.

What about couples who *weren't* sexually involved before they got married?

Cliff: If couples had very limited physical contact in the dating process, they may come into marriage with an expectation that because of their restraint, God is going to bless them with a wonderfully fulfilling sex life from the start. And they can be massively let down.

So you're saying that while some couples get false expectations from the media or from previous sexual experience, others get false expectations from adhering to Christian moral teachings?

Joyce: Many couples have gotten the idea that to obey God's commands by not becoming sexually active before marriage insures sexual satisfaction after marriage. But, in fact, those two factors don't automatically go together.

Cliff: The Scriptures teach that sexual intercourse is something God designed exclusively for marriage. That should be obeyed because it means being faithful to God, not because it will automatically make sex better in marriage. Obeying God's command doesn't come with a guarantee.

Everyone enters marriage with his or her personal baggage. Have you found more problems among people who had an overly strict upbringing or, at the other extreme, who had a promiscuous sexual history?

Joyce: Both can create problems. Some young couples come to us who have been taught not to do anything physical before marriage—no kissing or hugging, nothing. To control their behaviors, they totally shut down their sexual feelings—sometimes for years. Then they get married and those feelings don't suddenly come alive. They thought it would be so wonderful because they were obedient to what they believed were God's rules.

Cliff: In a home where nudity was totally shunned, for example, a person can come to marriage with an unhealthy view about sex and the human body. But, to cite the other extreme, the lack of privacy in a home—with the exploitation of nudity around the house—can cause incredible violation. Either extreme causes distortion.

Joyce: Those who live a promiscuous life come to marriage with so much confusion about the sexual relationship that they can't enjoy it within the confines of marriage. On the other hand, those who learned that the body was to be shunned and shamed cannot validate God's beautiful creation or enjoy freely giving themselves to one another.

It seems that even among Christians the old taboos against sex before marriage are eroding. However, there seems to be a continued stigma connected to adultery after one is married. Have you found that to be true in your counseling?

Joyce: It's absolutely true. Yet there is confusion about sex before marriage. Often, the couple's beliefs don't match their practice.

Cliff: For example, we were teaching twenty-three couples in a premarital class at an evangelical church. In our first session we gave them a survey asking how many had experienced sexual intercourse. All but two of the couples reported current or prior sexual involvement. So in our second session we spoke as if we were talking to people who were sexually experienced. Yet a number of the couples were offended that we would talk as if they had had sex.

Joyce: That seems a strange reaction, but it fits with what we've seen: Many times Christian couples have become sexually involved, but not intentionally. They never decide to have intercourse. They haven't discussed it; in fact they say they don't want to have intercourse. They believe it would be wrong to plan it, but they are constantly having sex "by accident."

Cliff: They put themselves in situations where they go away for weekends, spend time alone in each other's apartments, and so on. Then, SURPRISE, they find themselves having sex. Even though they believe they should save sexual intercourse for marriage, they have not actively decided how to adhere to that teaching. So they let sex happen to them. They don't distinguish between their desires, which are God-given, and their actions, which are their responsibility to control.

Young married couples with that kind of past experience would be prime candidates for the adjustment problem you mentioned earlier—a lot of guilt associated with the experience of sex.

Joyce: Right. Plus they have often developed unhealthy patterns of relating sexually. They haven't had the freedom that comes with the commitment of marriage to enjoy the pleasure of each other's bodies, which leads to a good sexual experience.

Cliff: They've tried to hold back the positive feelings while proceeding to do something they didn't feel right about doing.

Joyce: So, after marriage, they need to relearn how to make love. Even though they've been having sex, they don't have the correct attitudes, conditions, or skills necessary for truly satisfying sex. They need to learn to give and receive pleasure for the sake of pleasure. They need to learn to enjoy skin-to-skin contact, touch and sensation—without the conflict of those old, previously associated feelings. They need to invite God into the delight of each other's bodies.

Cliff: They need to learn a new way of connecting that is pleasure-driven, to replace the pattern they brought into their marriage that was adrenalin-driven. We try to teach couples how to be intimate, and in that intimacy how to enjoy giving and receiving pleasure. That's the new pathway to establishing long-lasting love, passion, and intimacy in marriage.

What steps do you suggest for couples who need help?

Cliff: They could start with self-help. There are good instructional books available, like our books *The Gift of Sex* and *Restoring the Pleasure*, with step-by-step instructions for overcoming problems. We find it makes a great difference if couples will read aloud together and then proceed with the exercises.

Joyce: If they decide they need professional help, they should ask someone they trust—a minister or physician—for the name of a trained sexual therapist. Ask the therapist how he or she proceeds in dealing with their particular problem. And compare that therapist's approach with that of our books to see if the suggested therapy fits with accepted practice.

Mary Ann Mayo

Inadequate Sex

The many causes of Inhibited Sexual Desire, and ways to restore sexual passion.

Interviewed by Janis Long Harris

*E*arlier in this chapter, Clifford and Joyce Penner identified premarital sexual experiences as one possible cause of sexual adjustment problems in marriage. But that doesn't explain why more and more couples are using their bedrooms just for sleeping.

In an era when American society places such a heavy (many would say disproportionate) emphasis on the importance of a good sex life, it's ironic that counselors are hearing so many couples complain of a lack of interest in sex. We asked Mary Ann Mayo, an author, counselor, and health educator, about the causes of Inhibited Sexual Desire, or ISD. Mayo is a columnist for *Virtue* magazine and the author of eight books, including *In the Beginning* and *God's Good Gift* (Zondervan) and *The Menopause Manager* (Revell).

In this interview, she explains what couples can do about Inhibited Sexual Desire.

What distinguishes Inhibited Sexual Desire from a naturally low sex drive?

ISD usually refers to someone who has had a fairly well-adjusted sex life in the past, but who now has difficulty feeling excited about making love. It becomes a problem when that person's spouse wants a more enthusiastic response to sex. That's what usually brings people into counseling for sexual problems.

But don't most couples notice a difference in how often they want sex?

I'm not talking about a simple frequency problem. Everyone is different as far as their sexual appetite is concerned. A difference in sexual appetite requires a lot of negotiation. It means saying something to the effect of, "I don't feel like having intercourse tonight, but what can I do for you to let you know I care?"

Someone with ISD is more likely to say, "I'm just not interested." They can't seem to tune in to anything that smacks of eroticism, anything that would turn them on. Sometimes they'll say to themselves, perhaps in the morning, "Okay, I'm going to be there for my spouse tonight." But as they get closer to the time to make love, a number of turnoffs may be at work.

What would make a person completely lose interest in sex?

A number of things. For example, you may be thinking positively about your spouse, but when you go to bed, you start thinking about the fact that your paycheck won't cover the cost of groceries this week. Or you might think, "Boy, he has really gained weight," or "Boy, she really has big thighs. What a turnoff." These turnoffs may have some legitimacy, but they are used to shut down any feelings that would lead to sexual intimacy.

Beyond that, work may need to be done about the way the affected person feels about sex. They may need to gain some insight into what kind of messages they received about sexuality as children or as teenagers that they have accepted now that they are adults.

Is this problem more common than it used to be, or is it just getting more attention?

It's becoming more common. When I first started doing counseling for sexual problems, I mainly worked with women who were having difficulty having an orgasm. Then it shifted to men in their fifties coming in with their wives who were saying, "Gee, he's not interested in me anymore."

They weren't understanding the natural aging process. Then there was a definite move toward ISD being the number-one problem.

It's one of the hardest things to treat. With some sexual problems, there's almost a cookbook technique to get things going again. But this is so nebulous. There could be thirty different factors that contribute to it. It could be a relationship problem, a communication problem, a motivation problem, fatigue, messages from the past, unresolved issues in the marriage. All of those factors, or any combination of them, can kill the desire to be sexual.

To what degree is boredom a factor?

Boredom can contribute to it considerably. But if we're bored, we'd rather not say that to our spouse. We'd rather say, "I don't feel like being sexual.""Or we'll stay up really late and make sure we're so tired that we can't be sexual and everybody will see how legitimate it is. If you're tired of always doing the same things sexually, you might not want to tell your spouse, "You're a lousy lover, you always do the same things." So you may say instead, "I don't know what's wrong. I just can't get interested in making love." People are reluctant to talk about their sexual feelings, desires and disappointments.

Who is most likely to be affected by ISD?

We see it often in young, up-and-coming people. But we also see it in mid-life and in every other stage.

Women are more susceptible, from women raising small children to women juggling twenty-six different roles. God made women more relationship-oriented in sexual functioning. The myth is that women don't like sex. That's not true. We're just more affected by external factors. A man can function to a greater extent if the right turn-ons are there. But a woman deals with so many other issues before she can function sexually. She has to be right in the way she feels about her life, right in relationship with her husband. Things have to be going right with the kids and on the job.

That's not to say that men aren't affected. Whenever I speak to groups, I always have a few women who say, "My husband just isn't interested." This problem is devastating for men. The male myth says they're always supposed to be interested in having sex. But, supposedly unlike other men, they're not. Men develop ISD for the same reasons women do:

fatigue, preoccupation, unresolved issues from the past, relationship problems, boredom, not making sex a priority, living life at a fast pace.

Is sexual experience prior to marriage a factor?

It could be, if guilt or unresolved issues are involved. For instance, if previous partners told you you're a lousy lover, either verbally or some other way. Or if you're in a second marriage, there might be a voice in your ear saying, "I don't want to be sexually involved or you'll find out I'm a lousy lover." But more often than not, it's that sex is ranked really, really low on our list of priorities.

What can be done about ISD?

Correcting false thinking is a first step. Examples of people who suffer from faulty thinking are the women who believe "ladies" shouldn't like sex too much. And if she does, she might be seen as vulgar. Or the couple in their sixties who believe they're not supposed to like sex anymore. Or the middle-aged woman who doesn't understand how sexual functioning changes with age. She thinks that, because her husband doesn't get erections as quickly as he used to, that he doesn't love her as much. In counseling situations, we point out these false messages to people and help them correct them. Getting a wife and husband to talk to each other about their concerns and desires is crucial.

And then there has to be a behavioral aspect. It doesn't help to just identify why you're having difficulty. If the problems are really bad, it may mean pulling back completely and beginning a new sexual way of being together, starting a new sexual life together. This may involve putting a ban on intercourse for a while and, instead, just approaching one another, knowing that your actions won't lead to lovemaking. Doing a lot of touching, for example, or giving each other a massage without pressure to have sex. After a husband and wife are comfortable with that over a period of time, then they can move back into a new sexual relationship.

What about things like time pressure, stress, and not getting enough sleep?

We need to evaluate all aspects of our lives. People are living at such a fast pace that they don't have the relaxed body they need for good sexual functioning. A typical scenario is that we go to bed and try to make love at the end of the day, a time when our energy is the lowest, when we've exhausted every other possible activity. Then we go to bed and are supposed to have this high-energy experience.

Also, talking to each other is extremely important. One of the best times to share what you need and what might spice up your sex life is right after you've made love, preferably after a time when things have gone fairly well. It's a good time to say, "You know, I was thinking about how I might get more excited." Or, "I think this would help me get into the mood faster."

For example, a mother with young children might say, "Maybe I could be more responsive if you could sit and hold me for 10 to 15 minutes before we get into the act of love." Sensitivity to her in that way could be a very arousing, erotic thing.

Planning sex is also important. It's funny a wife will put great effort and planning into meal preparation, but we think sex should be spontaneous. It's as if you were to go into the kitchen blindfolded and start taking things off the shelf and say, "Okay, we're going to have a spontaneous meal." It doesn't work that way. You have to plan for it, set an atmosphere for it. The same is true of sex, but we think that, without energy or planning, we can get into bed when we're the most tired and have wonderfully fulfilled sex. If we want wonderful sex, we have to plan for it and then communicate to our spouse what we think is wonderful.

At what point should a couple get some counseling?

If the problem has gone on for longer than six months, if you've really tried and nothing is working, it's a good time to see a counselor. If there's no intervention, frequently people just give up on sex. I hate to put numbers out there, because there are people who have great sex lives without making love frequently. But Joseph LoPiccolo, who is outstanding in the field of sexual counseling, uses the following guidelines to determine if a couple qualifies for counseling: If they're under forty-five and have sex less than once every two weeks, or over forty-five and have sex less than once a month, they are accepted for treatment.

How does Christian faith relate to the problem of ISD?

We are commanded in 1 Corinthians to be sexually intimate with our spouse. In essence, we're sinning when we choose not to be sexually involved. The only exceptions are those times when we agree together to abstain, for limited periods, in order to pray or fast. We could also make an exception for those times when one or both spouses is ill. But basically, married couples are to have a sexual existence. It's part of what marriage is meant to be.

It's interesting that the Bible includes an illustration of what could be ISD—or perhaps a frequency problem—and offers a solution. In Song of Songs, when Solomon comes to his bride at night, she says, "Go away." Solomon gives her a blessing and a present and tells her how wonderful she is to him. And then the woman allows herself to think of him in erotic ways and does a dance for him, wearing a see-through negligee, makeup, and jewelry.

The Bible teaches that each spouse reaches out to the other in ways that they find appealing. There's a message here for us. For women, it's getting in touch with their physical, sensuous side—allowing that to come out. For men, it's getting in touch with the romantic and verbal side, honoring and loving their wife and letting her know it.

When we look at the Song of Songs, we see the joy we're supposed to find in one another. That's the model we have to go by—not one of drudgery, but pleasure, joy and anticipation. If our sexual life isn't like that, we need to do something about it.

Stanton L. Jones

Appropriate Sex

When does legitimate experimentation cross the line into sexual immorality?

Interviewed by Ron R. Lee

Ask a group of marriage counselors what their clients struggle with when it comes to sex, and you'll hear the same issues coming up again and again: Why doesn't my wife (or husband) want to have sex more often?

Why isn't our sex life as fulfilling as it used to be? How much experimenting can we do without engaging in something the Bible forbids?

If we get our sex life straightened out, will it get our marriage back on track?

To find answers to these and other questions, I asked clinical psychologist Stanton Jones what he thought. Jones and his wife, Brenna, are the co-authors of *How and When to Tell Your Kids about Sex* and a four-book series for sex education in the family called *God's Design for Sex* (all published by NavPress).

As a counselor, Jones has seen the damage that is done when couples make false assumptions about sex. In this interview, he explains why more and better sex won't guarantee marital happiness.

What are the biggest obstacles that prevent couples from achieving sexual fulfillment?

The primary obstacles are two false assumptions that many people make: that sex can't become any better than it already is, and the other extreme—that sex ought to be perfect. Anyone who's looking for perfect sex will be disappointed. Sometimes the solution to sexual dissatisfaction is to grow up and realize that some of your hopes and expectations were naive, distorted or selfish. It's only after you accept the fact that you, your spouse and your marriage are imperfect that God can give you hope—and help—for becoming better than you are today.

So there's plenty of room for improvement, as long as couples aren't seeking perfection. Why do people expect so much from sex?

Too many couples have bought into the illusion that developing a great sexual relationship is the make-or-break issue for their marriages. People think sex should be a perfectly loving, beautiful, expressive experience, forgetting that it's a very human experience that invites all kinds of miscues. Good sex is important, but it's not the key to a good marriage.

Another false assumption is that sex comes naturally and doesn't require practice, effort, and learning. When I got married, I thought sex would be great right from the get-go. It was inconceivable to me that there was learning involved.

But why wouldn't we need to learn how to have a good sex life? You'd never walk onto a tennis court and expect to play Andre Agassi to a standstill in your first match. And yet in the area of sexuality we expect to completely satisfy our mate's every whim without first having developed and practiced the necessary skills.

The truth is, sex can become better as we learn to love each other more effectively. That's what makes the idea that "sex can never get any better" false. If you approach sex with the desire to learn about yourself and your spouse, and you're willing to devote the time and effort, that gives you ground for communicating.

If a husband and wife are dissatisfied with their sex life, how can they start talking about it?

By examining why they are unhappy. As a culture, Americans are infected with greed. And greed influences the area of sexuality just as it does materialism. The magazine headlines in the grocery store check-out line aren't limited to "Get rich quick." They also promise, "You can have the super orgasmic peak sexual experience every day!" Sexual greed makes us believe sex should be perfectly fulfilling—and if it's not more exciting with every passing week then something's wrong.

Sexual greed is also fueled by pornography, which sells sex from the standpoint of a male fantasy. Men who look at pornography develop a distorted understanding of female sexuality and end up feeling dissatisfied because their sex life bears no resemblance to what they've seen portrayed in pornography. So before they talk, spouses need to ask themselves, "Am I unhappy with sex because I'm greedy—wanting even more when what we already have is actually quite good?"

Are there any valid reasons to feel dissatisfied?

Sure. Many people suffer from various forms of sexual dysfunction, and they need to seek appropriate treatment. But beyond that, we all reach the point where things get stale. If a man and woman make love two or three times a week, after ten years of marriage they will have had more than 1,000 sexual experiences. It's not uncommon for couples to hit a plateau where sex becomes brief and perfunctory.

Let's say Beth and Nick have been married eight years. Nick's life follows a predictable routine. He comes home from work, eats dinner, plays with the kids, watches TV, and then goes to bed at 10:30 or 11. Beth knows that every few nights Nick is going to roll over and kiss her on the ear. It's always the same signal, and seven minutes later everything's over. Nick is lying on his side snoring, and Beth is left unsatisfied once again.

Actually, Nick's not happy with this arrangement either. He wonders why Beth always seems too tired for sex; and he can't understand why she just lies there on the few occasions when they do make love.

Sounds like Nick's a clod.

He may be, but it's also possible that he's just an uninformed husband. Too many man fail to understand that their wives view sex in the context of the entire relationship. Women link their sexuality with where they're at emotionally and relationally. If a woman is lonely for communication, romance, and nonsexual intimacy, she'll feel emotionally disconnected from her husband. And she won't be all that interested in sex.

Men are more fragmented in their experience of sexuality. They are quickly stirred up. If a guy gets the urge, he's ready for sex—even if he and his wife just had an argument.

What hope is there for couples such as Beth and Nick?

Nothing is going to change until they start talking. And when they do talk, they need to listen carefully and take each other's concerns seriously.

Let's say Beth initiates the discussion. What's the best way to introduce the subject?

She should avoid approaching it with a spirit of resentment: "I'm not getting what I want. Why can't you change?" Instead, she should put it in the context of what she hopes for their relationship: "Nick, I don't feel our sex life is all it could be, and I know I'm partly responsible. We've gotten into a rut. What can we do differently to help us both feel more satisfied? I'm willing to change, and I hope you are, too."

Her own willingness to change tells Nick he's not going to be judged on how well he "measures up" to his wife's suggestions.

Let's say Nick would like to experiment with some new approaches to sex, and Beth is willing to consider them. How can they determine what's permissible?

Many sexual practices that are commonly shunned really don't need to be, but there are lots of things that clearly violate biblical morality. Sex is meant to unite a husband and wife into one flesh. That means that while physical pleasure is important, it isn't the primary reason God created sex. The sexual relationship is meant to build up and enrich your marriage.

Since my sexual relationship with my wife is meant to be a personal encounter, any experimentation needs to be something that is "transparent," to use a metaphor. It should provide a window that allows me to see my mate clearly and emphasizes my love for her and her alone. We need to exclude anything that is "opaque," things that obscure our view of each other and make it easier to focus on ourselves.

What types of experimentation would tend to make us focus on ourselves?

One example would be using erotic materials to enhance sexual pleasure. How can a couple engage in foreplay while watching a video of other people having sex and expect that to draw them together? That is really drawing other people into your relationship and it obscures, rather than enhances, your view of your spouse.

Similarly, it's wrong to act out immoral scenarios. I've heard of couples play-acting that the husband has been arrested by a woman police officer who's into bondage. She puts him in handcuffs and ties him to the bed—things like that. If I'm doing that, am I really focused on a meaningful encounter with my wife or am I into a personal encounter with my fantasy? That sort of thing is not conducive to what sex is meant to be—to unite me with my wife. People can create a thirst for more and bigger thrills and desensitize themselves to practices they shouldn't be engaging in.

So anything beyond the standard missionary position in a dark room is taboo?

Not at all. Why should couples remain locked in the same old patterns? Assuming, for instance, that privacy can be assured while having sex in the back yard, why not give it a try? Also, flattering lingerie, soft lights, scented body oil, and beautiful music all enhance lovemaking. They are transparent windows—you see through those things to your partner. It's really a judgment call as to whether the techniques you're using help you focus on your mate or encourage you to concentrate only on yourself.

How do you feel about sexual fantasy? Is it strictly off-limits?

If we understand fantasy as the use of our creative imagination and memory, then not all fantasy is bad. One of the causes of low sexual desire can be a person's inability to think creatively about his or her sexual relationship. One type of fantasy is simply using your imagination to create scenarios about how your sexual relationship might be improved.

Part of "getting in the mood" involves thinking about what pleases you about your spouse. Let's get back to Nick and Beth. While Nick was at work one day, he was thinking about making love to Beth. He walked in the door that night with a smile on his face and a warm, rather than an obligatory, hug for his wife. Then he said, "You know, I was sitting at my computer today thinking about how much fun we had at the beach last month." Beth was pleased that Nick had been thinking about her. It fed her need for emotional intimacy, and it was the sort of thing that led to enjoyable lovemaking.

That's a pretty positive view of fantasy. What about its dark side?

Clearly there is bad fantasy, including mental images of having sex with people other than your mate. If you are dwelling on something that would be wrong to do in real life, it's wrong to fantasize it—no matter how much extra sexual spark or excitement it adds.

Let's say a couple feel their sex life is fine when they get around to it, but they're convinced everyone else is having more sex than they are. What is a healthy rate of sexual frequency?

Statistical averages really aren't that helpful. If the national average for people in their forties is twice a week, that means a survey showed that for every couple who had sex four times there was another couple who didn't have sex at all. Averages are made up of people at all different frequencies. The important question is, "Do you view sex as a God-given blessing that is a gift and blessing to your marriage?"

If couples see lack of frequency as a problem, why don't they just start having more sex?

Many couples aren't investing the necessary time and effort. Most people think good sex occurs spontaneously. But you need to plan for spontaneity. If a husband and wife fall into bed exhausted night after night expecting something spontaneous to happen, it just ain't gonna happen. But if they get to bed at a decent hour when they've still got some energy left, it gives "spontaneity" a chance.

So couples need to work at sex, be willing to change, and not expect sex to be the answer to the meaning of life. Does that about cover it?

One last thing. God created sex, but there are a lot of Christians who don't receive the gift of their own sexuality with gratitude. We have a hard time praying, "Thank you, Lord, for giving me this body. Thank you for giving me my partner's body. Thank you for giving us the opportunity to celebrate our sexual relationship." That spirit of celebration and gratitude for what God has given us is what Paul urges in 1 Timothy 4:1-5. That's an essential element in finding sexual happiness.

SOMETHING TO TALK ABOUT

1. Clifford and Joyce Penner identify several adjustments that take place early in marriage. How would we describe our sex life as newlyweds?

2. What experiences before marriage have had the greatest impact on our lovemaking? How have those experiences affected our level of sexual satisfaction?

3. How has our sex life improved since the early days of our marriage? What brought about those positive changes?

4. Mary Ann Mayo notes that couples have differing preferences on the frequency of sex. What would each of us say is an ideal— but reasonable—frequency for lovemaking? If our answers differ greatly, what would be a mutually acceptable compromise?

5. Does either of us have an exceedingly low sex drive? If so, what might be causing it?

6. On a list of our major involvements and commitments, including parenting, work, household chores, church, extended family,

hobbies, exercise, and outside friendships, how high would we each rank sex as a priority?

7. Stanton Jones says couples often make one of these false assumptions: that their sex life will never get any better, or that sex should always be "perfect." Have we fallen into either of these traps? If so, which one? How can we help each other overcome any misconceptions?

8. Have we expected more from sex than it's really supposed to deliver? What do we see as reasonable expectations for our sex life?

9. Do either (or both) of us have a problem with focusing on self during lovemaking? What could help us turn that habit around?

Chapter Five

VITAL FAITH

Spiritual Growth
Ruth Bell Graham

Prayer
Evelyn and Harold "Chris" Christenson

Shared Ministry
Stuart and Jill Briscoe

Ruth Bell Graham

Spiritual Growth

The role of prayer, praise, joy, and community. How Christian faith affects the way you approach life.

Interviewed by Ruth Senter

*F*aith is the basis of our relationship with God. And a shared faith in Christ is the element that binds couples together, from marriage's everyday challenges to the times of extreme crisis.

We asked Ruth Graham to talk about her own spiritual journey, which began in China where she spent her childhood as the daughter of Presbyterian missionaries—and which continues today after more than fifty-three years of marriage to the world's most famous evangelist, Billy Graham.

Your husband has spent a great deal of time traveling around the world preaching the Gospel. When your kids were young, you carried much of the responsibility for raising them. You must have had some needy times when you missed your husband. What did you do on those occasions?

In times such as those, it's important that we look to God, who is always there for us. He is our strength, our wisdom, our joy. Sometimes we let other people—friends, for instance, or our husband—become substitutes for God's work in our lives.

It's true that life has its problems, but I try to think of them more as priviledges than problems. I try to remember what one great missionary said: "Never mind how great the pressure is, only where it lies. Never let it come between you and the Lord; then the greater the pressure, the more it presses you to Him. When the pressures *do* come, if we're going to follow Paul's advice to "pray without ceasing," we have to pray as we move through the day. Pray "on the hoof", as it were.

When someone comes to my mind, or I've just told someone, "I will pray for you," I stop right then and pray. Or when someone writes to me about a need, I pray for that person immediately and then again when the Lord brings them to my mind.

Then, of course, there are times when I need others to pray for me. Several years ago I needed to go to England to be with Bill. But as the time drew closer for the trip, I just didn't feel up to it—spiritually, mentally, or physically. Not long before I was to leave, I had two dear couples up for lunch. I told them I was feeling swamped and had little in the way of personal resources to make a trip to England. That afternoon they prayed with me, especially about my trip. And they took my need back to their prayer circle and prayed me all the way to England and back. I was only there a week, but it was a heavy schedule. Yet I never even suffered jet lag. I got on the plane the day we left feeling stronger than I'd felt for a long time.

My prayer support sometimes comes in rather unusual ways. One day I received a letter from a woman in North Carolina who was on death row. She became a Christian in jail and started sharing her faith with others. She couldn't leave her cell, but other inmates would come and gather around her cell.

In her letter she said she got up every day at 4 A.M., before the noises of the prison began, to pray and read her Bible. She said she prayed for us every morning. I received her first letter in 1980, just before I had hip surgery. Then I received another letter from her just before my trip to England. The thought that Velma, who was facing her own execution, could reach out in prayer for me when I was facing a strenuous travel commitment was enough to bring tears to my eyes. It is people like Velma and my retired missionary friends who provide the support I need when I feel so acutely the limitation of my own resources.

You mentioned that your friends had shared your need with their prayer circle. Are you uncomfortable when information about you spreads, even in the name of a prayer request?

You need to be careful in asking for prayer. I feel that as Christians, we need to take very seriously the question of confidentiality. This may apply in a special way to prayer groups where people tend to confide in one another. Even under the name "prayer group," such a time can degenerate into a pious gossip session.

I know of a Christian father who shared freely with others about his son's problems. One day this man had his friends in to his home to pray for his wayward son. The son found out about it, and left home so fast you couldn't see him for the dust. Fortunately, the son is now back in the fold, but he still bears the scars of parents who didn't know when to keep quiet.

How can parents know when to keep quiet, and when to share their family struggles with others?

God knows about the needs of our children, and He cares about them far more than we ever could. So why not talk to Him about our children? Maybe we should learn to trust God more with our children; it might lessen our need to talk to others about them. One of the things that has kept our family together is that when our children came home they knew they could relax and be themselves. They knew they could trust us with what they did and what they said.

On the other hand, people who are close to us and know us best can tell when we're going through needy times. They're the ones who stand beside us in prayer and know what to do with the information we give them in the way of a prayer request. These dear people know how to pray, and they also know how to keep quiet. It is a marvelous gift to have friends like that.

How can a couple find trustworthy friends such as the ones you're describing? It seems we often learn too late who the people are that we should not have shared with.

Over the years you develop a sense of whom you can trust. If a person talks to you about other people, you can be pretty sure he or she doesn't know how to keep confidences. You can usually tell when a friend is sincere, when she is concerned about you as a person and not just what she can get for herself through this relationship. I've observed in my closest friends a spirit of gentleness and a complete lack of self-consciousness. They don't always have to be talking, sharing everything they know.

I'm a bit uncomfortable with getting together as a small group and "letting it all hang out." So often, it seems, our spiritual growth is based on someone else's experience, rather than on the Word of God. I've heard it said, "There can be a dearth of experience from living on experiences." We need to concentrate on being fed from Scripture, not from experiences. Years ago, when I was in college, we had testimony meetings and prayer meetings, but we shared what God had done for us, not how bad things were for us.

Nowhere is transparency more obvious than in the Psalms. David wrote what he was feeling. But he always ended on a note of gratitude and praise to God. I think the tendency today is never to get beyond the problems. We don't get around to praising God for all He has done. I think we need to concentrate on solutions rather than problems. It's a much more joyful way to live.

You've had your share of challenges—a husband who was gone from home much of the time, five children to raise, a public that can sometimes be overzealous in their interest in you. And now that your children are grown, you are slowed down by physical limitations. Yet you talk about joyful living and viewing life as a privilege. How did that outlook come about?

I grew up around happy Christians. We lived on a missionary compound in China, and there was not one grouch in that entire mission station. Our compound was not a small place; there were Presbyterian missionaries involved not only in the hospital work, but in evangelism, in education. They were highly qualified people: medical doctors, Bible teachers, evangelists, educators, and homemakers. And all of them were hard workers. But they recognized that an essential part of hard work is relaxation. That's why they built a tennis court and had socials once a week. We got together and celebrated everything that came along.

Another contribution to joyful living was that my parents always made us feel we were extremely privileged to live in China and be missionary kids. We knew they truly loved what they were doing. I have tried to provide that same spirit for our children. Home should be a happy place. Joy is one of the fruits of the Spirit. And it's interesting to note that in the Old Testament when the Israelites were walking with God, joy abounded. There were sounds of singing and celebration. But when they disobeyed God and were out of fellowship, there was silence. The joy was gone.

Evelyn and Harold "Chris" Christenson

Prayer

Why couples need to pray together. How to get started. And how to keep shared prayer a regular part of your married life.

Interviewed by Marian V. Liautaud

Several years ago, I read Evelyn Christenson's book *What Happens When Women Pray* (Victor). For the first time, someone gave me (and about 2 million other readers) permission to experiment with prayer and test its power. It was a turning point in my spiritual life.

That's why I was eager to meet Evelyn and her husband, Harold "Chris" Christenson. Yet as the day neared to interview them, my excitement gave way to anxiety. Guilt about the quality of my personal prayer life, not to mention the marginal one I shared with my husband, started creeping in.

As I drove to their home in St. Paul, I prayed that I wouldn't sound like a spiritual slug. But my fears disappeared the minute I met the Christensons. I was able to relax thanks to their gentle, humorous style of sharing their considerable spiritual wisdom and knowledge. I left their home feeling revitalized and more determined than ever to put into practice the prayer habits they teach to Christians around the world—the same prayer habits they continue to live out after fifty-five years of marriage.

Couples are bombarded with different ways to improve their marriages—learning how to fight fair or keep romance alive. Is praying together just one more "marital-improvement activity"?

Chris: Hardly, because shared prayer has the capacity to be so much more. Every marriage needs some commonality—a place where a husband and wife meet, heart and mind, to share the important things in their lives. With most spouses living in different worlds the majority of their waking hours, shared prayer provides that common ground.

Evelyn: That's so true. When I know Chris' heart, and he knows mine through prayer, we share a oneness that is a wedding of our minds and spirits—a sense of true intimacy.

That kind of transparency sounds great, but intimacy is tough for a lot of couples. What holds us back?

Chris: Often it's pride and the desire for self-preservation. When I choose not to communicate my thoughts and feelings to Evelyn, I'm able to protect myself. But when we pray together, we become vulnerable because we open ourselves up to God in front of each other. I know such openness seems threatening. But once you start praying, wonderful things happen that far outweigh the fear of being transparent.

How can two people work prayer into their married life in a way that seems natural?

Evelyn: Praying together is like riding a bike. You can read how to do it or have someone tell you; but until you try it yourself, you'll never learn how to do it. With prayer, it helps to start out simple. Ask the Lord for forgiveness out loud in front of each other. Or agree on one concern the two of you share—maybe it's a discipline problem with one of your children. In your prayer together, simply say, "Father, help our child in this situation." Chris and I don't pray aloud to impress each other, we do it to communicate with God. For that reason, I encourage couples to pray together at the level of the less-practiced spouse.

What is your daily prayer time together like?

Chris: We usually begin by giving praise and thanks to the Lord. A few nights ago we offered praise to God after we watched our son, who was nearly killed in an automobile accident two years ago, limping to catch a football. After the accident, we didn't know if he'd live, let alone walk again.

Beyond praise and thanksgiving, Ev and I pray for whatever tasks are ahead of us and ask for the Lord's wisdom on every detail of our ministry. Toward the end of our prayers, we focus on specific needs in our family. Finally, we ask for a good night's rest and God's forgiveness for any selfish actions we committed that day.

It seems the core of your shared prayers consists of the everyday events that make up life. When do you get to the nitty-gritty issues you have with God?

Evelyn: Our deepest praying is not done together, but on an individual basis. Ultimately, I'll stand before God alone and be called to give an account for my actions and how I used the gifts He gave me. So it's essential that I maintain a personal relationship with Him. It is this one-on-one time with God that produces who I am with Chris in shared prayer.

Was there ever a time when the two of you prayed earnestly for something only to receive no answer from God?

Evelyn: Our daughter Judy was born with spina bifida, which left her paralyzed from the waist down. For months we prayed for her healing, yet nothing happened. The night we learned she would never get well, I remember praying, "Lord, we've already lost two babies to miscarriage and one to stillbirth. Why do we need to go through this? What are You teaching us now?" Gradually, I worked through my anger and grief. And when Judy died several months later, I had already let go of her and opened my heart to let the Lord teach me through my sadness.

Sometimes when God doesn't answer our prayers immediately or in the way we would like, He wants to teach us something. I'm confident God never makes a mistake. The more I get to know Him, the more I trust Him no matter how things turn out.

You touched on the importance of listening for God's answer. How can I be sure it's God who is talking and not just my wishful thinking?

Chris: I've never had a voice from heaven say, "Hey, Chris, go do this." I've wished for a heavenly telegram many times, but it never comes. Yet when I say, "Lord, I'm going to be quiet before You. Will You bring to my mind the answer to this dilemma?" He starts flooding my mind with the things that He wants me to remember or be advised about.

Evelyn: As I'm waiting for an answer, I've found that God usually recalls Scripture for me. Knowing Scripture is key to discerning whether the voice you hear is God's or Satan's. The Holy Spirit can't recall what isn't there, so it's important to spend daily time reading the Bible.

What's the secret to enduring those tough times when God's answer is "wait?"

Evelyn: It helps to realize that waiting isn't a passive activity. Actually, "wait" as it's used in Scripture refers to the active work of participating with the mind of God. When we clear our minds of all the clutter, we can begin to hear God's voice. I find that a good night's sleep clears my mind best. When I wake up, I'm refreshed. Often, I just lie in bed, completely open to the Lord. Sometimes I speak to Him in prayer. Other times I'm silent and alert for the thoughts He brings to my mind.

Let's say my husband and I are facing a tough decision—one we've prayed about together. What should I do if he gets one answer and I get another?

Chris: Keep praying. You'll know it's the right answer when you both reach the same conclusion, and each of you has a sense of peace about the decision. You'll feel released from having to pray about it any longer.

You seem so blessed, as a couple and as a family. Is it even possible for my husband and our family to follow in your footsteps?

Chris: It's true we are blessed, but it didn't happen automatically. A lot of effort went into developing our lifestyle of prayer. For instance, we've worked to develop an attitude of praying without ceasing—always being open to the Lord and recognizing His hand throughout the day. You know that attitude is taking hold in your life when, for instance, after a close call while driving, your first reaction is, "Thank You, Lord, for keeping me and the other driver safe" rather than, "Why can't that guy learn to drive!" If your first reaction to the circumstances of your day point to God, that's a pretty good indicator that your lines of communication with Him are open.

Evelyn: When Chris and I finish our individual prayer times, we don't say, "Amen. See ya' tomorrow, Lord." We are constantly communicating with God, because in my mind there's no other way to live. I'm not smart enough to handle the work He's given me; I wouldn't dare live without His wisdom. There are things you know by the time you've been married for fifty-five years. We know, don't we, Chris? Nobody could ever shake our faith in prayer.

Jill and Stuart Briscoe

Shared Ministry

What it means to serve God as a team. How to encourage your mate to use all of his or her spiritual gifts. How to help each other grow spiritually.

Interviewed by Annette LaPlaca

*I*n the preceding interview, Evelyn and Chris Christenson underscored the importance of shared prayer. In this interview, Stuart and Jill Briscoe take things a step further by looking at other essential elements of spiritual growth and joint ministry in marriage.

Twenty-seven years ago, the Briscoes moved from England to begin a new ministry at Elmbrook Church in Brookfield, Wisconsin. Before his marriage to Jill, Stuart had been both a Marine and a banker. And in the thirty-nine years since they married, they have built their lives on service: in youth work, adult ministries, and preaching and teaching all over the world. The Briscoes have authored and co-authored more than sixty books and Bible study guides, including *The Family Book of Christian Values* (Chariot); *Marriage Matters* (Shaw); and *Life, Liberty and the Pursuit of Holiness* (Victor).

Here's what they have to say about how couples can grow together spiritually and minister effectively to others.

Both of you were Christians when you married. What kind of spiritual backgrounds did you come from, and how has being married shaped your own spiritual growth?

Stuart: Our backgrounds were extremely different. My upbringing was strict and somewhat separatist, while Jill's parents encouraged her to enjoy a broader Christian tradition, including some forms of sports, entertainment, and travel that my parents frowned upon. But marriage has changed both of us. In fact, marriage will always have a profound impact on the development of both spouses' spirituality. The great evidence of spirituality is love. Well, what better arena for practicing love than in marriage?

Jill: Being married can "grow you up" as a person. You don't have the luxury of being self-centered when you constantly have somebody else's personality and needs to take into account. And there are always a lot of adjustments when you get married.

Given the differences that exist between most spouses, how do two people come together to create a shared spiritual life?

Jill: A marriage has to have both unity and diversity. You don't have to think the same about Scriptures, pray the same way, or enjoy the same spiritual exercises. Husbands and wives are just too different: gender differences, personality differences, differences in background and experience. It's a mistake to think, "Now that we're married we've got to do the same thing spiritually."

Stuart and I discovered this by trial and error. We knew that couples are supposed to read the Bible and pray together. Our problem was that Stuart comes to the Scriptures exegetically, while I'm always brainstorming applications. If we read the same passage of Scripture, I might think,

"I know what Stuart is going to do: divide it into three points and put a heading over it. Doesn't he see the possibilities I see?"

Has it been beneficial to have both of these approaches in your marriage?

Jill: Yes and no. If you don't argue about it, it's beneficial!

Stuart: Jill's talking about how people think having mutual spirituality always means having a quiet time together, studying the Bible together, and praying together. For us, studying the Bible together was an unmitigated disaster, and we found that it led more to frustration than anything else. Now we study the Scriptures independently, but we talk about what we've been learning.

And we have always prayed together. One of the week's high points for me is early on Sunday morning when we're driving to church. We spend that time praying, and I find it a great time of preparation. And once we get to church, we spend another thirty minutes praying before the first service.

Jill: You have to find what meshes with your partnership. For us it's prayer because we both love to pray, individually and together.

What advice would you give to couples who have been married for years but haven't started praying together? Perhaps one spouse—or both of them—is very private about their spiritual life.

Stuart: There's often a shyness—especially when one spouse has been on the Christian pilgrimage longer than the other. The less-experienced spouse may feel intimidated about praying out loud with another person. And sometimes one spouse pushes the other one into spiritual exercises that he or she isn't ready for. This is unwise. Before they begin, both must recognize the value of praying together. If one person is not convinced it's important, then it's an imposition.

Jill: If a husband and wife have never prayed together, they should begin simply and practically. Over breakfast, he might say to her, "What are you doing today, Dear?" She might have a dentist appointment, work at the office, and tea with a recently divorced friend after work. The husband could then say, "Okay, I'll pray for you." He can pray about her work, the dentist appointment, and that she would be a help to her friend.

Then she might ask him, "What does your day look like?" She can pray through his day. Or they might do this at night, praying about what happened that day. Sometimes couples just don't know what to pray; this way, they're giving each other the specific things they need prayer for.

Stuart: If they have children or grandchildren, that's always a common area for prayer. Even if two people don't agree on how to cope with their kids, at least they'll agree that it would be good to ask for God's help.

When one spouse is growing spiritually and the other isn't, is there any sense that one spouse has a responsibility to take the other along as he or she grows?

Stuart: When one person is growing more rapidly, there's a danger of putting pressure on the other spouse: "She should say grace at meals." or "He should lead the family devotions." Most people resist being told what to do!

If one person is uncomfortable, then the spouse who is spiritually ready should go ahead and initiate these activities and lead them. The point is not to nag but to encourage. Encouraging literally means "putting the heart into people"—giving someone a heart or desire for something. A spouse may get encouraged as he sees the Holy Spirit work in his family. That's a better way of encouraging each other than imposing one spouse's desires on the other.

Jill: I think it begins in being responsible for ourselves, for our own growing love for God. As we're absorbed in the Lord, it should be catching! It makes our partners hungry for that experience, but it does so without admonishing or pushing.

Stuart: Also, timing has a lot to do with it. For instance, sometimes I'll come home from some long hours at church dealing with people on a spiritual level, talking about and studying spiritual things. Then Jill comes in ready to talk about something she's excited about spiritually. Quite frankly, another discussion about spiritual things may be the last thing I want to get into. At another time I'd be very interested, but right then it would just be a burden. And sometimes Jill will be busy or preoccupied with something else. So couples need to look for the right time and place for a spiritual discussion.

Have the two of you found a way to communicate "I don't feel ready to discuss this subject right now. Can we talk about it later?"

Jill: Well, even if we don't say anything to each other, we communicate. When you've been married as long as we have, body-language clues are enough. To read Stuart, I look at the corner of his mouth.

Stuart: She looks at my mouth, and I listen for "the sigh." That tells me she's tired or preoccupied, and I should wait until she's rested and ready to join me in a discussion.

With the crowded schedule of travel and speaking that the two of you maintain, you always have to be "on." How do you protect yourselves against spiritual exhaustion?

Jill: There's a difference between being tired *in* the work of the Lord and being tired *of* it. Sometimes Stuart reminds me that I'm just tired out—physically, emotionally, and spiritually. That keeps me from feeling sorry for myself; after all, being tired is normal, because there's too much work to do. But when we get tired of the Lord's work, or spiritually discouraged, that's when we help each other.

Stuart: We're sympathetic. We recognize the validity of what the person is saying or feeling. We listen. Sometimes, just when I need it most, Jill is able to point out something I've missed, or to give me new perspective in my work or in a troubling situation. That's one of the great benefits of an intimate relationship.

I've got to be especially sensitive to Jill. She gets very tired, while I have the constitution of an ox. I grew up in a disciplined home, I'm an ex-Marine, I worked in the business community. I have a tough-mindedness that could easily make me insensitive to Jill. I know I have to give others the freedom to get discouraged or tired at times. Jill helps me keep that balance of sensitivity.

Did you come into marriage with a clear sense of how you would work together in ministering to others?

Stuart: Not in a detailed way. But we knew we would use our marriage to serve others. By definition, a Christian is a servant. So by definition, a Christian marriage is a serving team. There is something greater than us or our marriage. The paradox is that we find fullness of life in being expendable and available. The prerequisite to a resurrection is the cross. There's no such thing as spirituality without some degree of cost.

Jill: Marriage, and the family, is the environment where the Lord's work is done. When children see their parents making room in their marriage and family for a hurting world that doesn't have good relationships, they learn that sacrifice is involved in drawing those people into God's kingdom.

Couples need to have a shared outward focus. It's a good idea to find a project at church that requires serving together—maybe on a missions or youth committee or a team project. That way, if each spouse has different gifts, they don't necessarily have to do the same thing. But they'd be out together on the same night, they'd share the same end goal, and they'd be able to pray about it together.

Stuart: One woman at our church got interested in creating props when her kids signed up for the drama team. The kids were great actors. Her husband was a very busy attorney, but he came along to see what they were doing one night. They needed a spear carrier, and suddenly the attorney found himself up on stage. He got excited about drama ministry. Now, if he's not careful he might give up practicing law and go into acting! People can look for these kinds of opportunities. There are lots of things that need to be done.

What have you done to help each other develop your spiritual gifts?

Jill: We have used our gifts to serve God's kingdom because it's part of the whole package of being a Christian. People often ask me, "How did you become a speaker? When did you get your call?" Well, I got saved. And then I couldn't shut up. One thing led to another, and here I am.

Since I never had a chance to train formally, Stuart helped me learn to study and prepare to teach, to do public speaking, and to do evangelism. He has taught others how to study Scripture, and he taught his wife. His encouragement and help have been valuable.

Stuart: I don't really think in terms of "Let's identify gifts and then figure out what to do with them." My approach is, "Let's figure out what needs to be done and get people doing those things." If they're any good at it, it's because they're gifted.

In Jill's case, I didn't initially discern a gift for teaching in her, but I did know her heart for serving. I saw a desperate need for more women to be taught the Bible, so I encouraged Jill to develop her ability to study the Bible and to teach it. She started the women's Bible studies, and she discovered her gift.

Jill had a reticence about attempting certain things. Sometimes I'd need to say, "You can do this!" I believe in Jill even when she doesn't believe in herself.

Jill: For example, I was asked to give a commencement address to a group of 300 students and their families at a secular school. I felt it was too much of a challenge. I hadn't been asked to preach. How could I give a speech that could still be used for the Lord and yet not overstep the boundary? But Stuart fished my declining letter out of my correspondence basket and said, "What a wonderful opportunity. You have to do this."

Stuart: She did such a good job that she was invited back for three or four consecutive years! And the head of the school came to the Lord, and also his wife. So don't think in terms of impossible situations. If God calls you to some work, He equips you for it. With God, you go ahead and work in the arena of impossibility, reckoning on His resources.

Have you ever reached a point where one of you felt strongly that God was taking you in one direction, and the other one disagreed? What happens when a tension like that occurs?

Jill: When we were living in England, I remember one time when Stuart was on the road, and I was on my own. I got excited about my involvement in a pub ministry. We'd go into pubs and talk to people about Christ. I found I had a gift for this work. But actually, that type of service was somewhat inappropriate and inadvisable; it was too dangerous for a woman to be doing on her own.

Then Stuart came home from a trip and came along with me in my pub ministry. Once he saw the atmosphere, he said, "I don't want you to do this while I'm away. Do whatever else you're doing, but not that." I didn't agree because I was having such a ball, but I stopped going into pubs.

What should a couple do if both spouses are seeking God's will, but they feel pulled in two opposite directions?

Stuart: Recently I was talking to a man who was excited about an opportunity to work in Saudi Arabia. Since I'd been there, he asked me about the situation and the lifestyle there. Meanwhile, his wife was standing nearby looking extremely glum. She was worried about living in another culture and moving her children overseas. But when I described Saudi Arabia as similar to a little piece of Arizona stuck in the middle of Arabia, she felt more willing to consider the move.

Sometimes the reticence of one partner can be alleviated with better information. And sometimes the spouse who is charging ahead is neglecting to consider issues of real concern. Clearly, they have got to talk about it. Assuming they've each got a willing spirit, these problems can be worked out. But one spouse should never push the other into something. They should go slowly, working together. They say the Atlantic convoys of World War II used to go at the speed of the slowest ship. That's the way to go.

How have you found ways to serve together?

Jill: The first time we did a marriage seminar, we'd only just come here from England. It was the first time we'd been asked to speak together to adults. I prepared months ahead of time. In fact, I over-prepared because I felt unsure of myself. And all the while I kept saying to Stuart, "When are we going to sit down and work on our message?"

Of course, the day came and we still hadn't gotten together. I was upset. I remember shouting upstairs, "Do you YET know what we're going to do today?" He came down and said, "I have been so busy, Jill. We'll talk about it on the way there." I cried most of the way there. I kept repeating, "What are we going to do?"

Stuart said, "Well, we'll just get up there and tell the people what has happened. And then we'll talk it out." And believe it or not, that's what we did. I still meet people who tell me how helpful it was to watch us talk through the problem of our differences and brainstorm ways we could adjust our approaches, ways we could do better the next time.

Stuart: Two things were clearly going wrong. One was that Jill hadn't accepted that I didn't prepare the way she did. The other was that I hadn't accepted the fact that she needed to do things differently from the way I did them. Since then, our preparation habits have not changed all that much, but our attitudes have. We're much more open and understanding of the other person's way of doing things. I make time to interact with Jill because she needs that to feel comfortable. And Jill prepares on her own, knowing that I'm giving it thought and prayer all along and that I will draw on resources from many years of teaching experience.

Jill: Stuart and I both have speaking gifts. It's harder when spouses have similar gifts to make them mesh than when they have opposite gifts that help fill up the other's gaps. It brings the challenge of finding a ministry place that's big enough for both of you to work together.

What keeps a sense of competition from creeping in?

Jill: Focus on the Lord. We're on the same team here. We're trying to bring the kingdom in and put a dent in the devil's territory together. There's no place for competition.

Stuart: Each spouse is contributing something of intrinsic value, something that the other cannot bring. We concentrate on that. Also, we feel free to evaluate each other. For instance, I enjoy listening to Jill teach. I derive great benefit from what she does. But I will point out things that I think could be improved or things that might be inaccurate. That's not competing, that's an attitude of "How can we get through this together?"

That requires a tactful and loving approach in the critic and a teachable spirit in the person receiving the criticism. Those can be rare virtues.

Stuart: Jill has an openness, a readiness to hear something that will help. I'm less ready to hear criticism, but I'm learning. I've learned to receive criticism from her because I know her heart. I know she wants the best for our ministry and for me. Knowing I'm not being attacked makes me open to what she wants to say.

Jill: It's like a game of tennis. We're on the same team and we both want to win, but his forehand is better and my backhand is better. Since the goal is to win the tournament, we're going to help each other practice. We're going to speak from our strengths in areas where the other could benefit. And we're going to listen because we want to be a team, a team that wins the game.

SOMETHING TO TALK ABOUT

1. Ruth Graham emphasizes the need for a deeper trust in God. In what areas has it been difficult for us as a couple to let God be our burden-bearer? How can we lean on the Lord more, together?

2. Do we know of other Christians who are praying for us? If not, which friends or family members should we ask to pray for us regularly?

3. If we measured our effectiveness as a couple by our joyfulness, how would we measure up? What tends to steal our joy? How can we guard against that happening in the future?

4. Evelyn and Chris Christenson have based their marriage, and their ministry, on a disciplined prayer life. What are the main obstacles that hamper our efforts to pray together? How can we remove those obstacles?

5. What could we do that would help each of us feel more comfortable with shared prayer?

6. What personal needs can we pray about for each other?

7. At the end of this chapter, Jill and Stuart Briscoe discuss the challenges of blending two different spiritual backgrounds in marriage. How did our backgrounds differ on matters of faith and spirituality?

8. What areas of ministry interest us the most as individuals? Are there ways to bring these areas together in a shared ministry, or should we focus on other areas of joint interest?

9. What do we perceive each other's spiritual gifts to be? Which of these are we already using in service to others?

Chapter Six

WORTHWHILE WORK

Career Dangers
Bill Hybels

Dual-Earner Marriage
Judy and Jack Balswick

Self-Esteem
Stanton L. Jones

Family Finances
Ronald Blue

Bill Hybels

Career Dangers

How overwork and burnout can destroy a marriage. And what it takes to turn things around.

Interviewed by Ron R. Lee

*I*n many circles, workaholism is an "acceptable" sin. Christians agree that there is dignity in honest work, so what's so bad about months, or even years, of working harder and longer than the next person? Plenty, if you ask Bill Hybels. And he should know.

Hybels is senior pastor of Willow Creek Community Church, one of the largest congregations in the United States with a weekend attendance in excess of 16,000. Willow Creek, which began in a rented movie theater in 1975, now operates from a 145-acre campus in the Chicago suburbs and has a staff of more than 300. Few people would dispute the notion that Willow Creek would not be what it is today without the vision, commitment, and hard work of its founding pastor. But as Bill and his wife, Lynne, wrote in their book, *Fit to Be Tied: Making Marriage Last a Lifetime* (Zondervan), Bill's overcommitment to his work at one time threatened the health of their marriage.

In this interview he describes the dangers of overwork, and then shares his solution.

You have written about the dangers of "crisis-mode living," which often results from overwork. How can we tell when we have crossed the line?

You have reached the point of crisis-mode living when you're spending almost every hour of every day figuring out how you're going to keep all your balls in the air and all your plates spinning. You're no longer being proactive about life—you're simply trying to survive. You're living just above the level of total exhaustion, and you don't really have a plan to change your circumstances.

From time to time, anyone with a challenging job and a demanding family life will experience what I've just described. The problem Lynne and I faced was that crisis-mode living had become a way of life for us. It didn't last just a week or a month. It was every week of every month of every year.

What signs should a person look for to determine whether he or she has crossed the line from short-term to "chronic" crisis-mode living?

It has to do with something I call "skimming." You find yourself taking energy away from other facets of your life to feed the one area that is driving you. The one driving force in my life was the task of keeping my ministry afloat. And to make additional energy available for that, I began to skim relationally, emotionally, and spiritually.

How do you know if you're skimming?

The first signpost would be that relationships that once were intimate become more superficial. You find you have less time for intimate conversations with your spouse, for example. There are fewer walks around the block; fewer phone calls from work; fewer candlelight dinners. And you realize you're not as in touch with your kids—what they're doing after school and who their friends are. You start losing touch with your colleagues at work, too.

The second signpost is that you're skimming emotionally. You experience disappointments, but you don't have time to thoroughly grieve over them. You experience victories, but you don't have time to celebrate them. You get bland emotionally, and pretty soon you're not feeling much of anything. You become a mechanical person who's just putting in time.

The third signpost is that you begin to skim spiritually. Your spiritual life becomes a cry for God to help you sustain the treadmill of activity for yet another day. This is dangerous spiritually because you don't have time to reflect or to worship properly. You don't have time to confess your sins deeply. Pretty soon you're involved in mechanical Christianity.

You have written about being consumed by the work of keeping your ministry moving ahead. Have you found that a person's career is the thing that most often pushes him or her into crisis-mode living?

In at least 80 percent of the cases it's career-related, because most of us derive our self-esteem from our work. But ironically there are other people who slip into crisis mode because of the combination of work and church involvement. They have a challenging occupation, and they're also fired up about being lay leaders in the church. When they add those two things together, they have a recipe for crisis-mode living.

A third area is perfectionistic parents who find that their entire life revolves around carting the kids from here to there. These folks skim in every other area of their lives but child rearing.

You have talked about a period when you were teaching regularly at five weekly church services. Then one Saturday it all came crashing down when you realized you couldn't keep up that pace any longer. So you came up with a plan to divide a year's worth of church services between yourself and three other teachers. Why did it take you so long to acknowledge that you couldn't do it all?

Back then, every person I respected told me that delegating out my teaching responsiblities would lead to the undoing of what I and others had spent fifteen years building up. It was a very high-risk move. But I finally took action because I was dying spiritually. I would have done almost anything—including leaving the ministry—to get back into a condition where I was relating to God and being compassionate to others the way I needed to be. I felt I'd be better off as a big-hearted Christian out in the marketplace than self-destructing in the ministry.

I could not perpetuate a way of living that was destroying my walk with Christ, my relationships, and my emotional life. If I had continued teaching five times a week, I would have self-destructed. This was a desperate attempt on my part to recapture spiritual and emotional authenticity and to become a growing, healthy person once again.

Many people living in crisis mode wouldn't have the staff available to delegate out part of their workload. How might people in other circumstances adapt your solution to their situation?

You can only do the best you can with the options that are available. But if you're as fiercely devoted to getting out of crisis-mode as I was, you'll be willing to make some difficult changes—even to seek a demotion or to renegotiate a job description for a lesser wage—if that is what's needed.

I have a friend who requested a demotion at work. It meant a huge financial loss—many thousands of dollars a year. But now his weekends are free, and he leaves the office at 4 o'clock instead of 7. He has his walk with Christ back. His marriage is growing. He's growing in his relationship with his kids. Those tradeoffs may cost you dearly, but they become non-issues when you consider the reasons why you're making the adjustment.

Many people are going to have to take the road of downward mobility in order to achieve what we're talking about here. And I would ask them to consider, "What are you going to be like two years from now if you don't do this?" In my own case, the answer to that question was very clear.

If a person is convinced that major changes at his or her workplace just aren't an option, what would you recommend?

If they're like most active, churchgoing couples with young children, they're very likely overcommitted. They are probably involved in church, as well as in a parent-teacher organization or a civic group like the Kiwanis or Rotary.

If that's the case, and if cutting back at work really isn't possible, cutting back on outside commitments is another option. A couple in this situation should begin to make the tough choices necessary to simplify their life's agenda. They need to strip it back to the absolute basics of what God requires of us: First, to love Him with all our heart, soul, mind, and strength; second, to treasure our spouse; third, to raise our kids. If you have to limit yourselves to those three things in order to lead sane, healthy lives while your kids are very young, then I would strongly advise you to do that.

There's a season of your life when you can only be marginally involved in the church. Later, when your children are older, you can take up some of the slack for those whose children are younger.

Are there other changes to be made in addition to keeping outside commitments under control?

Yes, but it's an option that people hate to hear. A lot of our crisis-mode living patterns come from a desperate attempt to lead a middle-class lifestyle. To address this, couples might need to downscale the level of their lifestyle.

We've had many people here at Willow Creek, for example, who have sold a four-bedroom home and moved into a two-bedroom house and cut their mortgage payments by 50 percent or more. Then the wife doesn't have to work that extra job, and everything relaxes a bit. We've even had people sell their house and move back into an apartment. It allows them to lead a more sane life. Most couples don't consider that option, but they really should.

You should know how much pressure you're going to create by mortgaging yourself up to your eyeballs. You know when you buy a second car on credit that it's going to mean that if you miss one day of work there is likely to be heavy financial stress. Couples need to bring a sense of sobriety to their financial decisions so they don't put themselves into anxiety-producing situations that will leave them stressed out.

Another aspect of your own solution to crisis-mode living was finding activities that replenished your energy. Your hobbies tend to be high-energy activities—sailing, learning to drive race cars, barefoot water skiing—that fit your personality. What might be some options for those who don't have a type-A personality?

It's whatever turns your crank—it doesn't have to be fast-paced or expensive. We have one couple in the church who say the most replenishing thing they do is ride bikes together. Other couples go jogging or take walks together. Another couple garden together. We have a couple who finish dinner and sit down in the family room and read.

Your wife, Lynne, has written about the things she finds replenishing—nature photography, bicycle riding, visiting relatives, and writing. It seems the things that replenish her don't necessarily replenish you. If a husband and wife are more opposite than they are similar in those areas, how should they deal with it?

First, it's all right for spouses to head out separately—either as individuals or with same-sex friends—to enjoy outside interests. Lynne tends to do her reading, photography, and nature walks alone or with friends. And certain of my higher-octane activities are not that exciting to Lynne, and so she allows me the freedom to pursue those alone or with friends. However, it is exceedingly important to identify some common ground and to make that a regular part of your married life. Couples need to have shared activities, as well as things they do as individuals.

Judy and Jack Balswick

Dual-Earner Marriage

When you have one marriage and two jobs, the solutions to some of your challenges take extra effort. But the payoff is a big one.

Interviewed by Louise A. Ferrebee

*I*nvesting too heavily in your career can endanger your marriage, as Bill Hybels pointed out. But there's another side of the story. Making use of your abilities in meaningful work can actually strengthen your marriage, according to educators and authors Judy and Jack Balswick.

The Balswicks are coauthors of *The Dual-Earner Marriage* (Revell). Not only do they research and teach about the topic (Jack is a professor of sociology and family development; Judy is associate professor of marriage and family therapy in the School of Psychology at Fuller Theological Seminary), but they've lived as a dual-earner couple for much of their thirty-six-year marriage.

We asked the Balswicks about the pros and cons of dual-earner marriages, and here's what they had to say.

Why do dual-earner couples often get such a bad rap?

Jack: We often hear from some conservative groups, "God doesn't want both spouses to work, He wants the traditional marriage." Our position is that Christians need to be careful in how they define a "traditional" marriage. Traditional doesn't necessarily mean biblical.

The model of the husband working outside the home and the wife staying in the home emerged as part of the Industrial Revolution in the 1800s. Prior to that, the family—not an individual worker—was the basic economic unit. Until this is understood in its historical context, a lot of dual-earner couples will continue to feel unnecessary guilt.

Would you say dual-earner marriages are here to stay?

Judy: While couples are very creative about how they approach the dual-earner option, I think many couples today perceive, for a variety of reasons, that both people working is an economic necessity.

Jack: These days, corporate downsizing and mass layoffs are a reality. People today are finding they have to retool and change careers.

Judy: The dual-earner marriage allows for a financial buffer while one spouse may be training for a new career. When you have both partners bringing in an income, one of them being laid off isn't such a blow.

That's true, but being in a dual-earner marriage myself, I know that having both myself and my husband working creates extra stress. Why are some couples able to handle this challenge while others seem on the verge of burnout?

Jack: The couples who successfully manage their dual-earner marriages exhibit certain personal and relational characteristics. For instance, if a man is secure in who he is as a person, then having his wife work or earn more than he does won't be a threat.

While the process is slow, I see men redefining themselves and rethinking what makes them feel good about themselves. For so long, we've accepted the secular model that you're a success if you earn so much money or get so many promotions. If men finally begin to say, "I'm a success when I have a vital, nurturing relationship with my wife and a strong, deep emotional bond my children," then we'll let go of some of the more superficial, and false, definitions of masculinity.

That may be true for men. But what about the women out there who secretly resent having to work outside the home? How does a

negative attitude toward working affect a couple's success at managing two careers?

Jack: What's happening in that case is what we call the "push-and-pull factor." Sometimes a spouse is pushed into becoming a second earner—the husband's wages simply can't meet the basic living expenses and so the wife must work as well, even though they'd both prefer that she didn't.

Other times, couples are drawn into a dual-earner situation. When our kids were in grade school, Judy really wanted to return to college to earn her doctorate. While she loved being an at-home mom, she also wanted to teach. We felt if we could divide up the household duties fairly and support one another, then Judy would feel more fulfilled as a person and ultimately that would improve the quality of our marriage and home life.

Judy: Even if there are a lot of stressors, there are also a lot of wonderful rewards for both partners since they have fulfillment in life outside the home. But if you have one spouse reluctant to go into a dual-earner arrangement, that couple will have more trouble dealing with the stress and pressures of both spouses working.

If one or both spouses are feeling uncomfortable with their status as a dual-earner couple, what changes should they make?

Judy: In that case, they should see if they can make do with less. For a while, when our kids were young, we lived on very little in a tiny apartment so I could be at home while Jack was getting his theology training. It was hard, but the sacrifice had meaning—it was more important for me to be home with the children when they were little and for Jack to get his degree.

What are some of the secrets you've found to keeping stress manageable?

Judy: In recent years, what has helped us the most is meeting regularly with other couples in dual-earner marriages. Sure, it takes time; but we know how important it is for us to not become isolated. We need to talk with others who understand the stressors we're facing. We hold one another accountable for the health of our marriages, the intensity of our emotional togetherness, and the fairness of the decisions we make.

However, I think women, especially, have to realize they can't be superhuman. One woman we know, who worked full-time, was able to arrange her schedule so she could help with her kids' after-school activities. She kept her house spotless, entertained a lot, and volunteered in her church. One day, when she was particularly exhausted, she balked at the idea of driving her teenage daughter and her friends to cheerleading practice. When she suggested that one of the other moms could drive them, her daughter exclaimed, "They all work!"

Her daughter's sobering statement made our friend realize she was living a charade—she couldn't do it all. And so, with the help of her husband, she cut back on some commitments and they divided up the household duties more fairly.

It would seem that dual-earner couples have more opportunities for conflict due to increased time pressure. Is that the case?

Judy: I wouldn't say there is more conflict, but because so much is happening, normal differences or conflicts blow up more quickly. So much of a person's energy is expended at work that often the family gets the leftovers. We're all kind of frayed at the end of the day—the kids have been in school, you've both been at work. At our house, when everyone got home we each needed our own space for about an hour.

Jack: When there are arguments, most often it's about roles and the feeling that there isn't enough time to do everything that needs to be done. Both spouses come home and think, "He should have started dinner," or "She should have taken out the garbage."

In a single-earner marriage, since the roles are more clear-cut, there isn't as much need for negotiation. But for dual-earner couples, there is greater role ambiguity. That calls for more negotiation, which then invites more opportunities for conflict.

People who grew up in single-earner families didn't have role models for how they should function in a dual-earner marriage. How can they work out roles without having a good road map to follow?

Jack: Who does what in a marriage evolves over time, and it may take years to perfect the roles—if you ever do perfect them. Dual-earner couples need to do a lot of experimentation—trying it this way and that way, sometimes failing until you gradually get it right.

But accepting and then following through on a certain responsibility won't work unless both the husband and wife are willing to make adjustments. The adjustment we see men making most often is moving from merely helping out at home—like when his wife asks him to lend a hand with dinner—to being the one who makes the dinner start to finish.

What adjustments are you finding women having to make?

Jack: Women have to realize they can no longer be the only one who sets the standards in the home—usually for household chores or parenting. The standard is now open for negotiation, as was the case in our marriage. When we decided I'd take over the vaccuming, I set the standard at once a month.

Judy: And I decided that wasn't acceptable.

Jack: Judy said, "I've always vacuumed every week, and that should be the standard." After some discussion, we finally compromised at every two weeks.

What kind of changes happened in your parenting?

Judy: Relaxing my parenting standards didn't come easily. I kept trying to tell Jack how to parent. Finally, he looked at me like, "Butt out of here." He said, "Unless you let me be the father I want to be, this co-parenting thing won't work." I was getting in the way of him establishing a relationship with our children.

But once I admitted he had the capability to parent—admittedly different from my style—I started to respect our differences. Only then did our kids became very much connected and attached to Jack. But I had to be willing to leave a gap and then let Jack fill it in his own way.

In a dual-earner family, the husband isn't the only one who needs to take on additional responsibilities, right?

Judy: Right! Don't forget the kids. When I went back to school, our kids were at the age where they could share in the work of running the household. They started doing the laundry and more of the cleaning. We began to think as a family how we could make it all work.

How did you manage to work out the details and keep everyone happy?

Judy: What helped us keep things on track was our weekly family council meeting. We had a certain time we'd meet each week—usually for fifteen or twenty minutes. We'd look at how things were going. Who was discouraged with the chores they were doing. We considered roles and duties interchangeable. Knowing one person didn't have to be stuck with something all the time was helpful.

When I was working on my dissertation, the rest of the family would say, "Since you're so busy, we'll take on some extra duties."

Jack: Not feeling locked in is important; and so is not feeling locked out of something. For instance, if we realize we're not entertaining as much as we once did because of hectic work schedules, we know the situation isn't permanent. Schedules and responsbilities will change and open up free time again later on.

Obviously, a sense of flexibility and adaptability is essential. What else comes into the mix?

Jack: In a dual-earner marriage, where work roles are separate and spouses function independently, they're less likely to depend on one another. And while this fosters healthy autonomy, it can also make it more difficult for you to develop a sense of emotional closeness.

Judy: You have to work intentionally to develop a sense of cohesion so you won't be pulled apart. For some it might be family vacations, a birthday celebration, or a certain holiday ritual.

So when my family watched "Babe" on video last night we weren't wasting time—we were building a stronger family.

Judy: Exactly. And, in a sense, our family councils were a way to do that. We were connecting every week. When our kids were younger, they even said, "We want you to be committed to Friday night as our family time."

Whenever Jack and I were invited out on a Friday night and we didn't meet that commitment to our kids, they'd call us on it. Following through on our commitment, especially when we had to turn down an exciting business engagement, required some sacrifices. But we knew if we wanted to build a sense of closeness we'd have to stick to our family traditions.

I've read that intimacy is one of the first things to go in a dual-earner marriage. Why is that?

Jack: The time factor is what most frequently erodes all types of intimacy. You ask most couples how their intimacy was when they were on vacation, and they'll say, "Great!" That's usually because they were finally together.

Spouses in dual-earner marriages need to intentionally allow time for, and even work on, building a sense of intimacy. If you're not finding time to be alone, then you've got to be adamant about scheduling it. Just say, "Saturday morning is ours. We're going out for breakfast."

Judy: The wife and husband are the architects of the family. If the marriage relationship doesn't stay strong, you've got problems. Your relationship has to be a priority. God wants you to keep the boundaries of your marriage intact, which means making time for emotional and sexual intimacy.

We know that's important, yet we tend to put nurturing intimacy on the back burner—especially if we have kids at home. Why is that?

Judy: One reason is that people are afraid of intimacy. The fear is this: If I let my partner know the "real me," I might be rejected. So it's easier just to go about our busy lives without really connnecting. It feels safer.

Jack: On the other hand, research shows that intimacy doesn't happen automatically in the marriages where only one spouse works outside the home. In fact, some studies indicate that when the economic burden is solely on the husband, the wife complains much more about intimacy.

I could build the case that there's a greater potential for intimacy in the dual-earner marriage because couples are encouraged to get away from the control issues. We're convinced that to the extent that one spouse controls the other, rather than empowering one another, you erode the basis for true intimacy. One strength of a dual-earner marriage is that a lot of these control issues have to be worked through when spouses are negotiating new and changing roles.

Judy: Instead of unhealthy dependency, dual-earner marriages help husbands and wives develop a healthy interdependency. There's a deep sense of fulfillment when couples figure out together what it will take to make their dual-earner marriage work.

Stanton L. Jones

Self-Esteem

Why we tend to derive our sense of self-worth from our work, and what to do about it.

Interviewed by Lynda Rutledge Stephenson

*I*t's easy to fall into the trap of basing our self-worth on what we do, rather than on who we are as God's children. Basing our self-esteem on what we do creates an unavoidable problem: We all fail from time to time, and failure can make us believe we're not worth much.In contrast, God says we all have great value because of who we are—His creations. And He calls us to be much more than just productive employees. He commands us to excel as husbands and wives. So why are we tempted to overinvest in our careers, often at the expense of our marriages?

Educator and clinical psychologist Stanton L. Jones says maintaining a healthy self-image is one of our most difficult challenges. In this interview, he explains how working at marriage can provide the sense of accomplishment that we all need.

Why do so many people base their view of themselves on how well they perform on their jobs?

Psychologists say one of the most basic human drives, after the biological needs, is the need for significance—and we derive a large part of that significance from what we contribute at work. It's hard for a person to have a well-developed sense of maturity without the sense of accomplishment gained from contributing productively to the world around us.

But there are many ways people contribute to the world around them, other than what they do at work.

Certainly, and marriage is one arena in which our contributions are the greatest. As both partners contribute to the joint task of marriage, they feel a sense of competence through working out the details of life together, contributing to each other's lives, and supporting one another in God's unique call on each spouse.

So in a very real way, marriage is work?

Yes. For instance, wives and husbands can derive a great deal of significance from the work of parenting.

And if they don't have children?

In that case, there is probably less overlapping of marriage and work. A marriage that doesn't have something that parallels parenting probably will suffer from that lack. But there are things that can take its place, especially some form of ministry.

By "ministry" you mean something spouses do that benefits the world around them?

Exactly. They share a task that contributes to the betterment of future generations. It's ministry in the broad sense, contributing to God's kingdom.

Is it safe to say that most men's self-images are tied closely to work, and many women, even if they are career-oriented, still find their fulfillment in relationships at home?

Yes, although some of those distinctions are becoming blurred. But my sense is that it's harder for women to find their needs met in a vocational area.

Men can more easily tune out the needs at home; they don't feel as much guilt about not excelling in domestic tasks. But many women can't tune out the demands of the home. So when their husbands don't pitch in, they try to do it all.

How does this difference between men and women typically affect marriages?

This differing attitude between men and women can be seen in a recurring theme in many of the couples I have counseled: The husband builds his identity by overinvesting in his career. Then he comes home without a need to interact with his wife on the level that she desires.

This dynamic is especially poisonous when they don't see it coming. There's a slow accumulation of bitterness and coldness between them, a recognition of things not going well, but they don't know why. Over time, the situation can devastate a relationship. The wife reaches out to have her needs met, and the husband can't make the stretch.

Sometimes this pattern will change. Over time, the husband realizes he needs to find fulfillment outside work and in the marriage relationship. But by that time his wife has already given up on him and found other relationships that will fill her deep-felt needs. That's when affairs often happen.

So you're saying spouses' self-images—and their respective needs—change over the years, and often they don't intersect.

Yes. I see that happening all the time. When a husband and wife hit a rough spot in their marriage, they find it easy to invest even more energy in their work because that's where they're getting their strokes. Then slowly they draw away from the marriage relationship, where the strokes are harder to get. We live in a time when relational accomplishment is minimized. It would take a rare person to look back and say, "We didn't get that promotion or that big house, but we had a great marriage!"

What about workaholics?

These people usually feel incompetent in other areas of life, so they throw themselves into what they know they are good at—which is usually their trade or profession. The stereotypical bitter forty-eight-year-old man who's working seventy hours a week usually is a person who feels a lack of control in every other area of life. Often, workaholics are those who felt such a sense of failure when they tried to gain fulfillment in other relational areas that they turned totally to their work, which they know will make them feel good.

How can men and women achieve a healthy balance between work and other areas of life?

Cliches such as "God first, family second, work third," while grounded in truth, can't capture the complexities of working these things out. Couples should sketch out what they want their lives together to be like in terms of time investment.

Is it okay for the husband to work all day every Saturday? To get home every night at 7:30 and leave the next morning at 6? Is it okay for the woman to do the same? And what form should their parenting take? These rules should not become inviolate or guilt-producing, but they should provide some standard by which the couple can reassess their use of time after several monthly intervals.

We need subjective standards as well. We need to ask, "Do I like the way my life is going? Do I feel the sense of God's contentment with what I'm doing?"

How then can spouses combine their marriage needs and their work needs to produce something positive in their lives?

Couples can have a complementary relationship in which each spouse is an asset to the other's work. For instance, the spouse can become a resource person to talk over decisions and problems.

Too often people are passive. They allow themselves to be drawn toward the area where they get the most strokes and away from what might prove difficult. But avoiding the things that are difficult leads toward a breakdown in marriage. No intimacy can survive that.

Instead, we should be more active. Asking and answering such questions as "What form should my life take?" and "How do my relationships fit into my work?" give us ways to be called back to what we originally committed ourselves to at home.

Ronald Blue

Family Finances

Couples are working harder to earn money to support their families.
But what's the best way to manage our money once we bring it home?

Interviewed by Ken Sidey

As Stan Jones noted in the previous interview, men and women derive a great deal of their self-esteem from their careers. But there is a much more basic reason people get up and go to work every day: to earn money to support their families. And while couples seem to be working harder these days to pay their bills, it doesn't seem to be any easier to make ends meet.

That's why we asked financial adviser Ron Blue for honest answers to some real-life money dilemmas. Blue is founder and managing partner of Ronald Blue & Co. in Atlanta, Georgia. He is also the author of several books, including *Master Your Money* (Thomas Nelson) and *Taming the Money Monster* (Focus on the Family).

Here's what he had to say about managing your money when finances are tight.

Conflicts over money are often cited as a primary cause of divorce. Why do couples find it so difficult to deal with finances?

Money is the reason given in 50 percent of the divorce cases, but I believe money problems are symptoms of an inability to relate on other levels. How you use money reflects your priorities. For example, one spouse may want to furnish the house, while the other wants to take a vacation. They call it a money problem, but it's really a priority problem, or a problem of communicating about their priorities.

Couples come up with lots of excuses for not discussing money. The problem is that when we talk about priorities, there are bound to be disagreements. So usually, to keep peace, we just don't talk about it.

What can couples do to improve their communication about finances?

It begins with commitment. Unless a husband and wife have a mutual commitment to work together on their finances, they will probably stop doing it when the going gets tough. That's why, once a year, they should set aside an hour or two to set new goals. Each spouse should write on a sheet of paper every financial goal they can think of. Next, they should put their individual goals in priority order.

When they're done with that, they can get together and compare their lists. At that point, it's important to develop a third list of shared goals. That's where they work through the priorities of life. They need to do it on paper so both spouses can see it, agree to it, and avoid misunderstandings later on.

Sounds like we're getting close to the "B-word"—budgeting.

That's right, but a budget is nothing to be afraid of. It's nothing more than a predetermined spending plan that puts into practice the goals you have developed together. A budget gives you tremendous freedom. For example, if you have budgeted $1,000 for a vacation, when you go on vacation and spend $1,000 you don't have to feel guilty about it.

Does every couple need a line-by-line, ledger-type budget, or are there more flexible approaches that accomplish much the same thing?

The line-by-line approach is wise for first-time budget users. It takes two years for a couple to create a budget and then develop discipline and good financial habits. After that, they'll find the line-by-line approach is less important.

My family has a budget, and my wife, Judy, has responsibility for buying the food, clothes, gifts, and gas for her car. She also handles entertainment expenses. Let's say, for the sake of using round numbers, those expenditures total $1,000 each month. So on the first day of the month, she enters $1,000 in the check register. I don't care exactly how much she spends for gifts or clothes or whatever. I'm really only concerned that she stay within the predetermined amount for the month. We no longer live according to a line-by-line system, but we don't overspend our budget either.

You say an itemized budget is important for beginners. Yet it seems that drawing up such a budget is the scariest first step to ask couples to take.

You're right, it is scary. But couples should approach it like climbing a mountain, one step at a time. You don't need to go back through all your receipts to figure out how much to budget for each category. You can estimate your expenses, and you can probably come pretty close to the actual numbers.

After living with those figures for six months, compare your actual spending with your estimates. After that, adjust the numbers and repeat the process for the next six months. It may take a year to figure out exactly how much you are spending. The second year is when you can begin to live within the budget and determine whether it's realistic. By the third year, you've developed the needed discipline and habits—budgeting, watching your spending, communicating about money—that will help you gain real financial freedom.

In your books, you mention that financial troubles usually are not caused by an earning problem, but by a spending problem. As a result, you counsel against looking to a second income as a solution. But with many people's earning power shrinking, has your thinking on that changed any?

No, it hasn't. I have found time and again that when a second wage starts coming in, the expectations of a family's standard of living rise by 100 percent of that wage. And then you're dependent on two incomes. People tend to overlook the fact that out of two incomes you have to deduct higher taxes; a higher tithe; additional work-related expenses such as childcare, clothing, and transportation; and other increased costs. And if either spouse is out of work for even a short time, they can get into financial trouble by depending on both incomes.

Second, I warn against having a second income at the expense of some other priorities, like time with your children. As children get older and are in school, there may be more time available for working outside the home. But I tell couples to do a thorough analysis of their financial situation to see how much money the second income will really contribute, and what it will cost.

Third, when couples are in a better position for both partners to work, say when the kids are in school, I ask them, "What are you going to use that extra money for?" Maybe it's for college tuition, or a vacation. Plan how you are going to use the money before you go out and earn it. Don't just assume you have to have a second income to cover your expenses.

But there must be some cases where the problem really is an earning problem, not merely a spending problem. At what point should a couple consider boosting the "earnings" side of the equation?

It's hard to give one answer that fits all couples. One time to look at increasing your income might be if your earnings have leveled off. It may be time to change your position within your field, or change careers altogether.

But here's the dilemma on earnings. Typically if you're going to increase your earnings it means taking on a second job, or your spouse going to work or taking a second job. There's a price to be paid for that: namely, time away from your family.

Whereas, if you look at reducing expenses there's almost no cost, other than giving up some of the things you might want out of life. But that's a much better price to pay than the cost of additional time away from your family.

Having said that, there are cases in which a job change or location change is legitimate, but you need to be careful. If you change locations you may be disrupting your kids' school experience, disrupting church relationships, disrupting family relationships, and that's a big price.

More couples than ever have accumulated debt before they even get married. Maybe it's a loan that helped pay for their college education, or a loan to get a reliable car to commute to work. What do you say to couples who want to follow the best advice, but right off the bat they've got debt to deal with?

They should begin by defining reality: Where are they financially, and where they want to go. As simple as that sounds, few couples can do it. They just don't think that far ahead.

I hate to keep going back to the budgeting idea, but a couple in these circumstances needs a budget or financial plan. That way they are putting into writing the sequence of steps they plan to take to get from where they are to where they want to go. Creating a budget begins the process of working out of debt.

How about couples married ten years or so who still have not been able to get out of debt?

My suggestion is, don't try to cure the past. They need to start where they are and move ahead. They may have to work themselves out of a hole, or to relearn how to communicate about their financial priorities.

Incidentally, I believe that the ten-year mark is a dangerous time in a marriage anyway. That's often the time when couples enter a period of disillusionment, when they realize many of their dreams aren't going to be fulfilled. Trying to redo your family financial plan at that time can be difficult. I recommend getting help from others if that's the situation you're in.

For a lot of couples, even basic goals such as avoiding debt or accumulating a small savings account remain far from reality. They feel they've done the right things, but they're still not getting ahead. What do you say to couples who are discouraged by their lack of progress?

First, they should do a thorough analysis of their financial situation: what they owe, what they own, where they are spending their money.

Second, they shouldn't try to solve everything at once. If they take small steps, they will begin to get the positive reinforcement that they are making progress. For example, say you want to save for your child's college education. Start saving five dollars every week, or even every month, in a college fund. By doing that, you establish a disciplined habit of saving. Later, you may be able to increase the amount. And it's amazing what compounded interest can do to a savings fund. No step is too small to take.

Third, I encourage people to set goals and then make themselves accountable to someone. For example, I share my financial plan with a friend. Periodically I tell him where I stand relative to that plan. It's high risk, but it's high reward, too. If you try to deal with financial problems without that accountability, you're probably not going to do much.

Fourth, measure periodically how you're doing relative to where you started. If you take those four steps, I think you'll find you are making progress.

Let me pose a case study. A couple is living on one income; they don't have a problem with debt or overuse of credit cards. They're making ends meet, but they look at their situation and say, "It's going to take us thirty years to accomplish our goals. By the time we're able to save enough for college, our kids will be parents themselves!" What encouragement would you offer them?

This is one area where faith comes into play. If it doesn't appear that you're making progress, yet you're being obedient to God, then you're placing your confidence in God to provide when the time comes.

I think of a seminary professor who retired with $9,600 in savings, which is not enough to provide an adequate retirement income. When I counseled with him almost twenty years later, his $9,600 had grown to about $1.6 million. God had provided for him through an investment in a stock that did phenomenally well. My point is that when it doesn't look like you're making progress, but you're being obedient, then God has promised to provide for your needs.

Of course the temptation is that we expect God to provide by an envelope full of money arriving mysteriously in the mail.

But that's not what I mean. I'm not saying how God is going to meet your needs. It may be that He provides a son or daughter who invites you to live with them after you retire. Or He may provide a job for you during your retirement years. He doesn't necessarily provide money in a lump sum or by way of a huge return on some investment you've made. People have misconceptions about this.

How do you define debt?
Debt is being in a position where you cannot repay an amount that you have borrowed. For example, if you buy something with a credit card and can't pay the full amount when the bill comes due, you're in debt.

Do you believe it's possible to live in today's economy without having any debt at all?

It's not wrong to be in debt, but most people could do without debt, with the exception of a home mortgage. And whether a mortgage qualifies as debt is debatable.

One rule to follow in considering whether to borrow money is, "Will I have a growth in value greater than what it is costing me to borrow this money?" With a home mortgage, let's say you have an 8 percent loan and your home is appreciating at 10 percent a year. In that case, you have an economic return that is greater than your cost. You could sell your house and pay off your mortgage, and thus eliminate that debt if you needed to.

How does that rule apply to auto loans?

People often ask me that. The point I try to get across is that if you can afford to borrow money to buy a car, you can afford to save for it ahead of time. Yes, that probably means giving up your desire to drive a new car right now. It may take you several years to save and trade your way up to that top-of-the-line model. But over that period of time you need never pay a dollar more than that car's price.

But you need to realize that when you choose to live without debt, you will be living a lifestyle that is lower than what the world says you can afford. We tend to define poverty as having only one television, or one car. But that's a fallacy. People spend a lot of money on things they consider necessities that could easily be cut from a budget.

Do you use credit cards?

Yes, but I use them like a check. When I charge something, I enter in my checkbook "VISA" or "Chevron" and the amount, and then I deduct that from my checking account balance. So when the credit card bill comes in I've already got that money set aside to cover it.

Are there any good alternatives to using credit cards?

If you can anticipate expenses, save ahead for them. For example, if you suspect it might cost you $1,200 for car repairs next year, set aside $100 a month in a separate account, or separated out from your normal spending, so when that expense comes you already have the money available. There may be times when you have to use a credit card. But when that happens, pay that credit card off just as quickly as you can.

Are there other ways families can avoid credit card use?

Basically, they need to exercise self-discipline in their spending. To help develop discipline, try going on an envelope system. On each payday, put cash in envelopes to cover expenses like groceries, entertainment, and other areas that tend to get out of control. When you pay for things with cash, you think more about what you're spending. When the money in a particular envelope is gone, it's gone. You stop spending on that category for the rest of the month.

What other general advice do you give couples?

They need to establish a habit of tithing, because there are two "givens" related to money. First, all uses of money are really decisions about priorities. And second, God owns everything. My income is a gift from God. In tithing I put money—and more particularly my income—in its proper perspective. Right off the top, I recognize God's ownership of all things. Until I do that, I can never really be financially free. When you establish giving as a priority, even when you're in debt, you tend to keep your other priorities in better order.

SOMETHING TO TALK ABOUT

1. At the beginning of this chapter, Bill Hybels explains what leads to "crisis-mode living." At what points in our marriage have we lived in crisis mode? Has crisis-mode living become a way of life for us?
2. Is our relationship suffering because of some other driving force, such as a job, a ministry, or a hobby? If so, what do we need to do to restore biblical priorities?
3. What do we do together that energizes our relationship?

4. Judy and Jack Balswick point out that prior to the Industrial Revolution, families essentially operated as small businesses with each member contributing in a significant way. What aspect of our life do we feel suffers most because of work commitments? What can each of us do to change or improve that situation?

5. Are we doing a good job of distributed duties such as house-work and childcare, or do we feel the load is distributed unevenly? What would make us a more effective team at home?

6. According to Stanton L. Jones, people base much of their self-esteem on career accomplishments. What are the things that make each of us feel significant? How are they different? How are they similar?

7. How do we feel about the way our life is going? In an ideal scenario, what would be different? What can we do to work toward achieving that dream?

8. Ron Blue says the missing element in many approaches to money management is open communication. Let's recall a recent conflict we had over money. Was it actually a disagreement over financial priorities, or did we have a communication problem?

9. Do we have clear financial goals? If not, when can we set aside time to discuss them? Do we need a budget to enable us to achieve our goals?

Chapter Seven

SOLVING STRESS

Balance
Louis and Melissa McBurney

Rest
Ben and Lauretta Patterson

Recreation
Jay Kesler

Having Fun
Dave and Claudia Arp

Louis and Melissa McBurney

Balance

Feeling guilty because you're not getting enough things done? It might be time to re-evaluate your priorities.

Interviewed by Elizabeth Cody Newenhuyse

Time. We all have twenty-four hours of it every day, but it never seems to be enough.

Making the most of every minute has become a national pastime—and a lucrative one, as the makers of cellular phones, microwaveable pancakes, and television remote-controls have discovered. It all feeds our urge to cram more into every day. Jobs, kids, houses. Each could easily consume all of our waking hours. Add to that church commitments, yard work, exercise, sleeping. And we haven't even touched on friendships or hobbies or fun. Then there's taking the kids to and from tee-ball, music lessons, and Boy Scouts.

Time out!

Psychiatrist Louis McBurney and his wife, therapist Melissa McBurney, know all about the time problem. They work with stressed-out couples at Marble Retreat, the counseling center they founded in western Colorado. Their clients are members of the clergy, some of the most driven, and most image-conscious, people around.

Over the years, the McBurneys have developed some unexpected ideas about stress, the choices we make, and the guilt we endure. They have achieved a balance in their own lives, and we asked them to share their experience with you.

People feel like their lives are out of control, that they have to meet a schedule and get everything done, which leaves them drained at the end of the day. If you feel as if you've totally lost control, where is the best place to start?

Louis: Most people don't realize it, but they actually exercise great control over their lives. It's just that the way people choose to use their time makes them feel that they're being squeezed by some outside force. So, as a starting point, it's important to look at the kinds of choices we're making. Most people don't stop to do that, partly because they're driven by inner conflicts.

In the past, I was driven by the need to please others, and particularly the need to serve people. I felt that I had to be available to everybody. My problem was that by saying "yes" to everything, I ended up feeling angry and manipulated. But whenever I mustered the courage to say "no," I felt guilty. Both caused inner conflict. But since then I've come to realize that saying no is not the end of the world.

But we can't say no to everything. How do we deal with all the time-consuming "givens" of life?

Louis: I'm not sure I have the answer to that. It's true that there are responsibilities you can't let go of. But you need to look hard at each one and decide whether it's critical.

I think we make a lot of our obligations worse than they really are. We had a married woman here at the retreat not long ago who had two or three small children. This was the first setting where she had ever heard other women say they hated taking care of kids all the time. She thought she was supposed to not only do it, but to always love doing it. It was liberating for her to find out she didn't have to love changing diapers. The lesson is that we need to evaluate the attitudes we have toward the givens in life, and recognize how much pressure we feel from them. It's very freeing when some of the pressure is alleviated.

Another point is the need to understand life's stages. Take the conflict between work and family. In the younger adult years, one of life's givens is proving yourself in the world. It's an important psychological task, and it connects with your work. Many people feel guilty because they enjoy their work more than they do spending time with their family. Naturally you have a responsibility to your spouse and your children, but simply recognizing and acknowledging this preference will help ease that sense of feeling guilty and torn.

One thing my husband and I struggle with is the feeling that we are helplessly mired in the day's routine. How can you break out of that?

Melissa: It's something like taking medicine. You have to intentionally force yourself to do it. Likewise, you have to force yourself to do some things that seem unproductive.

About ten years ago I went to a fat farm called Canyon Ranch. I was determined that I was going to lose a lot of weight there, so I signed up for everything they offered—aerobics, walking, swimming. But at the end of the first week somebody said to me, "You can't keep up this pace. Part of the program is rest." So I had to force myself to rest, and after a while I learned to enjoy it.

Apart from life's routine obligations, there are other time-consuming activities that don't seem all that productive. How can people feel like they have more time simply by learning not to waste it?

Louis: I'll give you an example. Since Melissa and I live on a mountain, we don't get good television reception. So we don't have a TV, and I've never missed it. Basically, it's a time-waster.

A lot of people feel like they have to be in front of the tube when a certain show comes on every week. I used to be that way about sports events. But you know what I discovered? I have seen all the possible plays that can happen in football. I've seen 100-yard kick returns, intercepted passes, amazing fumbles and tackles and sacks and all that stuff. Now if I see a game—and I still enjoy watching football—I'm amazed at the commentators' hype. I just sit back and chuckle to myself. But if you get caught up in it, you start thinking "Here's something I can't live without."

What about other unproductive uses of time? I'm thinking specifically of people who spend more time than they need to in order to do everything "perfectly." The drive of perfectionism just seems to increase their stress level.

Louis: You're right. But making a few changes can turn that round.

The Marriage You've Always Wanted

First, perfectionists need to work on their self-image. Many times they are working so hard on everything in order to feel they're "all right," that everything's morally ordered. This can come from the family system they grew up in. For instance, we see many people who are driven to prove to their parents that they are worth something.

We have a woman at the retreat now whose mother was highly organized, and she has a hard time seeing anything that is disorganized as being "right." But this woman's husband came from a family that was disorganized and spontaneous. And as a result, they're driving each other crazy.

How does a couple deal with such a contrast?

Louis: Each spouse has to recognize that his or her own system is not morally superior, and realize where their attitudes come from. Then they need to meet each other halfway.

Another important point is the fact that couples sometimes use "time" as a copout. The kind of relationship they have colors the kind of time they feel is available. Melissa says when she knows that she's Number One in my life, I can be as busy as I have to be; she doesn't feel threatened.

One woman who came for counseling was struggling because her husband wasn't paying enough attention to her. But it wasn't a lot more time she needed—just a little, and the right kind of attention. When she shared this with her husband, he was surprised; he thought she needed a lot of time that he was unable to give.

Melissa: Where perfectionists also struggle is with forgiveness. Sometimes Christians look in the wrong place for forgiveness. They think they need God to forgive them, when what they really need is forgiveness from their parents—permission to be themselves.

What tension points do the two of you face?

Louis: We disagree about what it means to be "on time." My basic idea is that you get there thirty minutes early. Hey, something might happen on the way there! Melissa used to tease me, saying, "What if an alligator came out of the swamp and bit you?"

I know Melissa gives up a lot of things in order to relieve my anxiety about being on time. It's been a real conflict for us. You can talk all you want about "embracing the differences," but when you get right down to it, it ain't so easy to do.

It seems that easygoing people and driven people both feel guilty, but for different reasons. Do you think there is ever a time when people *should* feel guilty?

Louis: If a person is not taking care of his or her basic job or family responsibilities, perhaps that person should feel guilty about it. But what one person would define as "taking care of his job" would be different from the next person. I find that high-energy, highly motivated people tend to tire me out. Melissa, what's "lazy"?

Melissa: That's a hard one, because some people feel guilty even when they're going ninety miles an hour. They feel guilty because they're sure they're just not doing enough!

We often hear the advice that couples should "pencil each other into their calendars." Does that work for most people, or is it just another guilt-inducer?

Louis: A lot of people are so enslaved by their schedules that they won't spend time with their spouses unless it's on their calendars. But it's not healthy to have every fifteen-minute period of your life accounted for.

Ben and Lauretta Patterson

Rest

Why we'll never get all our work done, and why it doesn't matter.
What God meant when He commanded us to observe a day of rest,
and how to apply that principle in our overcrowded lives.

Interviewed by Ron R. Lee

Work and rest are two recurring themes in Scripture. Both are essential, but it's not easy to keep them in balance. How can you just turn your back on your responsibilities in order to engage in restful, yet "unproductive," tasks? To answer that question, we went to two of the busiest people we know, Lauretta and Ben Patterson.

The Pattersons got married when Lauretta was still in college, and it wasn't long before Ben got a job as a youth pastor. Four years later they moved to Irvine, California, where they helped found a church. While Ben pastored that growing congregation and wrote magazine articles and a book, he and Lauretta added four children to their family.

Then, in 1989, they moved across the country to New Jersey, where Ben pastored a historic, 253-year-old church. He also got involved in a radio ministry and worked with an outreach to Manhattan professionals. Meanwhile, Lauretta directed a 120-member children's choir and served on a committee that reviewed the local public school district's sex education curriculum.

Several years later, the Pattersons made their latest move—to Holland, Michigan. Ben serves as dean of the chapel at Hope College, and continues to write. His latest book is *Serving God: The Grand Essentials of*

Work and Worship (InterVarsity). Meanwhile, Lauretta stays busy teaching, writing, and being a mother.

Through the Pattersons' many changes, there has been one constant: They make times of rest and creative fun a central part of their relationship. Here are some of the things they have learned about "keeping the Sabbath."

For a couple committed to rest and relaxation, you are both incredibly busy. How do you maintain your high level of activity while still making rest and play a central part of your marriage?

Ben: That has never been easy for us. Our commitment to the Sabbath was never tested more than it was while we were living in New Jersey. Lauretta was heavily involved with the curriculum-review committee, which required a lot of her time and put her under a lot of stress. At the same time, I was busier than I had ever been. I was pastoring a difficult church, and then I got involved in a businessmen's ministry and a radio ministry.

The incredible pace of life on the East Coast and the cultural obsession with work and visible achievement was something we had never faced before. It was absolutely exhausting. And as opposed as I was to getting frantic, I grew frantic. But Lauretta and I maintained our commitment to the Sabbath: It was the lifeline we held onto during those four difficult years.

What does the "Sabbath rest" look like in your marriage?

Lauretta: Because Ben was in the pastorate for the first twenty-two years of our marriage, Sunday was a workday for him. So Monday was our Sabbath. Ben and I would get the kids off to school in the morning and then we'd settle in for a second cup of coffee. During the day, we'd go for a walk, listen to music, or read. Some Mondays we'd just fall asleep on the couch.

During our Sabbath, we talk about anything we want to, but we don't feel an obligation to solve anything. With busy lives and four kids, it's easy to fall into a pattern of always discussing logistics, or character issues or whatever concerns woke you up the night before. To avoid that trap, on the Sabbath we agree that we don't have to solve anything.

Ben: Actually, we have found that that approach ends up giving us better solutions. Couples often feel pressure to wrap things up, to get everything in their marriage or their family life "solved." As a result, their solutions are usually premature.

But if you let it drag on a while, you can take the time to think things through. That gives you the freedom to be more creative, and you arrive at better solutions.

Lauretta: Instead of trying to solve problems, we often discuss our dreams. We'll write out what we'd like to do on vacation, for example, or jot down other grand thoughts that may not be related to any sense of reality in our lives. We enjoy thinking about things on a grand scale.

Ben: So much of life is "micro living"—the stuff that is right in front of you. But couples need to do more "macro living"—they need to spend time getting the big picture. It doesn't have to be practical—it's fun to just dream about things together.

The idea of a couple carving out time every week for just the two of them sounds great. But how did you pull that off when your kids were preschool age?

Lauretta: We often traded childcare with friends who had young children, and we had a neighbor who would take care of one of the kids for us. During the time when we had two toddlers, we often just took them with us when we'd go out for breakfast on Monday mornings. We'd bring along a bucket of Legos, and they would sit at their own table and play. That allowed Ben and me to talk. Even having two hours of good time together sometimes felt like a week's vacation.

With everyone's life so crowded with demands and responsibilities, it can be difficult to justify devoting one day a week to "nonproductive"activities. Is there a way to view a day of rest as having some sort of payoff?

Ben: There are a number of benefits, but looking for a tangible payoff isn't the right way to approach the Sabbath. In Deuteronomy 5:15, the Hebrews were commanded to keep the Sabbath in light of the fact that they had been freed from slavery in Egypt. And even today, the rationale for keeping the Sabbath is to help us remember that we're not slaves to our work or the demands of others. We belong to God, which means we're free.

For me, the great payoff for observing the Sabbath is that it reminds me that I'm more than my work. And because I tend to be a driven person, I need to be reminded on a weekly basis that I'm not defined by my work. I belong to God, not to my work.

But don't you pay a price the next day when you've got two days' worth of work waiting for you at the office?

Ben: The Sabbath wasn't designed to enhance productivity, but I have experienced its practical benefits in my work. When I was in the pastorate and taking my Sabbath on Mondays, I was always astonished that the work I thought I'd have to do first thing Tuesday morning frequently resolved itself while I was gone on Monday. My practice of taking a day of rest set up an opportunity for God to show His sovereign and gracious hand to get things done through other people—or sometimes by issues simply resolving themselves—without my involvement.

If a person is a hard-driving type who thrives on accomplishing things, how can he or she make the transition to the more hang-loose approach you're describing?

Ben: One way is to realize that the Sabbath is both a gift and a command. I'm one of those driven, goal-oriented people you're talking about. And I know I wouldn't force myself to stop working unless God told me to. That's essentially what the Sabbath is: One day a week when your duty is to stop. It's a command that saves people like me from ourselves.

Lauretta: It's like we're all two-year-olds who have to be told to take a nap. No two-year-old wants to take a nap. But when you take one, you feel so much better. You emerge with a whole different outlook on life.

How do you avoid feeling guilty for taking one day a week to rest when there is always so much to do?

Ben: It's easy to feel guilty or irresponsible, especially if you're under pressure because of tight deadlines or a staff cutback at work or whatever. That's why it's important to remember that all of God's commands are about freedom. And it's an act of faith to believe that obeying God by keeping the Sabbath is going to set you free.

It's similar to the problem a man faces when he's caught in the grip of lust. He feels a compulsion about a certain woman or a certain immoral sexual practice. He is convinced that he's "got to have" that woman or he's "got to have" that forbidden sensual experience. But to overcome that, he has to believe he will be a freer, happier man if he doesn't give in to the destructive compulsion.

This obsession with time management and productivity and schedules and busyness is no different. One person's compulsion to work is just as much slavery as another person's compulsion to abuse alcohol or indulge in pornography. They all make slaves out of people. And if I have become a slave to something, whether it's my work or something else, I need to break free. How do you do that? It's a matter of believing God. It's faith.

Lauretta: It helps if you stop to consider who the boss is when you're enslaved to something. For example, I'm real keyed into other people's expectations of me. I hate to disappoint them. I look at a stack of papers, and I see each one representing a person who needs something from me. Not getting all of that work done means I won't be getting back to people who have a need.

Ultimately, it comes down to the question of "Who are you going to disappoint?" The realistic answer is "You're going to disappoint some-body." That has been the hardest thing for me because I don't want to disappoint anyone. I will just keep churning and producing and doing whatever it takes to meet the expectations that other people have of me. However, if I'm driven to accomplish a certain amount of work to preserve relationships with people, it's just another type of compulsion to keep working and neglect rest. And that's where getting up early to have some coffee and read the Bible transforms and renews my thinking.

If taking time off every week means you'll end up disappointing some people, how do you decide who you will disappoint?

Ben: There is no simple formula that will solve that dilemma. Earlier this year Lauretta and I were speaking at a conference with Stuart and Jill Briscoe. Jill was talking about Matthew 6:33: "But seek first His [God's] kingdom and His righteousness, and all these things will be given to you as well." She was talking about the hierarchy that is involved in seeking God's kingdom first. Is the proper priority God first, then family, then work? Or is it God, work, family?

Jill said a wise thing: Seeking God's kingdom involves doing whatever God is urging you to do at the moment. Sometimes it means your family is last. Other times it means your family is first.

The question, then, is "How do you get to the place where you can discern God's direction on a day-to-day basis?" Maybe God is nudging me one day to drop my work so I can spend time with one of my kids. But the next day I've got to put my family on the shelf and really concentrate on work. It gets down to listening on a daily basis to the voice of God. And that only comes after a lifetime of cultivating an ear for God's voice.

That sounds great in theory, but how does that help a person who finds him or herself falling farther and farther behind at work?

Ben: Well, I'm sure of one thing: I can't get all my work done. There are simply too many things coming at me. So when I reach the end of the day I've got to ask the Lord, "Have I done what You've required of me today?"

By saying that, it might sound as if I don't care about getting things done. But for someone like me, who has so many things going all at once, I've never been able to satisfy all the requests of people who need me to do something.

So I have to throw myself on God's mercy and say, "Lord, I know I'm way behind on my work commitments, but I'm going to go home and have dinner with my family." Then I leave the work until the following day and pray that it somehow will work out all right.

What have you done to help your children place a high value on rest and creative renewal?

Ben: If you boiled it down to a family credo, it would read something like this: "The skills we need to be a success in life are learned while fooling around." It's a matter of following your own giftedness, your own love.

We're willing to let the house be a mess. That's one price you pay if your kids are creative and playful. If they have to clean up every project before bedtime, it will take the fun out of it. So we let them keep the project going over a long period of time.

How do you view the current parental preoccupation with giving kids every opportunity to maximize their talents and abilities— either athletic or musical or academic—which creates more work for the parents and leaves less time for family togetherness?

Ben: I would never say that kids shouldn't take music lessons or be in gymnastics or whatever. But we need to put in a good word for the value of boredom. Boredom gives people, kids included, a wonderful opportunity to become creative.

Most people medicate their boredom with television or spectator sports or some other form of entertainment. But when our kids come to us complaining of boredom, we tell them: "Now you have a chance to figure out something to do." Bored kids are potentially very creative kids if you can live with the pain of their boredom for a while. With a little adult supervision, they will come up with amazingly creative ways to fill their time.

Lauretta: God has called Ben and me to invest a lot of time and effort in our children, and also in the lives of their friends. Our home is a place where children feel comfortable. There's even a rock band that practices in our basement.

How do you maintain your sanity amid all the chaos and disorder?

Lauretta: I think my upbringing had a lot to do with it. Most of my siblings got awards and honors in academics and music, and our parents were happy for us. But one of my sisters struggled with a chronic health condition. My parents refused to compare our awards and honors with my sister who was struggling just to get to school each day.

My parents' attitude did a lot to keep me from developing a compulsive pursuit of over-achievement. And that has carried over into the way Ben and I approach our marriage and our family life. The daily struggles of work and parenting keep us both on our knees in prayer, and they help us keep the atmosphere of our home fairly light.

Jay Kesler

Recreation

Why marriages can't remain healthy if they are all work and no play. How to relearn the art of having fun together.

Interviewed by Lorraine Mulligan Davis

As Ben and Lauretta Patterson mentioned in the preceding interview, God commands us to rest. But what are we supposed to do with that prescribed "downtime"?

If you ask Jay Kesler, a former pastor and former president of Youth for Christ, he'll say "have some fun together!" In other words, all work and no play makes for a dull marriage.

Kesler is the author of nineteen books, including *Raising Responsible Kids* (Avon), and he speaks on the "Family Forum" radio program, broadcast on more than 250 stations across the country. In addition, he carries a heavy load of responsibilities as president of Taylor University in Upland, Indiana. Yet his attitude toward life, and especially his forty-year marriage to Janie, reflects his goal of trying to include fun and play in virtually everything he does. Here's what he has to say about couples working hard at having fun together.

What exactly *is* fun, and what makes it so elusive?

Fun is intensely personal. One person's fun can be terminally boring to someone else, but most would agree that fun has certain attributes. Fun is a voluntary and often spontaneous way to provide relief from routine or stress. Couples often say fun occurs when they can be together, rather than separated by various work or role demands. Sometimes when I need to put in overtime at work, Janie goes to the office with me, and she'll sit nearby reading. Just being together makes the extra hours at my desk seem fun to me.

Sometimes fun involves forcing troublesome things to the back of your mind. When I fish, for example, I think about very different things than I do when I'm conducting a meeting.

Our personality types and the context of our lives also affect our definition of fun. I'm a workaholic by nature, so my fun activities have to have a goal, but that goal can't be seen as a duty. However, I can turn most anything into play if I want to. For instance, I'll be dog-tired at the end of a week, but I'll still plan to build a garage on Saturday. I'll get up at 5 in the morning and work all day and into the night. Though I'm exhausted physically, it's still a relaxing day for me.

Is fun different from recreation? Building a garage or cleaning the house may be fun for some people, but is it recreation?

Depending on the persons involved, either of those activities could be both "fun" and "recreation." I see fun as a spontaneous activity that requires little if any planning, and recreation as a change of pace, a break from the routine.

Why is fun something that everyone seems to crave, especially in marriage?

Anything that is done routinely becomes monotonous. And for many people, there is a sense in which monogamy and monotony mean the same thing, because they're both repetitious. A couple might kiss good-bye every morning before going off to work. Even if the kiss is heartfelt, there's an element of duty—and therefore monotony—present. Or maybe you have a tradition of eating pizza and watching video movies every Friday night. After a while that will get stale, no matter how good the pizza!

In courtship, of course, we do unexpected, spur-of-the-moment things. A healthy marriage relationship needs to maintain that surprise element by doing things that are serendipitous.

So it's not immature to have a high need for fun and play.

On the contrary, it's good! There's an argument that would say that virtually all of the human race's great inventions are the result of play rather than effort. Originally many of the most useful tools—probably even the wheel—were invented as toys. The slingshot came before the catapult. Airplanes were flown as toys before they were ridden in, and so on. Progress comes through play.

What should spouses do when they don't define fun the same way?

In the context of marriage, fun involves commitment. Each spouse has a duty to try to understand the other person. We're called to this because Scripture tells us to love each other and to prefer one another (Rom. 12:10). Often when spouses try to explore the areas of fun that the other person enjoys, they learn to enjoy it too.

My daughter's husband is caught up in sports, and she decided that if she couldn't fight him, she should join him. Now she's somewhat of a sports addict herself. Of course, sharing interests ought to be a two-way street. Often after doing a new or unusual activity with their spouses, people say, "I didn't know this could be so much fun!"

What do you recommend when spouses find that each of them has a deep need for areas of fun that are incompatible, and they can't enjoy doing those things together?

It's imperative that they find a third thing they both enjoy. Often you have one person leading the other person into personal territory. For instance, a husband might lead his wife into the adventure of golf. But there are women who simply cannot enjoy it. They might tolerate it, but it doesn't fulfill their need for fun.

Or sometimes a woman might lead her husband into the adventure of collecting antiques, an area where he feels very much the amateur beside an expert. In such cases couples need to find alternative ways to be together. Not just the man doing his thing and the woman doing hers.

The process of finding enjoyable activities that can be shared by both partners is one of the ways we deepen the marriage relationship. We create a world where we get to do things we've discovered together. Many times, this happens through travel. By going to a place new to both spouses, couples become novices learning something together. Often their mutual enjoyment overcomes even the fears and apprehensions connected with new experiences.

Isn't there another alternative, that of keeping your separate pastimes?

Sure. For example, one spouse shouldn't let his or her body go to pot just because the other spouse disdains exercise. I'm not saying spouses should share *every* activity. But they should try to avoid developing interests that cause them to derive most of their fun in an environment away from their spouses. Doing fun things together draws the couple together.

There is a volitional side to fun in marriage. We agree to give up some of our former fun in order to have enjoyment together. Somewhere in the first two or three years of marriage, most people discover they can't maintain both their single and their married lives. Those who are unwilling to give up their single lives to develop married lives often run into great trouble.

If you asked couples why they were initially attracted to each other, most would mention that their prospective mate was a lot of fun to be around. If that's the case, why do couples tend to lose a sense of fun in marriage?

Courtship almost always involves planning and plotting. In fact, some anthropologists would say courtship is a highly socialized form of stalking. A hunter never catches anything without thinking about where the game goes, what it likes to do, what its habits are, what bait to use, and how to set the trap to capture the game.

Often, after people get married, the stalking is discontinued because the individual has already been caught. That is the precise opposite of the way spouses ought to think. They ought to continue the stalking, the courting, the planning, and the thought and effort that's put forth in courtship.

Courtship is a demanding process. People pursue it while sacrificing their rest and everything else until the capture is made. Then they somehow feel no more need. They think they can relax and just enjoy things. But that's when they actually do need to continue the process. It's what makes marriage fun. Who can resist the element of surprise and the fact that your spouse is plotting to make you happy?

So there's an anthropological basis for fun and recreation. Is there a biblical basis?

Jesus certainly provided recreation for Himself and His disciples, and He did it by changing location. He pushed the boat away from the shore and went to the other side of the Sea of Galilee to get away from the press of the crowd. But today, many highly motivated and guilt-ridden Christians don't feel they can ever get away from their jobs because they have a sort of messianic view. If they would look at the Messiah Himself, they would discover that He left some of this to His Father while He re-created His own person. Jesus' trip across the sea and His going to Bethsaida with His friends gives me the feeling that He had favorite places, retreat centers if you will.

Following Jesus' example, I think there is legitimacy in going away on vacations, seeking a change of pace and a change of scene. That sort of recreation is not only enjoyable, it's biblical.

If it's so enjoyable, why aren't couples spending more time at it?

Most couples fail to plan recreation into their lives. The truth is, unless they plan ahead, busy couples won't have any time left for each other. There have to be some X's in your calendar that mean "this time is reserved for family." I encourage couples to reserve at least one night a week when they get alone to do something by themselves that draws them together.

Plus, you get more mileage out of an anticipated activity. Having plans for a vacation, or even an evening out, can make the days of routine work seem more tolerable. But it's important not to over-plan to the point of rigidity. Fun is easier to pull off when you're flexible, willing to change direction. Most people tell me the real fun stuff happened when they were carrying out a plan and then decided to try something different from that. Take a risk! It throws both of you into the unknown.

Many couples seem to have a "Fantasy Island" mentality regarding fun. They somehow feel they can't have fun unless they go somewhere and spend a lot of money. They feel the need to step outside reality in order to enjoy themselves.

That idea is all right, but it doesn't have to cost money. Many couples are too commercial in their understanding of fun. They watch television and see people doing things—the lifestyles of the rich and famous—and don't realize that fun, really, is more related to giving oneself and one's full attention to the other person.

One time I said to my children, "I'm going to talk to parents about their kids. What do you think their kids would like me to tell them about having fun?" They replied, "Tell them to go to the park and jump in the leaves; tell them to go climb trees" and so forth. Their list was twenty-five items long, and not one of their ideas cost a dime. So the idea that we're not going to have any fun until we go to Hawaii is not true. We can have fun at some local greasy spoon where we find a booth in the corner and enjoy being together.

Ultimately, I'd say fun is tied to faith. If we believe the Father cares for us and that somehow life will turn out all right, then we don't have to feel so tense. Uptight people don't seem to have fun. They fear rejection and failure. For the Christian, fun and play ought to come easily.

Dave and Claudia Arp

Having Fun

How to recapture a sense of lightness and enjoyment in your marriage.

Interviewed by Annette LaPlaca

Claudia and Dave Arp have devoted their lives to marriage ministry. They are co-founders of Marriage Alive Seminars and host the nationally syndicated radio program "The Family Workshop." In their work as family-life educators, they hear it all. But the most common complaint they hear from couples has nothing to do with money, sex, or the kids. Instead, it's the problem of not having fun together.

The Arps, coauthors of *Where the Wild Strawberries Grow* (ChariotVictor) and *Ten Great Dates to Revitalize Your Marriage* (a book and video resource published by Zondervan), take this complaint seriously. We asked them how couples can succeed at making fun a higher priority, and here's what they said.

It's easy for the pressures of life to crowd out the fun. How can couples regain a sense of enjoyment in their marriages?

Claudia: We encourage couples to take the things they are already doing and find ways to make those things enjoyable. For example, Dave and I—like any couple—have to get groceries on a regular basis, so we go to the grocery store together and turn it into a date. The free food samples we get at the store are our hors d'oeuvres for the evening.

Dave: Women often tell us, "I can't get my husband interested in dating." But frequently that's because they have defined a date in terms of a romantic, expensive evening out. But a date can be almost anything. A woman might get the dating habit started again by surprising her husband with tickets to a ball game.

Claudia: She might get the tickets even though she doesn't really enjoy baseball. But on the way home from the game they can stop for coffee and conversation. That's what she was longing for in the first place. This way, both partners get to do something they enjoy, and they're doing it together.

Dave: By doing something simple like going to a ball game, they discover a way they can enjoy spending some time together. And they plant the seed for a new dating habit. Since they enjoyed their "experimental" date, they'll be more likely to plan similar activities into their schedule in the future.

Claudia: Sometimes, to help couples get started, we ask each spouse to write out a list of things they would like to do with their mate. We have them discuss their lists with each other, identify any areas of commonality, and then set an actual time to try doing something new. The lists give them a place to start, and assigning an actual time and date helps make the goal measurable.

Also, we encourage couples to have fun with other couples. In our society, we tend to "cocoon" in our own homes or within our own marriages. I recently read that the average couple does something social once a month. That's only twelve times a year!

It takes some concrete goal-setting to prevent a life of isolation. Every couple could use the support of another couple. And sometimes, when the fun has been going out of your own marriage, it's good to be with other people who can help you relax and laugh a little. Having fun in your marriage creates positive memories, and those memories can help carry you through the hard times.

Have there been times when the two of you struggled to find a way to restore a sense of fun to your own marriage?

Claudia: When Dave left the business world to enter full-time Christian work, it was scary. But I supported him in his initial decision to quit his job and start working for Campus Crusade for Christ. Then, when we had three small children, Campus Crusade asked us to help start a ministry in Switzerland. If we accepted that offer, we'd be moving to Europe in just six weeks. That was a time of real crisis, and I didn't feel very supportive.

Dave: Claudia and I got the issues out on the table. The more we talked and prayed about taking our family to Europe, the more peace I got about going ahead.

Claudia: And the more fear I got. Finally, we agreed to go because Dave's feeling that God was leading us to Europe seemed stronger than my fears. I hated to leave our ministry here—and all our friends. Then we got to Europe and we had no telephone, we had only one car, and we lived in a little village with no English-speaking neighbors. Since Dave and I hadn't been making a habit of spending time together—especially fun time—those early months were even more stressful. We recognized a number of problems that had been building up in our marriage, so we began to talk about them and to chip away at them.

Dave: It almost seems that God, in His wisdom, said, "It looks like Dave and Claudia are not quite getting their act together. I'll just pick them up, move them to Europe, and see what happens." The problems we discovered in our marriage weren't that major, but we hadn't been making time for each other.

Our ministry in the United States had been busy and exciting, but we had developed what we call a "front-door relationship." I'd leave the house to teach a morning Bible study. Then I'd come back home and Claudia would hand the kids off to me, and she'd go teach her Bible study. We were missing each other. We had no time to talk about things, or to set goals.

Claudia: But undergoing the major change of moving to Europe—and entering a life that was a little less comfortable—helped bring some issues to light. We started setting goals for our marriage and for the time we spent together. Our desire to help other couples grew out of that experience.

What are some of the goals you're working on these days?

Claudia: We've been trying to find a better focus in our life together. We hope to reorganize our commitments in such a way that we'll make sure to take time for some fun even if we have to snatch moments of fun out of our hectic schedule.

Dave: Sometimes when things get too heavy, we look at each other and say, "That's enough." And we just take off for a couple of hours. At other times, one of us will say, "Let's go walk around the block." That gives us a few minutes away from the telephone, our work, and the house.

Fun is a crucial ingredient in a strong, healthy marriage. If you're having fun and your spouse becomes your friend, you'll want to be together. Having fun is divorce prevention. Have you ever seen a couple having fun on their way to divorce court?

Claudia: Life in the '90s is accelerated; everyone is too busy. We've got to find those moments of fun and relaxation, or the stress will overpower us. And sometimes a "moment" is all you can find. We keep looking for a whole weekend or a whole week, and it rarely happens. But fifteen minutes of fun here or there can make a world of difference.

In our book *52 Dates for You and Your Mate*, we developed a number of "Just-Too-Tired Dates." One of our favorites is to turn on the answering machine, pop in a video, order pizza, and agree not to say a word. That way, we've lowered our expectations for that time together. We know up front we won't be concentrating on communicating or working on our relationship, we're just going to relax together.

How important is it to maintain a sense of humor when life starts getting too stressful?

Dave: It's vital for spouses to laugh together and not take themselves too seriously. Looking for the humor in any situation is a habit that should be cultivated. In the middle of the hard times, you'll be glad you learned to laugh together. A good example from our own marriage was parenting—especially when our boys were teenagers.

Claudia: During those years, I relied on Dave's laid-back nature and his sense of humor. We promised each other that we'd laugh whenever we could, and our boys captured a sense of that.

Once, we were deep in a heavy discussion over a problem with one of our teenagers. We were trying to talk with him, and the tension was really thick. Finally, our son looked around and said, "Humor! Where are you, humor, when I need you?"

Dave: His comment made us all laugh—and it helped break the tension. The same thing can happen when the conflict is between spouses.

Claudia: We have a family motto: "Every family needs a little insanity, to keep their sanity." It also helps to "put on the rose-colored glasses." In many families, there's sort of a taboo on showing tenderness. If someone has strong negative feelings, they speak up. But too often they keep the warm, loving feelings to themselves. But a mate who learns to look for the positives can become the most positive reinforcing agent in his or her spouse's life.

In addition to doing things that are "fun" together, joy is an important part of the Christian experience. How does joy relate to fun in building a healthy marriage?

Dave: As Christians we're instructed to be joyful in times of difficulty. That doesn't mean we should say, "Hey, isn't this horrible circumstance just great!" But it does mean that we have the assurance that the Lord is there with us in all circumstances. This same thing holds true in marriage. In times of difficulty, there's joy—and peace—in knowing your partner is there with you. The two of you are in it together.

Claudia: Joy is more like an attitude, while fun is something we can—and should—plan. The fun times can contribute to the joy, but the joy goes much deeper. I have a peaceful joy knowing that whatever I'll face in life, Dave will be there with me. When you know that one other person understands and cares how you feel, you can face anything more easily.

Couples get married and think, "Oh, we love each other. That's all we need." But marriage is the hardest thing any two people will ever attempt. The good marriages are the ones that continue to grow, and that includes putting the other person first. It means not just thinking about what I want for me, but considering what I want for you and what we want for us.

Most young couples don't receive much help getting ready to deal with the tough parts of marriage. That's why Dave and I want to help couples grow—and keep growing—and never lose their sense of joy or fun as they grow together.

SOMETHING TO TALK ABOUT

1. Louis and Melissa McBurney, at the beginning of this chapter, identify the choices couples make as the source of much of life's stress. What makes us feel that our lives are sometimes out of control? In what ways have our choices contributed to that feeling?
2. What obligations do we feel we were pressured into? Can we legitimately disengage ourselves from those commitments? If so, what is the most gracious way out?
3. Ben and Lauretta Patterson underscore the benefits of observing the Sabbath. How would each of us describe an ideal Sabbath?
4. What tensions do we feel in trying to balance work and times of rest in our lives?
5. Jay Kesler talks about his goal of incorporating an element of fun into everything he does, including his work. Where do our respective definitions of "fun" coincide? How do they differ?
6. When was the last time we enjoyed some spontaneous fun together? How could we include more "planned spontaneity" in our relationship?
7. According to Dave and Claudia Arp, "Fun is a crucial ingredient in a strong, healthy marriage.... Having fun is divorce prevention." How can we make some of the things we're already doing together more fun?
8. What are our favorite memories of enjoyable times in the past? Could any of those events or activities be incorporated into our current lifestyle?
9. This week, where could we fit in an extra fifteen minutes of fun?

Chapter Eight

POSITIVE PARENTING

Becoming Parents
Merton P. Stromen and Irene Huglen Strommen

Demonstrating Love
Gary Smalley

Raising Teenagers
Dawson McAllister

Teaching by Example
Jim Burns

Merton P. Strommen and Irene Huglen Strommen

Becoming Parents

How to deal with the pressures your marriage will face from the birth of your first child all the way through to the empty nest years.

Interviewed by Dave and Neta Jackson

*N*othing changes your marriage as much as having children. No longer can you focus solely on one another's needs— even after your kids are grown and out of the house.

No one knows this better than Merton and Irene Strommen. They raised five sons to adulthood and then lost their youngest in a tragic accident. They are now the grandparents of ten children ranging in age from two to twenty-two. From their own experience, and through their work in psychology, research, and education, they know the most effective ways to respond to the pressures of parenthood.

Merton Strommen is founder and former president of the Search Institute, a leading research organization based in Minneapolis. He is also founder of the Augsburg College Youth and Family Institute in Minneapolis. He is the author of several books, including *The Five Cries of Youth* (HarperSanFrancisco). Irene Strommon is a retired secondary school teacher. She and Merton are co-authors of *The Five Cries of Parents* and *The Five Cries of Grief* (both published by HarperSanFrancisco).

What can husbands and wives do to keep the pressures of parenting from pushing them apart? Here is what the Strommens advise.

It shouldn't come as a surprise that children will radically change your marriage. But couples still seem to be blindsided by all the changes that a baby brings. Why do the demands of parenthood catch people offguard?

Merton: Couples know that having kids will change their marriage. But they aren't prepared for the extent of the demands that are placed on them, and the abruptness of all these changes.

After the first baby comes, most couples are simply too tired to do much more than say "hello" in passing, grab a sandwich, and fall into bed. That's a big switch from what they've been accustomed to. The most stressful years in our marriage were when our first three boys were small. And that's not a unique experience.

What are the biggest changes that occur in the early years of marriage, when the children are young?

Irene: A number of factors come together to create stress, and sometimes intensify it. One of the first major stressors in our marriage came when Mert was in graduate school. We already had Peter and Tim, and when Jim, our third baby, was born, I experienced postpartum fatigue and depression for six to eight weeks.

Merton: And she was exhausted to start with.

Irene: I had been working on a book manuscript during my pregnancy, among other things, so when Jim was born, nervous fatigue paralyzed me. Everything seemed to make me cry. I struggled alone for a while because I felt that Mert was so busy that I couldn't burden him with my problems.

Merton: I had a psychosomatic reaction to all the stress, and my face broke out in a rash. I couldn't shave, so I grew a beard—evidence of all the strain we were under.

What did you do to cope with all that stress?

Merton: I knew from my psychological studies how valuable it was to talk during stress times. Once I realized what a difficult time this was for Irene, I encouraged her to keep talking to me, even if it was the middle of the night. Talking was like a pin bursting a balloon—the tension eased and eventually the load seemed to lighten. But the talking we did was not all catharsis; we also made some important decisions.

What kind of decisions did you make at that time?

Irene: A big one was that when Mert realized my struggles, he cut back on his classes so he could help me out more.

Merton: Actually, I took incompletes in all my graduate courses that quarter. Another decision we made was to get records that Irene could play to fill the house with music. She has always loved music. We also decided to give her a change of scenery by going on frequent drives around the city.

Irene: We thought we knew each other before this time, but through those long hours of talking and driving together we came to know each other in new ways.

What types of things did you begin to learn?

Merton: We started discussing my childhood, and I began to realize how much it was affecting my parenting and my marriage. I was brought up by a very strict father, and I responded by becoming overdemanding myself. My talks with Irene helped me to unhook myself from my drivenness and my inflexibility, which I'd inherited from childhood.

Irene: Mert began to enjoy the children once he realized that he didn't have to respond in the same way his father had.

The important thing in those early years was learning that whatever the stress, we needed to talk it out. This became a pattern for our marriage, and we viewed our children as happy additions to our marriage—not detractors.

Merton: When the children came along we had to find a new balance. When I first started in the ministry, I was so caught up in the concept of Francis of Assisi— "sacrificing all"—that I burned the candle at both ends. Not only was I a pastor, but I was youth director for a national church body and college pastor at the school where I taught. I also did workshops on weekends and traveled all summer with a quartet, which meant I saw Irene and our sons only a few times during the summer. I finally came to the place where I knew I had to make some drastic changes.

Irene: Mert cut way back on his outside involvements. But I also started going with him more on speaking engagements. Up until that point I had almost always stayed home with the children. It was difficult leaving the children, but I decided that it was more important for me to make some effort to go with Mert.

You're touching on a big stress point—not having enough time to do all the things you need to do as a spouse and as a parent.

Merton: There's never enough time. Even after I cut back on outside commitments, things still got too tight. Irene and I would have to get out our calendars and cancel some of my appointments so we could spend more time with each other and with the children. I suppose as long as there are children in the home, time is a point of tension.

Irene: The important thing, no matter your children's ages, is that you give your marriage priority.

What changes come about when the kids enter the teen years? Does marriage become more difficult at that point?

Merton: Yes. Parents of teenagers face more stress than they did when their kids were younger. As a result, they don't hug and kiss each other as much as they used to. Even their children notice the difference. During the adolescent years, there is a general decline in family closeness, coupled with declines in parent-child communication, parental control, and nurturing.

Why does that happen?

Irene: One reason is that teenagers bring about new parenting challenges. When our sons were teens, Mert and I discovered how differently we thought and felt about rearing children. We talked through our differences, but situations still came up where we responded differently. Kids learn pretty quickly where their parents differ on issues.

Merton: Our boys knew Irene tended to be more lenient on some issues than I was. So they would ask her permission in those areas while I wasn't home. But she could see what they were doing, and she often foiled their efforts by postponing a decision until I got home.

Irene: We felt it was important for our sons to know that we didn't always agree. So when we came up against a matter in which Mert and I didn't agree, we often used the line, "We think a little differently on this, but for now we've agreed to do it this way."

Can you think of a specific time when that occurred?

Irene: Before the kids learned to drive, I was more willing to run them around to their various activities. So when they got their licenses, they would come to me for permission to use the car.

Was that an area in which you two differed?

Merton: My natural reaction was to be more cautious. I visualized them in an accident. In fact, one of our sons took the car and went for a joy ride. In the process, he and his friends began throwing tomatoes at other cars. One driver got so mad he began to chase the boys in his car.

Our son tried to outrun the irate driver, screeching down the street and shortcutting corners. Four very scared boys finally drove into our driveway with the other driver still in hot pursuit. He drove by with some menacing glances.

That was when the issue of using the car came to a head. And since this was one area where Irene and I differed, we talked it through and came to a compromise. After that, when the kids asked to use the car, I would usually say, "Yes, but the car is to be used for transportation only—to and from wherever you are going. No joy rides or tomato chases!"

Irene: One of our boys, more than the others, really pressed against our rules. During a family vacation he took the speedboat out onto the lake without our permission, with two of his brothers along. We saw him out there, cutting the waves at full speed, but we were helpless to do anything about it.

When he brought the boat back in, Mert confronted him. But he was very defiant. Finally, I was the one who got angry and came down hard on him. Usually Mert was the strong disciplinarian. But this time, I was the hardliner. The speedboat experience turned out to be a watershed for that son. He really turned around in his attitude.

Children, especially adolescents, need the security of knowing that they can't come between their parents. They need to know that their parents, though they may not always agree, are a united front.

What are the biggest changes later on, after the kids leave home? Do marriages become stronger then?

Merton: Couples need to understand that their children will continue to affect their marriage, long after they move out of the house. Wise couples plan ahead for the empty-nest years.

Irene: I had always been involved in activities outside the home. But as our boys got older, I began to think about entering more fully into a career. At first, I went back to substitute teaching. That made the transition to working outside the home quite easy. Mert and I worked together on my professional portfolio, and I felt his support in a new way.

Merton: We've had one advantage, though. We have had more opportunities than most couples to work together in writing our books, leading seminars, and so on. When the kids were gone we still had something that drew us together. We had our work.

Irene: Praying together has been a unifying part of our marriage, especially when the children could have divided us. Since we had established a habit of praying together, it was a natural thing to continue when the children left home. These are happy years, and we're glad we laid the foundation for them early in our marriage.

What other advice do you have to help couples protect their marriage during their parenting years?

Merton: Sometimes the balance in a family tips too much in favor of the kids—and against the marriage. We encourage couples to keep a sharp lookout for when the scale is weighted toward children. Spouses need to keep each other—not the kids—their top priority.

Irene: For instance, a marriage may be headed for trouble if one spouse wants time alone as a couple but the other consistently refuses "because of the kids." Another warning sign is a spouse's inability to relax with his or her mate—again, because of worry over the children.

That's a common struggle. How can couples with children keep their priorities in balance?

Irene: My primary advice is "talk, talk, talk!" Even if you don't have answers to the problems you are facing, keep talking anyway. As a husband and wife discuss the impact their kids are having on their marriage, for good or for ill, they will gain new insights into themselves and each other.

Merton: Communication—or the lack of it—affects the way couples handle crises. Most of us hope that, should tragedy strike, our spouse will be a comforting anchor. But our research indicates just the opposite. We did a study of forty families who lost a child to leukemia. Within a year after the death of a child, 70 percent of the parents showed evidence of serious marital difficulty. Lesser crises, such as unemployment, also can affect a marriage adversely. In almost all these cases, improved communication between husband and wife will help the situation.

Irene: We also emphasize the importance of building memories that include only the two of you—without your kids. Couples need to intentionally create a shared life. It could be a sport or hobby that you both enjoy, or a service project that you do together. Whatever it is, find something to do together.

With the right approach, your children won't come between you and your spouse. Instead, children will help make the love relationship between you and your mate even deeper and more fulfilling than it was before.

Gary Smalley

Demonstrating Love

How to show your kids—in a visible, memorable way—that you love and value them.

Interviewed by Ken Sidey

In the previous interview, Merton and Irene Strommen explained the many ways being parents affects your relationship as husband and wife. But how do things look from your children's perspective? In other words, what do your kids need most from you?

We could come up with a long list, including affirmation, security, love, acceptance, and a sense of self-worth. All those things and more are wrapped up in what family counselor Gary Smalley calls "the blessing," an age-old custom with a much-needed, modern-day application. Without it, Smalley says, children can wither in adulthood into anger and heartache.

Smalley is a popular speaker—both in person and on video—on marriage and family topics. He is also the author or co-author of fourteen books, including *The Key to Your Child's Heart* (Word) and, with John Trent,

The Gift of the Blessing (Thomas Nelson). Smalley and his wife, Norma, have three children and four grandchildren.

Here is his advice on how to show your kids you love them—and why.

How would you define the "blessing" in contemporary terms?

In the Old Testament, the word for blessing literally means "bending the knee." It refers to bowing in the presence of someone who is valuable and significant. Nowadays, I may not kneel down in front of my family, but I bow my heart before my children and say, "You are very significant to me. You are highly treasured." That is the attitude I want to convey.

People often talk about loving their kids as if it's merely an attitude. But love is far more than an attitude; it's something you do. It's an action that grows out of an attitude that says "I value you." If we value our kids, the loving is easy. We will have a natural drive and desire to do things for them because they're so significant to us.

How do you express that attitude, in practical terms?

In both the Old and New Testaments, when someone in a family received a blessing, several elements were present. One was touch: A parent placed his hands on the child's head, or gave the child a hug. Another element of the blessing was a spoken message: words of love and encouragement that communicated the value parents placed on their children. That message also included a picture of what the children would do in God's kingdom in the future. We can give our children the idea that they are not only valuable now, but will be valuable in the future. We can tell them they have a special future.

Can you explain that a little more?

I'll give you an example. You could say to your child, in so many words, "We have observed you as our son or daughter, and we think you would be great as . . ." Fill in the blank. It could be one thing or ten things in which you feel your child could be outstanding.

But how can a parent know what his or her kids will excel in when they are adults?

You start by observing your kids. Pay attention to how they react and interact with other children, what they do in school with their teachers, how they do their homework, what kind of grades they get. And look at their natural interests, their hobbies, what they enjoy doing. Then suggest some careers or roles that would fit their natural interests and abilities. But tell them anything is possible—they can rest assured that their parents believe in them, no matter what they do.

When our daughter, Kari, was young, she could gather little kids in the neighborhood and captivate them by telling stories. So we used to say to her, "Kari, you'd be a great teacher." At the same time, we said she could do anything she wanted. But Kari is now an outstanding elementary school teacher.

How do you do that and yet avoid becoming a pushy parent?

Don't say, "You're going to do this because your father did this, or because your older sister did this." Recognize and reinforce your children's natural likes and abilities, and tell them you'll help them do whatever they desire.

Another element of the blessing in Scripture was the responsibility of the one giving the blessing. He made an active commitment to the person being blessed. Words alone don't do it. The words need to be backed up with a commitment to do everything possible to help your child succeed.

So the blessing isn't a one-time event, it is really an ongoing process.

Absolutely. It's the sum total of lots of little things. When our kids were younger, once in a while when I'd walk through a room I'd drop my jaw and say, "Unbelievable! I can't believe I'm in the same house with you. You are the most incredible kids!" They'd say, "You are the strangest dad in the world." But I could tell they really liked the attention.

What's the most difficult aspect of the blessing to communicate to our children?

A sense of value. The materialism in our culture creates pressure to work long hours to pay the bills; it results in tiredness and stress. All those things can cause us to devalue our children. Sometimes we need reminders of how valuable our kids are.

For example, take a picture of what you consider your most important material possession. Put it on your wall or your desk, but right above it or beside it put a picture of your children. Let that remind you of what is really valuable.

How does it affect me as a parent if I don't have my own parents' blessing?

If you never received the blessing from your mother and father, then you probably feel you're not valued very much yourself. And you tend to project that onto your children. People usually give away what they get.

When adults haven't received the blessing from their parents, I suggest they become the "blessers"—they bless their own parents by placing value on them. That often means they have to bless their trials, because growing up in a home without the blessing can be very difficult.

What do you mean by "bless our trials"?

I call it "treasure hunting"—finding something of value in our trials. I once talked to a single man in his early twenties who was extremely angry at his parents, especially his mom. I helped him realize that his mom had blessed him by her mistreatment. She actually had made him one of the most sensitive men I knew, because he was so aware of what it feels like to be hurt and rejected.

Eventually, he was able to say, "I'm going to bless my mom and dad. I'm going to value what they did for me." I've seen many relationships restored when a grown child returned to his parents and blessed them. If not for the way they treated him, then for the positive result he's been able to discover in his life.

Does "treasure hunting" have other applications?

I help my children value or bless the trials they face, because those trials will create more worth within them. Trials are inevitable, so we might as well find value in them.

But my reaction as a parent is to protect my child from trials, rather than value them.

You can't protect your kids from everything. Let's say my son breaks up with his girlfriend. He comes home, doesn't talk to anybody, and walks upstairs to his room. I don't rush up there and hug him and say, "Let's find the good in this situation!" That would be inappropriate at that time.

Instead, I grieve with him for a couple of days, or a week, or a month. Then, when he's ready, we start treasure hunting. I might ask him: "What character quality has this built in your life? Is there something you can be thankful for? How can I help you?" Until he starts becoming grateful for the trial, he won't grow. The exciting thing is that our kids now know there's nothing they face in life that eventually can't produce something valuable.

How can I know I've communicated the blessing to my children?

From time to time, in a casual way, ask them, "On a scale from zero to ten, how valued do you feel?" Whatever they say, ask them what it would take to move the score all the way to a ten. I also ask my wife if I'm communicating value to each of our kids.

You have to brace yourself when you ask those questions. But I ask them because I can always improve, and I want to keep working on valuing my kids.

Dawson McAllister

Raising Teenagers
How to understand the problems your adolescents are facing, and how to love your teenagers in a way they'll understand.

Interviewed by Ron R. Lee

Earlier in this chapter, Gary Smalley emphasized the importance of making sure your kids know you love and value them. In this interview, youth expert Dawson McAllister helps parents understand that once kids enter adolescence, they need to know they are loved more than ever.

Over the past twenty-eight years, McAllister has spoken to more than 6 million teenagers. In addition to conducting student conferences across the country, he hosts the weekly "Dawson McAllister Live!" program, broadcast on more than 400 radio stations. Every month he receives thousands of calls and letters from teenagers requesting help and advice.

We asked him what teenagers need most from their parents and how parents can best prepare their kids to deal with the pressures of being an adolescent. Here's what he had to say.

You talk to more teenagers in one month than most of us do in a lifetime. What do kids say are the biggest problems they face?

A great many pressures face kids today, and I identified eight of the most common ones in my book *Please Don't Tell My Parents* (Word). High on the list is the misuse of sex. By their senior year in high school, some 72 percent of today's kids have had sex. Related to that is the high incidence of teen pregnancy—3,000 girls are getting pregnant every day.

Another widespread problem is the damaging effect of kids seeing their parents' marriages disintegrate. And related to the high divorce rate is the high incidence of kids being sexually abused by a stepparent or even their own parent.

Of course, drug and alcohol abuse are rampant. About one-half of all high school students admit to having tried illicit drugs, and alcohol abuse is an even greater problem. Also listed among the top eight problems are the damaging effects of verbal and emotional abuse in the home and involvement in the occult.

All of these factors feed the growing problem of teen suicide—about one out of three teenagers has thought about it; 15 percent have come up with a plan; and 6 percent have actually attempted it.

It's hard to pick up a newspaper without reading about these problems. So in a sense, shouldn't parents already be well-informed on these issues?

It's not that parents are unaware of the problems on a broad scale. It's more that they aren't tuned in to the problems, struggles, and needs of their own kids. And there are reasons for this.

First, many parents of teenagers are themselves dysfunctional. Their marriages are either on the rocks or they're already divorced; or they're alcoholics; or they haven't figured out how to show their kids love and affection; or they're physically or emotionally absent from their families. Those adults have issues in their own lives that prevent them from being effective as parents.

Another thing that happens when adults read about the problems of teenagers is that they assume these are problems that other people's kids are facing. We prefer to think that our own kids would never contemplate suicide, take drugs, become promiscuous, or get involved in the occult. But it's time for all parents to face the facts: These problems are as likely to affect your kids as anyone else's.

When today's parents were in high school or college, drug and alcohol abuse and rebellion against authority were already widespread. Shouldn't that experience help parents understand the temptations their kids are facing?

Actually, the parallels you're suggesting aren't all that close. It's true that drugs, promiscuous sex, and open rebellion became much more widespread in the '60s. However, today's teenagers are living in a very different culture from the one we grew up in.

For example, in the 1960s fewer teenagers came from broken homes. But today it's common for a teenager to be living in a single-parent home or with one parent and one step-parent. That trend alone is having far-reaching adverse effects on teenagers.

In addition, today we have the destructive influences of occult involvement and the growing tendency to view suicide as a solution to a kid's problems. These are big changes from what was happening in the '60s.

But having said that, there are ways the '60s ethos continues to have a major effect on parents. For example, too many adults are allowing the relativistic values of the '60s to influence the way they raise their teenagers. Too many parents feel that their teens need to make their own decisions and set their own boundaries. And kids are suffering as a result of this "anything goes" attitude.

The fact is, kids don't need "hip" parents. They need loving, consistent, caring parents. Kids are searching for direction, for meaning, and for someone who loves them. Their parents should be the source of these things, but too often that isn't the case. That's one reason teenagers get caught up in drugs, promiscuous sex, and, in some cases, the occult. They aren't getting the love, attention, and support they need from their parents, so they resort to all these damaging things that stand waiting for them with open arms.

Are you saying teenagers are messed up because their parents aren't willing to enforce some hard-and-fast do's and don'ts?

Exactly. Permissiveness is a widespread problem. Most teenagers won't come up to their parents and say, "Hey Dad and Mom, you know what I really need? I need you to buckle down and enforce a strict curfew on me. And I also need for you to do a better job of monitoring my friendships. And while you're at it, why not ground me for a week or two whenever I blow off my schoolwork?" Kids are never going to say that, of course, but they're feeling it. And let's face it, they shouldn't have to say those things. The parents are the people God made responsible for the welfare of these kids.

Parents need to show consistency. They need to enforce moral standards and foster a sense of order, discipline, and trust. A teenager wants to know that his parents love him enough to be involved in his life. He wants his parents to show interest in his friendships, to be concerned about his schoolwork, and to love him enough to correct him when he shows signs of getting involved in self-destructive behavior.

I know parents who are reluctant to clamp down too hard. They don't want to be so unyielding that their kids overreact and get involved in things they might otherwise not even consider. Isn't it possible for parents to be too rigid?

Yes, it's possible to be too strict. That's why parents need to achieve a balance between the two requirements of good parenthood: The need to be consistent in enforcing the rules, while at the same time obeying God's command that we love our kids. When parents become too strict and the teenager rebels even more, it's usually because the parents are failing to love the child with the same passion and level of dedication that they employ in disciplining the kid.

You can't be a stickler on grades, curfew, and being drug- and alcohol-free and expect it to work if you're not also listening to your kids, devoting a lot of time to them, and getting involved in their lives. If you don't have love and discipline working together hand-in-hand, your kids will probably get involved in things you don't want them involved in.

Parents wonder why their teenagers won't talk to them. Well, if you're a kid you might be wondering, "Why bother talking to a brick wall?" To be a good parent you have to love your kids. And loving them means, in part, that you put them ahead of other concerns you might want to invest your time in.

What sorts of things might have to take a backseat to your teens?

Things like work, accomplishments, hobbies. Too many adults are caught up in getting ahead in their careers, buying a bigger house, playing golf every weekend, or any number of other self-centered pursuits. They devote so much energy to those things that they fail to free up the time necessary to really listen to their kids. And as a result their kids are adrift.

Parents often fail to realize that in order for their kids to open up to them, they need to spend blocks of time with their kids. A teenager needs a block of time to feel assured that he has his parents' attention. They need to be sure that you are concerned enough that you're willing to take time to really listen to their concerns.

Why do teenagers talk so candidly with you when they are often reluctant to talk to their own parents?

Part of it is that a lot of kids don't think their parents really care. And sadly, they are often right. If they don't see their parents making certain sacrifices in order to work at being good parents, or if they have already tried to talk to their parents and have been shut out by them, then they aren't going to keep trying. They'll either seek out another adult who will listen to them, such as me or their youth group leader at church, or they'll buy into whatever the youth culture is telling them to do.

That's part of the reason the rate of sexually transmitted diseases— and the rate of teen pregnancy—is rising. Kids are not being loved by their parents, so they accept a cheap substitute. Looking at this from the outside, we can see it's a poor counterfeit of genuine love. But these kids feel that it's better to accept a substitute than to face the hurt of not receiving love from their parents. The same dynamic is at work with teenagers who abuse alcohol and drugs, or get involved with the occult, or any other self-destructive behavior. If their parents aren't doing their job, kids will look for a substitute.

We frequently hear that parents who were in agreement on disciplining their kids when they were young start disagreeing when the

kids get older. One parent thinks their teenager needs more freedom, while the other parent feels it's time to really clamp down. What advice would you give those parents?

I would begin by saying that parenting problems sometimes uncover what has been a problem in the marriage all along. And that problem is a lack of communication between husband and wife. It's amazing how often you'll have a strict person marry a more laid-back person. I believe that God, in His grace, allows that to happen so we can balance each other out.

But it can create a lot of friction when the children reach adolescence. Of course, the basic answer is whether you agree or disagree over how to raise your teenager, you need to work out your differences away from the kids. You need to agree together that you will never sabotage one another in front of your kids.

If you fail to work out a united front, your kids will play one of you against the other. And a lot of times, the parents will end up turning against each other. The father might say to the child: "Well, I would let you go to the party, but you know how strict your mother is; and I'm not going to hassle her on this." This puts down the mother in front of the children, and it makes the kids insecure.

Instead of doing that, the couple should arrive at a decision together, but apart from the kids. Then the father should tell the teen: "Your mother and I have spent time praying and talking about this, and this is our answer. Now we're not going to argue with you about it." Taking that approach makes kids feel secure.

Do you agree that teenagers need more freedom as they grow older?

There is some truth to the idea that parents need to be more laid-back and give their children more freedom as the kids approach adulthood. As our kids get older we have to let them go.

But we don't just say to our kids: "Well, you're fifteen now, so Mom and I are going to back off. We've done our job, so now we'll wait and see what happens." You can't do that because the teen years can be dangerous, volatile times. You can have an unwanted pregnancy from just one quick one-night stand. And that one mistake will cause heartbreak and emotional scars for the rest of your and your child's lives. And that's only one example of the minefields in which kids are expected to make responsible decisions.

Have you ever thought about the critical decisions that a boy or girl makes in their teen years? They're thinking about the type of person they're going to marry, what kind of college they're going to go to, how they will develop a life philosophy. They know just enough about sex to get pregnant. They know just enough about driving to drive recklessly and get themselves killed. They know just enough about friends to latch onto the wrong ones. So, in a sense, kids need their parents as much when they are in their teens as they do when they are young children.

We've heard other experts say the best thing parents can do for their kids is to love each other—that the marriage relationship has to be primary. Do you agree that the parenting role should be subordinate to the marriage relationship?

Yes. In fact, that's true in more ways than one. For example, teenagers are self-centered in the sense that if there is a problem in their parents' marriage, the kids will almost always blame themselves for being the cause of the problem. And the opposite is also true. When their parents' marriage is healthy, the teenager is likely to feel good about himself or herself because they feel they are responsible for their parents having a good marriage. The teenager will think: "Maybe there's something good about me that's helping this marriage do so well!"

A second thing is this: If the child sees love and care between his parents, then he has a sense that he can go out and take on the world because as a family unit they stand strong. A loving family can overshadow all the negative, destructive influences in a teenager's world.

On the other hand, there is nothing more destructive than two parents who aren't walking with the Lord and loving each other in front of their kids. When that happens, your teenagers become fair game for drugs and alcohol, the misuse of sex, and all the other lies our culture tries to sell them. When parents are at war with each other, it plays on their child's insecurities. He doesn't know from one day to the next if his parents are going to be together, and that affects his entire sense of well-being.

We always hear that things are so bad in the youth culture that parents can't really comprehend the pressures their teenagers are facing. Have things really gone that far downhill?

I believe things really are worse today. As our culture turns further away from God, we need stronger Christian families. Unfortunately, some parents see how bad the youth culture is and they panic and overreact. Or else they go to the other extreme and deny reality by saying, "No one in our family ever got pregnant out of wedlock, and our kids aren't going to either."

We need to avoid both of these extremes. Parents need to face the facts head-on. Talk with your kids. Spend more time with them and not less. Love them more, not less, because the culture is constantly chipping away at the kids' self-esteem. Hug your kids, build them up with your praise, and spend extra time with them.

Given that things are this bad, how well are parents doing to help ground their teenagers in the faith?

Frankly, most parents aren't doing a very good job, and there are two main reasons why. First, too many parents don't think it's important enough. They haven't realized how powerful it is to help kids really walk with God.

And second, you can't give away what you don't have. Kids will watch their parents closely to determine if Mom and Dad really are people of God. Kids want to know if the Christian faith actually works, and one way they can be shown that is to observe it working in the lives of their parents. In the end, Christianity is not simply taught, it's caught. And if you don't have it, children won't catch it.

So I say to parents, "Get right with God. Live for God not simply for yourself, but also for your children and your children's children." God didn't put us here to win a popularity contest. He entrusted us with the task of raising godly children. And He gives us the power to make good on that responsibility.

Jim Burns

Teaching by Example

How to make your marriage a powerful source of moral instruction and development for your children.

Interviewed by Mark Moring

As president of the National Institute of Youth Ministry, Jim Burns insists he's no marriage expert. But if there's one thing this youth specialist does know, it's the power of a loving marriage.

"We need to kiss in front of our kids," he says. In Jim's case, the woman he's kissing is his wife, Cathy. And it's often done in the presence of their three daughters.

Burns is the author of several books, including *Drug-Proof Your Kids* (Regal) and *Steering Them Straight* (Focus on the Family). Having worked with teenagers and their parents for more than twenty-five years, he knows what types of marriages produce young people who grow into healthy adults with their spiritual lives intact. Here's what Burns has to share with couples who want their marriages to send the right messages to their kids.

You've met a lot of kids over the years. Think of the ones who turned out well, and describe their parents' marriages.

One characteristic is that the parents continue to court each other. It's great for kids to see Mom and Dad putting their relationship first—sometimes even ahead of the kids. Most of the time the opposite happens: Parents make their kids such a priority that they don't have any time left for each other.

What do you mean by parents "courting" each other?

Part of it is affirming each other—in front of the kids. Even if it's just "thanks for a great meal!" Or, to say to one of your kids, "You know, I think your mom is the most beautiful woman in the world." Yesterday I told the girls, "Okay, you guys do the dishes. Mom and I are going to sit on the couch." I put my arm around Cathy and we had a great talk.

I try to show Cathy love and respect. The byproduct is that my kids are seeing their parents "date." When they see their parents give each other time, affection, and respect, they feel more secure.

What else does courting involve?

When we're out in public, I like to hold Cathy's hand. That says, in the midst of other women, I'm still choosing her. For Valentine's Day, I wrote fifty affirmation/thank-yous to Cathy. I printed them out from the computer and put them in a box. Our girls were so interested they read all of them. One says, "Thanks for being the world's greatest taxi cab driver," since Cathy chauffeurs our girls, and sometimes me, all over the place. Another one says, "Blue Lantern Inn." Our oldest daughter saw that and asked, "Hey, what did you guys do at the Blue Lantern Inn?" She doesn't need to know, but she gets the point that I'm in love with her mom.

Where does the oft-recommended "date night" fit in?

Cathy and I are obsessive when it comes to keeping our commitment to have a weekly date. There was a time, even before we had our girls, when Cathy had to tell me, "I resent the fact that you give your best time to the church."

We came up with three solutions: We'd have a regular date night; Cathy would have veto power over my schedule; and I'd try to be out only three nights a week doing youth work. Part of the reason our marriage is strong today is because we've been faithful to have a date night.

So good parents keep on dating each other. What else makes for healthy kids?

It seems obvious, but just do things with them! Pray together, play together, take vacations together. They don't have to be big-deal outings like a trip to Disneyland or a night at the movies. Our best communication times happen when we're out cruising on our bikes or walking on the beach.

Once a month Cathy and I let the kids plan a Family Fun Day. Our oldest daughter will say, "Hey, let's go into L.A." But our eight-year-old wants to go to McDonald's every time. Whatever we end up doing, Family Fun Day has become a meaningful tradition.

Your description makes it sound like a lot of fun. So why is family togetherness so hard to pull off?

One of the biggest problems is overcommitment—which is connected to fatigue. We live our lives at a breathless pace, and that hurts kids like crazy—more than parents realize. It's that old story where the dad says, "I work two jobs because I love my kids so much." Meanwhile, the kids are out doing drugs because they have no relationship with their dad.

When I graduated from college, a friend wrote me a note that said, "Jim, if the devil can't make you bad, he'll make you busy." If I'm not careful, I can become so busy that the most important things get run over. I'm a lousy husband and dad when I'm fatigued.

Little choices make a big difference. Cathy and I decided years ago that I would quit making early-morning breakfast appointments so I could get breakfast ready for the kids and take them to school. I work major hours now, but I don't work that early-morning shift. It has been such a joy for me to have those mornings with our kids. Perhaps it costs me, work-wise. But it's worth it. While kids and parents are together, the kids are learning—how to live a life of faith, how to live together in a family, how to fight.

Um . . . you're teaching your kids how to fight?

Every marriage has conflict, and kids need to see conflict being resolved. Parents often go behind closed doors before they really let it rip, and the kids never see them work through the tension. Cathy and I try not to leave the girls hanging. If we have a disagreement that can't be worked out in front of them, we say, "We need to go settle this, gang, and then we'll come back."

So after the argument is over, do you explain to your daughters how you and Cathy worked things out?

Well, take yesterday. We had just gotten home from a family trip, and our flights were delayed so we were running late. I was getting ready to go out of town again. Then I found that a family friend was coming over. I wanted to call her and say, "Hey, Pam, things are nutso around here. The kids have homework to do. We still haven't had dinner. Can we reschedule?"

But Cathy really wanted Pam to come over, so eventually she said, "So are you telling me what to do?" Our kids were in the room, and Christy, who's thirteen, said, "You know what, Mom? Dad's right." But the other girls insisted Cathy was right.

Sometimes we let our girls give input; that's part of learning how to resolve conflict. But this time I said, "This is not about you guys. Mom and I are going up to our room to discuss this." Cathy and I had ten minutes to iron out the problem. We ended up doing what Cathy wanted because the visit from Pam was so important to her. We told the kids what we had decided and, generally, why. Pam came over, we made a Taco Bell run, and Pam ate with us.

The point is, the kids saw Cathy and me each being intense about what we wanted, and then they saw that it could be worked out. Cathy and I don't resolve every issue, but in those instances the kids see us "agree to disagree" and move on.

And I hope my girls noticed that I love Cathy like crazy. Because that's life—conflict and love and appreciation. Kids need to feel that. Way too many kids have this idealistic view that they're gonna fall in love with Prince or Princess Charming, ride away on a great white horse, and live happily ever after. Okay, life is passion and love, but it's also conflict and give-and-take.

Did you and Cathy learn how to solve problems from your own families?

I was raised in a family that avoided fights. So when Cathy and I had our first argument, I didn't have a clue how to handle it. And get this: We were on our way to a youth-group meeting to talk about the joys of marriage! I can't even remember what that argument was about. But I remember feeling like a hypocrite while I gave that talk.

Today, I'd handle it differently. I'd tell the students, "Look, Cathy and I had a disagreement on the way over here." Young people should know that adults don't have it all together, but God's principles can help us make it.

When we got married, we had no idea we'd have so much conflict. But early in our marriage we agreed divorce was never going to be an option. That decision brought security. We said, "If we're gonna have conflict for the rest of our marriage, how can we work through it instead of running from it?"

We believe God has kept us together. Now we're quick to say, "Look what God has done for us."

That fits in with your commitment to live out your faith in front of your daughters.

You know, of all the students I've worked with since 1971, probably 85 percent of the young people who are thriving came from homes where there was an active faith. When parents have a solid faith, the kids often follow suit. Cathy and I believe our primary reason for living is to instill our faith into the lives of our children. Christian education takes place first at home, not in the church.

Cathy and I know that our Christian commitments are the only reason we're still together. We want our kids to have the stabilty that comes from giving your life to God, so it's good for them to see us praying—to watch us give our problems and issues and conflicts and joys and everything else to God. Our active faith teaches them how to have an active faith.

Cathy regularly takes the girls with her to a nursing home. She is also the most disciplined person I've ever seen when it comes to having devotions. One day when our middle daughter was four, I found her sitting in the chair where Cathy reads her Bible. She had a Disney book—and it was upside down because she couldn't read yet. "I'm doing 'votions," she told me. Our kids know that Mom values her time with God.

Do you have formal "family devotions"?

We started with traditional devotions when our girls were young, but it didn't work very well. Now we have a family meeting—we try to do it weekly. Sometimes we do skits and let the kids act out passages of Scripture. A while back, we did the story of Adam and Eve. They made me be the serpent! No one wanted to be Adam; I had to talk Christy into it. She drew a mustache on her face and put on a flowered shirt—you know, the garden motif. Rebecca, who's eight, played Eve, and she showed up without any clothes on. She said, "Well, Eve wasn't wearing anything, was she?" Cathy and I looked at each other and said, "Nope!" The play must go on! Later I told her, "Rebecca, just don't do that in Sunday School!"

Sometimes we do "affirmation bombardment," where we say, "Heidi, the thing I appreciate about you is ..." Each person does it for every other family member. Or we play a thankful game: "I'm thankful because ..."

This week we tried a game called "Start, Continue, and Stop." I said to the girls, "Fill in this blank: I'd like us as a family to start . . ." And then, "I'd like us as a family to continue . . ." and then "stop." Heidi said, "I'd like to continue our devotions." And when we got to "stop," the conversation revolved around conflict: "I'd like us to stop arguing so much." It was great to gauge how the kids were feeling about our family life, and then we prayed together.

There's no magic formula that works for every family all the time. If traditional devotions don't work, we keep trying other books, other activities until we find something that does.

What do you hope your marriage is saying to teenagers in general and to your own kids in particular?

A healthy Christian marriage provides a lot of hope. In a recent poll, 74 percent of teens said they'd live with someone before marriage or instead of marriage. The majority of kids also said they didn't think their parents had a great marriage.

However, more than 90 percent of them still said they want to get married someday. Fifty percent of today's kids don't live at home with both parents, yet the majority still want to marry. They need hope and role models. Folks like Cathy and me and others are trying to make that happen.

SOMETHING TO TALK ABOUT

1. Irene and Merton Strommen describe some of the ways marriages are altered by having children. What were the biggest changes, both good and bad, that we experienced when we first had children? What are the current trade-offs, the lifestyle losses versus the blessings and gains of parenting?
2. Is our personal time weighted more heavily in favor of our kids, or toward time with each other? Do we feel the current balance is appropriate? If not, what changes do we need to make?

3. Gary Smalley is a big believer in honoring and valuing each member of the family. How is expressing "value" different from expressing "love" to those closest to us?

4. What are the "great things" about each of our kids? Do we regularly praise them for their admirable qualities?

5. What difficult experiences from the past call for the practice of "treasure hunting"—that is, looking for the positive results or blessings that came from the trials?

6. Dawson McAllister pulls no punches when he details the temptations facing today's teenagers. What fears do we have regarding our children's teen years? How can we pray and work together to offset certain temptations that confront them?

7. Is our parenting style too permissive, too strict, or a good balance of reasonable discipline in the context of clearly expressed love? If changes are needed, how can we begin that process?

8. Do our kids feel the freedom to talk to us? Why or why not?

9. Jim Burns, at the end of this chapter, makes a strong case for parents romancing each other in front of their kids. How does each of us like to be "courted?" Do our children see us showing affection to each other?

10. In what ways is our faith being communicated to our kids? What wisdom and life skills do we think our children have picked up from observing us interact as husband and wife?

Chapter Nine

REDEEMING FAILURE

Forgiveness
Lewis B. Smedes

Betrayal
Donald R. Harvey

Anger
Gary Smalley

Starting Over
Walter and Thanne Wangerin

Lewis B. Smedes

Forgiveness

When it's better not to forgive. A thorough analysis of forgiveness and its application in marriage.

Interviewed by James D. Berkley

Even when we're trying not to, we all mess up. And it's never easy to go to your mate and apologize. But it's even harder to humble yourself and ask your spouse for forgiveness.

It's no wonder, then, that so many people struggle with anger and resentment toward their spouses. If a wrong is committed and isn't made right, it doesn't just go away. It spreads beneath the surface to infect the entire relationship.

Since forgiveness is essential to overcome the damage of sin, we asked ethicist Lewis B. Smedes to explain how both the offender and the offended can seek and find forgiveness in marriage. Smedes is professor emeritus of theology and ethics at the Graduate School of Psychology at Fuller Theological Seminary in Pasadena, California. He is the author of a number of books, including *A Pretty Good Person: What It Takes to Live with Courage, Gratitude and Integrity* (HarperSanFrancisco) and *The Art of Forgiving* (Ballantine).

Smedes and his wife, Doris, have three grown children, and they lost another soon after birth. In this interview, he explains why spouses need to go beyond the cheap apology, and he shows us how to get to the core of the crisis of forgiveness.

We each have our share of flaws, so how can we best deal with the nettlesome shortcomings of a spouse?

It's interesting that we're talking about marriage, since there is no other relationship in which our personal flaws become more transparent. Given the intimacy and relentless routines of marriage, our own flaws not only are revealed as we become transparent to each other, but they also are exacerbated, because they're in constant conflict with our partner's flaws.

What do you mean when you say "flaws"?

Let's consider flaws as gaps in our character, the habitual patterns that annoy others, and the potential for hurting other people. Sometimes these character flaws become confused with disappointments in the relationship. For instance, someone expects to enjoy a lifetime of happiness and wakes up to the fact that his or her partner has a disabling, long-term illness. Or a husband and wife expect to have children, but discover that one partner is infertile.

One of my disappointments in marriage was our failure to bear children. And then, after years of praying and trying, when we finally had a child of our own, he died. I found it hard to keep our inability to have children in perspective. Even though we may know infertility isn't a character flaw, we can easily experience our disappointment as a "flaw" in our mate.

It's important to sort out personal flaws from things that disappoint us—things like a person's low energy level, neuroses, anxieties, or depression. Living with a depressed person, for example, is extremely difficult, and the spouse may begin to view the other's depression as a character flaw. But it is, in fact, a tragic dimension in which the depressed person is a victim.

What about failings that are more volitional in nature?

Certainly each of us has moral flaws. Take, for instance, the flaw of selfishness and insensitivity to another's needs, of lack of respect for the partner's boundaries, of constant teasing, or of emotional infidelity—having friendly relationships that have an intimacy that is not sexual but still inappropriate. And then, of course, there's out-and-out physical infidelity. These are not mere disappointments. They are moral failings serious enough to violate a marriage.

What should the formerly idealistic spouse do when harsh reality takes over? When is it time to forgive?

We mustn't begin talking about forgiveness too quickly. First, each of us needs a "conversion"—a reorientation—of the spirit that will lead us to live creatively, graciously, and patiently in a flawed relationship.

That sounds great, but how do we go about being converted?

It often requires a profound reorientation of one's expectations toward life. It's a conversion from an egoistic, hedonistic ethic (which many Christians have without knowing it) to an ethic of willingness to suffer, an ethic of accommodation to others' weaknesses, an ethic of patience with the other person's inability to provide you with all that you need.

This is particularly true of aggressive people as they move toward middle age. I went through a period in my own marriage where a voice deep within me complained, "I'm not getting out of this marriage what I'm putting into it, or what I assume I have a right to expect from it." In short, I tended to concentrate on what I was missing. I became, for a while, in my discontent, a "hedonistic egoist."

The only way out of that kind of attitude is a renewed spiritual conversion that opens our eyes to the inevitability of pain and gives us a new willingness to accept our portion of suffering in life.

But in our society we're immersed in the expectation of self-fulfillment. Isn't there some value in becoming all we can be?

Self-fulfillment is important, but as a means, not as an end. As important as psychological fulfillment may be, to make our self-fulfillment our ultimate goal in marriage makes putting up with each other's flaws that much more difficult. It is a mistake to think of our marriage as a means to our own fulfillment. Instead, we should think of our self-fulfillment as a means to a better marriage.

What can we do to be converted away from such self-centeredness? Is it a matter of shifting our thinking?

Thinking isn't enough, although right thinking and understanding are important. We need to experience—no, appropriate—grace, so that we base our lives on God accepting us in spite of what we are.

How have you made that work in your marriage?

I've been married for forty-eight years, and I can testify to the truth that self-fulfillment is reached most surely and most richly by not seeking it. Remember the hedonist fallacy: Happiness is a good, but you don't get happiness by seeking it; you get happiness by seeking that which brings good?

I went through a period in my forties and early fifties when, if it hadn't been for Doris' patience, and loyalty, and love, our marriage would have dissolved because we were at such loggerheads in our feelings about life. At that time our daughter was an adolescent hothead, a volcano of anger toward the mother who gave her up for adoption. Both Doris and I were deeply pained and frustrated, each of us failing to understand how the other was handling the pain.

At the same time, I was prey to the feeling that I was being cheated out of some of the happiness I'd dreamed of having. I became an angry person, and my need to appear the "sanctified professor of ethics" made my anger more inwardly destructive. Thankfully, Doris believed in God and in God's patience with angry fathers. Her patience with me and her faith in God made my own recovery possible and preserved our marriage.

We've talked about failure. Now what can you tell us about forgiveness?

Let me reel off several points. First, don't forgive everything that annoys you. There are some pains that we ought not to forgive for two reasons: (1) they're not serious enough; and (2) they're not things for which another person is responsible, such as depression.

A man once came to me and said, "My wife has been depressed for three years. Now she's just a couch potato who leaves the couch only to fill her stomach. I can't take it. How can I forgive her?"

So I asked, "Would you forgive her if she broke her leg? It's the same thing. You don't forgive. You bear, you wait, you suffer along with her."

Patience is not the same thing as forgiving. We ought to pray for an unsung gift: the gift of magnanimity, the gift of being willing to accommodate, cope with, and endure each other's weaknesses.

Some things are too trivial to forgive. Everyone has annoying behavior patterns that are better accommodated to than forgiven. For example, I have a habit of channel switching on the television. It's very annoying to my wife; it grates on her, and she tells me so. But she doesn't forgive me for that. While I'm trying to improve, she basically says, "I'll put up with that."

And Doris has nettlesome, but trivial, faults that I need not forgive but rather put up with. She's a perfectionist, for example, and I find it annoying that her perfectionism keeps her from doing little things that I wish she would do quickly because she can't get to them until she's in a position to do them very well. Again, I don't need to forgive her for that.

How do we know what needs to be forgiven and what merits only acceptance?

We have to develop the gift of discernment to recognize the flaws that should be put up with and the things that need to be forgiven. In general, you need to forgive the things that (1) your partner does for which he or she is responsible, and (2) cause deep hurt such that the partner is not only pained but wronged. To be hurt and to be wronged is a moral offense that forces us to say, "Our relationship cannot go on as it has been unless something happens to overcome the wrong and heal the pain." This is the crisis of forgiveness.

What else can you tell us about forgiveness?

To mention just one thing, it's important to be concrete. Forgiveness must be so specific that before we even think about forgiving, we should write down the exact thing we need to forgive. We should only forgive for something specific that a person did. We should not forgive someone for being a bad person.

In other words, forgive what somebody does, not what he or she is. Piece by piece, one thing at a time. Don't forgive a spouse for being someone who always does something wrong. I once had a habit of saying, "You always do this!" It made things difficult for Doris, because if I tried to forgive her, I would be accusing her of being the kind of person who always did something that hurt me. God can forgive wholesale, but we have to do it retail—one thing at a time.

Should forgiveness be spoken?

Not always. Not everybody is skilled at telling other people what they're being forgiven for. Often if you tell somebody, "I forgive you," it's an invitation for the other person to say, "What should you forgive me for? You had it coming!" So instead of making things better it just reopens the controversy.

Now I'm not recommending this as a hard rule. I'm only saying that we can forgive in silence, doing the work of forgiving, which in itself tells the person that you have forgiven him or her even though you haven't spoken the words.

How does forgiveness enter into the process of reconciliation?

In the suffering of serious wrong, there can be no reconciliation until there is forgiveness. But there can be forgiveness without reconciliation. Forgiveness, which happens in the mind and heart of the injured person, opens the possibility of reconciliation. Reconciliation is the ultimate goal. But sometimes we need to forgive even when we cannot be reconciled.

What, in the final analysis, is forgiveness?

When you forgive someone, you do three basic things: First, you surrender your right to get even. If you have been wronged, getting even is the natural impulse.

Second, you revise your caricature of the person who hurt you. When you've been deeply wounded by your spouse, you redraw your picture of that person, making him or her not primarily your husband or wife, but rather "the person who hurt you." So in forgiving, you need to reconstruct that image and see your spouse as a flawed, weak human being—not much different from yourself—who hurt you as much out of weakness as out of ill will.

And third, you revise your feelings. Gradually your feelings of rage are transformed into a desire for that person's blessing and for that person's change.

I suppose that's a gradual process.

Definitely. God can forgive in a single swoosh, but we are finite, temporal creatures for whom almost everything takes time. Some people—sometimes—can forgive in an instant. But most of us need a lot of patience with ourselves, especially when we forgive for deep hurts.

The biggest rub in many marriages comes at the point of repeated failure. How should we handle the mistake that won't go away?

The worst thing we can be is legalists, saying we should stop forgiving at such and such a point, or that we should keep on forgiving no matter what. Jesus said, "Forgive seventy times seven," but He didn't mean to count. What He meant was, "Be the kind of person who doesn't ask the question, 'How many times should I forgive?' Just be a forgiving person."

The proper question is not, "How often?" but rather, "Under what circumstances can I forgive?" Let's take a marriage in which there is savage and persistent brutality. I don't believe a spouse can forgive while the brutality continues. The spouse must first get out of reach and then begin a process of forgiving.

A second consideration is this: Repeated forgiving should not be confused with toleration of what's going on. We must be intolerant of evil of any kind, whether it happens to us or anyone else. We must signal that forgiving is not the same as being a fool, and forgiving is not the same as being a doormat.

You can forgive me almost anything, but if you tolerate everything I do you will make matters between us worse. Sometimes there comes a time when one spouse will say to the other, "I cannot forgive you while this continues. It must stop or I must get out, so that I can begin to forgive."

You're talking about clear-cut sins. What about the more prosaic scenarios in marriage when, say, one person just will not bother to keep the checkbook balanced? He or she keeps saying, "Honey, I'm sorry," but the behavior doesn't change.

Forgiving is a private activity, as is a sense of injury. I may think when I see this happening in someone else's marriage, "Well, that isn't deep enough to need forgiving. That just has to be worked out."

But the person involved in the situation has every right to say, "How do you know? You're not experiencing this. I sense that my partner is doing this not simply because he's a math klutz, but rather to spite me." At that point, it becomes a wrong in the feelings of the person who feels the pain.

Most of the time, I'd rather have somebody enter the process of forgiving when it's not in some objective sense called for than to keep the grudge or nourish the rage. But, again, we need a lot of discernment to tell us when to forgive and when to forbear.

Why not just go ahead and forgive? What's the harm?

There's a subtle danger in forgiving somebody, since forgiving always means blaming—holding the person responsible. So if we forgive too much, we load too much guilt and blame on the other person. That's what I worry about, because that could just make matters worse.

Another problem with forgiving too much is that forgiving can be a self-righteous act: You have done wrong, and I, a wonderful person, am willing to forgive you. Forgiving can be a way of getting an advantage, of making the blame unilateral, when forgiveness should usually take place in a context of shared blame.

Many people who need to forgive a mate have contributed to that for which the partner needs forgiving. Take infidelity. It may well be that the partner who is sinned against has been aloof, afraid of intimacy, or a carping critic. So when the spouse commits adultery and the "innocent party" forgives, that "innocent party" needs to forgive out of a context of shared blame.

There is, however, such a thing as a "guilty party;" the inadequacies that have contributed to the infidelity do not undo the fact that the infidelity was a sinful response and therefore needs to be forgiven.

How can a person forgive something as damaging as infidelity?

The most effective, and sometimes the most necessary, first step is to get on your knees and let God's forgiveness of you seep into your feelings—not into your intellect—but into the deepest recesses of your emotions. That's what's powerful.

You may have to get alone and give yourself time—maybe several weekends—in which you do nothing but wait for God to get through to your deepest feelings. It's when you become overcome with gratitude for being forgiven for your contributions to whatever went wrong—even if you don't know what those contributions are—that the power of resentment and rage gradually erodes, and it becomes much easier to forgive.

So far we've been talking about responding as the one who has been wronged by a mate. How about when we are the "wrongdoers"? How should we proceed?

The number one question to ask ourselves is: Have I done this for selfish reasons? And second: Am I rationalizing, deceiving myself into thinking that in my case the wrong is excusable? Sometimes we do seemingly "virtuous" things that actually have an underbelly of malice. If I'm really doing something "to get her," then I well need to be forgiven.

For example, during my angry period, I would do things like jump up from the dinner table to do the dishes before Doris got to them. I'd put dishes in the dishwasher with a rattle and clank, just to let her know I beat her to it. I didn't understand it then, but my secret motive was to make her feel incompetent, to make her feel pangs of failure that she wasn't taking care of things the way she should. I was flaunting my "virtue," flaying my wife with my goodness.

Our ability to deceive ourselves is almost unlimited, and self-deceit is difficult to recognize because we don't set out to deceive ourselves. I may get up in the morning and think, "I'm going to lie to my wife today," but I never get up in the morning and think, "I'm going to lie to myself today." We bamboozle ourselves without a conscious awareness of it.

Because of that, we need somebody who will say, "Buddy, what you're doing is wrong." We need a spouse who will say, "I don't want to tolerate this. You are doing something that is impermissible."

When a mate says that, how do you avoid becoming defensive?

Part of it is your spouse's approach. When my wife says, "Honey, I just can't take this," rather than, "What you're doing is totally wrong!" it helps me feel less defensive.

A lot of what we've been discussing requires a willingness to apologize. Is there any way to make that easier?

One approach is to remember that only the person who gets hurt knows how much it hurts. To you, it might be a triviality. But what you cannot do, then, is say to your spouse, "Oh, come on! I know it didn't hurt that much." What that is really saying is, "I didn't do anything that bad," which is not for the offender to say.

It takes discernment and empathy to feel along with your mate's hurt. Then you can repent not in terms of your estimate of the wrong you did, but in terms of the hurt it actually caused the other person.

Any final advice to give us?

When forgiveness is necessary, don't wait too long. We must begin to forgive, because without forgiving, we choke off our own joy; we kill our own soul. People carrying hate and resentment can invest themselves so deeply in that resentment that they gradually define themselves in terms of it. The offense and the resulting anger begin to possess you, until your identity is practically demonized by resentment.

So when forgiveness is truly necessary, forgive as quickly as you can, because forgiving has two good results: The first is your own release, and the second is the possibility of reconciliation.

Donald R. Harvey

Betrayal

How to identify patterns of betrayal in your own behavior and in the life of your mate. How to put a stop to those subtle betrayals, confess your failures, and start rebuilding trust.

Interviewed by Ron R. Lee

*E*arlier in this chapter, Lewis Smedes underscored the importance of forgiveness in preserving the health of your marriage. The obvious reason forgiveness is essential is because we all fail our mates, sometimes without even knowing it.

In fact, the sins we're blind to might very well be causing the most damage, according to Donald R. Harvey, Ph.D., author of seven books on marriage, including *I Love You—Talk to Me! A Change of Heart*, and

Surviving Betrayal (all published by Baker). Most people think of adultery as the greatest betrayal of the marriage vows. But Harvey, a marital therapist and graduate faculty member at Trevecca Nazarene University in Nashville, says most betrayal has nothing to do with sexual misdeeds.

We asked him to expose the hidden dangers of betrayal and to explain how couples can rebuild their relationships once the damage has been done. Here's what he had to say.

What are the most common ways spouses betray each other?

Much of the time, betrayal results from inaction rather than deliberate deeds. For instance, too many people neglect their spouses because they're overinvolved in their work or in parenting the kids. Or a person might betray his marriage vows by being insensitive to his mate's need for conversation, for companionship, or for sex. Either deliberately—or often quite unknowingly—people are betraying their spouses by failing to address their mate's needs.

Most spouses realize they could be doing a better job, but isn't "betrayal" too strong a word to describe the failure to meet your mate's needs?

For most people, the word "betrayal" conjures up thoughts of extreme wrongdoing, such as a secret addiction, habitual lying, or carrying on an affair. But betrayal actually covers a much broader scope of actions: It's anything that violates the marriage vows.

When couples stand at the altar, they commit themselves to love, comfort, honor, and cherish each other, and to forsake all others. In general, a person promises to "leave and cleave"—to make his mate a priority over all other earthly concerns. However, if a married person is paying more attention to his work, his friends, or the kids, he is actually betraying the vows he made.

Are there degrees of betrayal, or is every act equally destructive to a marriage?

Betrayal, by its very nature, has the potential to destroy a marriage. But it's important to understand that the failure of a marriage is a process, not a sudden event. It's like traveling from Nashville to Chicago. You could take a plane, a car, or a bicycle. Your destination wouldn't change— you'd still be headed for Chicago. The only thing that would change would be the amount of time it would take you to get there.

It's the same with the destructive effects of betrayal. Some behaviors, such as sexual infidelity, can get a marriage to the point of failure more quickly than others. But any act of betrayal, even a seemingly benign one, will create a lot of havoc if it becomes a pattern.

When you talk about a pattern, are you making a distinction between a person who slips up only once in a while and a person who makes a habit of violating the marriage vows?

Exactly. When I work with couples, I don't get concerned about isolated incidents of neglect or insensitivity. But I do get concerned about a pattern of betrayal. Let's say a woman is tired of eating cold dinners while she and the kids wait for her husband to get home from work. So they agree that, to ease mealtime stress, the husband will call if he's going to be late. Then, just a week after they reached this agreement, he's late for dinner again, and he failed to call.

If it was an honest mistake and he doesn't make a habit of forgetting to call, it's of little concern. But if it becomes a pattern, it will lead to trouble. When this sort of behavior—in this instance being insensitive and inconsiderate—becomes a pattern, it tears down the assumption that you can be counted on. It also communicates to your spouse, "I really don't care about you, because if I cared I'd stick to our agreement."

A person doesn't lose hope because of a single incident; he or she loses hope because of repetitive behavior. It eats away at your marriage, and eventually a mate will reach the conclusion that the future is going to be no better than the past. When that happens, a person loses hope in his or her mate and in the marriage. That's when people start thinking about divorce.

But life is unpredictable, and reality dictates that your job or the demands of raising kids have to be made a high priority. How can a person determine when his or her commitment to other responsibilities becomes a betrayal of the marriage vows?

It's obvious that things like holding down a job and raising children are quite demanding, and we have to devote large amounts of time to them. All of life's external issues are important, they're just not all-important. We need to strive for balance, both outside and within the marriage. Your outside involvements and responsibilities must not be prioritized above your marriage relationship.

The balance we all need to strive for can be described as "his, hers, and theirs." Each spouse needs his or her own set of outside interests, as well as separate peer support networks. These "his" and "hers" realms help each spouse maintain some emotional balance. It's unrealistic to expect your mate to meet all of your social and emotional needs.

However, if the separate "his" and "hers" realms become more important than the realm the couple share together in marriage, their relationship is being neglected. This often builds gradually, so that its effects aren't seen immediately.

If a marriage has been damaged due to a pattern of betrayal, what can a couple do to restore their relationship?

It depends on how badly their relationship has deteriorated. With isolated incidents of neglect or inattentiveness, for example, about all they need to do is acknowledge the problem and agree to do things differently in the future. Then, of course, they need to stick to their agreement.

But when repetitive behavior has caused what I call a "pattern wound," significant damage has occurred and three things must happen before the marriage can be restored: resolution, reconciliation, and restoration.

To resolve the betrayal, couples need to identify the problem and acknowledge their own contributions to it. They can't continue to deny that anything is wrong or pretend that once the problem is out in the open that everything will be okay. It's impossible to "just forget it ever happened." Betrayal is laden with all kinds of emotion, so there must be an airing of past actions, feelings, consequences, motivations—all the things that contributed to the destructive behavior.

Once the problem is out in the open, the next step is to reconcile the relationship. If there has been significant betrayal, reconciliation must include an admission of guilt on the part of the offender; genuine remorse for the pain that his or her actions have caused; a recommitment to the marriage; and a demonstrated change in behavior. Repentance and forgiveness—both sought and extended—bring healing to a relationship.

For the final step, restoration, to take place, both spouses need to be committed to positive change. Having already laid a foundation of healing, they need to deal with the dynamics in their marriage that led to the problem occurring.

I have a saying: "What was still is." The natural tendencies, characteristics, and dynamics that allowed the relationship to deteriorate are still there. And now, with reconciliation achieved, the husband and wife are ready to deal with those issues.

We've been talking mostly about everyday issues like staying late at the office or being overinvolved with your kids—not the "biggies" like adultery or a secret addiction.

Part of the problem is that confronting even these everyday issues makes people feel uncomfortable. And too many people are unwilling to do things that make them feel uncomfortable, even if that would be best for their marriage. People let their emotional comfort level control what they do, and actually that's another type of betrayal.

Let's say I'm frustrated with something my wife, Jan, has done, but I fail to deal with it because conflict makes me uneasy. When that happens, my behavior is being controlled not by my commitment to my wife, but by my comfort level. By choosing to avoid discomfort, I am eliminating the opportunity to resolve an issue in my marriage that is causing dissatisfaction.

But if I'm committed to my wife and my marriage, I'll be willing to suffer some discomfort in order to do what is in the best interest of our relationship. To have closeness in your marriage, you have to be willing to deal with problems. And you also need to be open and vulnerable with each other.

Now you've introduced another wrinkle, the need to be vulnerable. Is that as important as the need to address problems as they come up?

The two go together. To achieve intimacy in marriage, you and your mate both need to be vulnerable—to share what you think and who you are. This involves sharing weaknesses, fears, and feelings of inadequacy or neediness. But it also includes sharing the things that aren't so threatening—your dreams and joys, for example. That type of openness allows two people to bond together, to be intimate.

Admittedly, most people find it difficult to reveal this much of themselves, even to their spouse. But if you take the easy road and remain closed, you are betraying your marriage. If you go ahead and take the risk of opening yourself to your mate, warts and all, you'll enjoy greater intimacy.

We all know that confronting problems and admitting weakness aren't easy. In fact, most of what marriage requires of us isn't what anyone would call "easy." But the good news is that doing the things that contribute to health and intimacy in marriage does become easier with practice. It's really a matter of getting started and then keeping at it. Over time, your marriage will become more intimate and you'll see that all your effort was worth it.

Gary Smalley

Anger

Fear, frustration, and unmet expectations create anger that many of us try to bury. But buried anger comes back to haunt us. Here's what to do about hidden anger.

Interviewed by Ron R. Lee

Anger and intimacy don't mix. In fact, when it comes to relationships, anger has the power to kill, says relationship expert Gary Smalley, the author and co-author of fourteen books, including *Making Love Last Forever* (Word), *Hidden Keys of a Loving, Lasting Marriage* (Zondervan), and, with John Trent, *Love Is a Decision* (Word).

Smalley speaks not only from what he has observed in his thirty years as a teacher and counselor, but also from his own experience of reaching the melt-down point. That's why he is devoting much of his current work to solving the problem of anger.

Here is his strategy for disarming your anger before it explodes and hurts someone you love.

People seem to be reacting to situations with an intensity that is way out of proportion to their circumstances. Why do relatively insignificant events trigger such extreme reactions?

People have a tendency to avoid dealing with hurtful situations when they occur. Instead, they try to bury the pain. But it just builds up inside them and eventually turns into anger. Anger is a secondary emotion, which means it begins as something else—usually fear, frustration, hurt feelings, or major disappointment. We can try to bury our anger, but it's always buried alive. And it's just a matter of time before it comes out.

When I explain this to people, they start looking back over their lives and a lot of issues come into sharper focus. They say, "Wow, I was hurt by something my parents did years ago. I didn't realize it, but I'm still really angry at them."

What made you decide to focus much of your recent work on combating anger?

It was two different things. First, I've seen too much damage done in the lives of the couples I've counseled over the years. And the other reason is that I have suffered the devastation of anger in my own life.

When I was in my thirties, I was working on the staff of a para-church ministry—a job I really loved. I started noticing some things in the ministry that I thought needed to be addressed, so I challenged the leaders on a few matters. But instead of welcoming my input, they rejected me.

Up until then, I had never known what it felt like to be rejected. And since I didn't understand it, I responded by pressing a little harder, thinking they just weren't hearing what I was trying to say. But the more I pressed, the more negative they became toward me. I ended up being squeezed out of that organization.

You mention feeling rejected. Was that an instance of anger growing out of another emotion?

Clearly, my anger was produced by the rejection I was feeling. It hurt me deeply, and I became so angry I actually wanted to have a fistfight with one of my bosses. At the time, I didn't understand all that was going on, but I was sure experiencing the symptoms.

What were the symptoms?

A big one was that I lost interest in spiritual things. I didn't want to pray or read the Bible. My anger was diminishing the importance of God in my life.

Another symptom was that I started rehearsing the pain. I was convinced my bosses were planning to fire me, which made me feel like a victim. It was like I had a videotape that kept playing in my mind. I'd mentally berate them: "You're going to deny me the work I love. You're going to prevent me from supporting my family." I'd rehearse all of that over and over.

I even started having physical symptoms. I tried to stay away from my bosses because I'd literally become nauseated whenever I was around them. I realized I couldn't stay there, so I quit.

How did all that turmoil affect your marriage?

Well, I left that organization with a tremendous amount of bitterness. And it created a lot of distance between Norma and me. I started saying and doing a lot of hurtful things, and I didn't even know where they were coming from. I would try to excuse my behavior by saying I was upset or stressed out.

How did Norma react?

She didn't understand what was happening, and she took a lot of it personally. She tried to get me to talk about what was going on, but I was in the dark. I didn't make the connection between my anger and the emptiness I was feeling.

Things got so bad that I finally started crying out to God, asking Him to release me from the burden I was under. And little by little, from reading books and talking with a lot of different people, I began to get insights into what was going on.

What was the most important thing you learned?

One of the most important lessons was that my anger was tied up with a lot of unforgiveness. Jesus told His disciples: "If you do not forgive men their sins, your Father will not forgive your sins" (Matt. 6:14-15, NIV). There are dire consequences for the unforgiving person, and that's what I was back then.

What helped you get over that hurdle?

I had to put everything in context. I'd been sinned against, to be sure.

But I realized that my sins against God greatly outnumbered the few offenses that others had committed against me. I could identify only about ten offenses I had suffered at the hands of my former bosses, yet I was unwilling to release them. That's when I told myself: "Smalley, God has forgiven you of all this junk you've done against Him. So you have to forgive these other guys whether you like it or not."

If you didn't want to forgive them, how did you get yourself to do it?

One thing that helps is to understand that people who offend us usually carry around a lot of pain in their own hearts. When I found out that my former bosses had both been deeply wounded by others, my compassion for them started building. After that, I committed the matter to prayer. I confessed my sin of not forgiving them, and then I said out loud, "I release you. I forgive you. God forgives you." I pictured the Lord hugging my former employers, and I just started weeping. I was a basket case for about five hours.

So forgiveness is a big part of conquering anger. What else can we do to keep anger in check?

One of the biggest causes of anger is disappointment over not getting what we expect. We expect life to work out in our favor—we want to be loved and appreciated and all that. But the truth is we'll never get everything we want or expect. If we can accept that fact, it will do a lot to minimize our big disappointments.

Second, we can't choose what others will do—we can't keep someone from hurting us. But we can always choose how we will react. We can prevent adverse circumstances from controlling us by choosing a road away from anger to forgiveness and healing.

It's not easy to choose not to get angry when every fiber in your body is gearing up for a good venting. How do you flip the "off" switch?

Part of it is realizing that you're not being singled out as a victim. We all get blasted by life—that's true no matter who we are. But we won't grow spiritually from these experiences unless we look for the good things that can come from the pain.

What's so good about pain?

It's not the pain itself that's good, but the things pain can produce in our lives. It can make us more loving, more sensitive, and more empathetic if we really search for it.

No one would naturally be thankful for being rejected or for losing something they deeply value. But the Bible says "give thanks in all circumstances" (1 Thes. 5:18, NIV). As we start to become grateful for circumstances that hurt us, we'll see a change in our attitudes. Our motivation changes, our self-confidence rises, a lot of things improve. One of the best ways to overcome anger is to be thankful for everything that happens.

How does this apply to marriage?

Well, we all need to start focusing on honor, which means placing a high value on your spouse. It's the opposite of being angry, and it's another of the choices we make.

When Norma does something I don't like, I may react negatively at first. But as soon as I can, I start honoring her in my mind. I pray, "God, would You help me be a source of encouragement to my wife—this woman I value so highly? Will you show me how I can help her?" It's a matter of taking control of your attitudes and emotions and steering them away from an angry response.

What are some ways you can help your spouse, especially when you're so mad you can't see straight?

One way is to control how we talk when we're mad, which not only defuses the anger but helps us arrive at solutions much more quickly. Norma and I have found a way to have an argument that brings honor to our relationship. It's based on a communication method developed at the Center for Marital and Family Studies at the University of Denver. I like to call it "drive-through talking," because it's similar to what happens when you order fast food at the drive-through window.

Are you saying you argue with your wife the same way you order fast food?

Something like that. Think about what happens in the drive-through lane at a burger place. You pull up to the speaker. The person inside asks for your order. Then it's your turn to express your "needs." You recite the complete order, without being interrupted. When you're done, the person inside repeats what you just said, to make sure he or she understood it.

You listen to the person repeating back your order, and you either say, "Yes, that's right" or "No, I ordered two burgers, not one."

That's great if you want lunch. But how does it solve the problem of anger?

If you're really mad at each other, you need a way to keep things under control. This method controls what you say, and how you say it. One mate "stays in the car" and expresses his or her needs and feelings. The other spouse stays inside the burger place and has only one purpose, to understand the person who is placing the order.

When the first speaker is satisfied that his or her mate understands what has been said, they trade places. Now the second spouse is in the drive-through lane, explaining his feelings and needs, and the other is listening and repeating back what is being said. They keep switching back and forth until they both feel understood. When you take the time to really listen to each other—without judging each other's feelings—you'd be amazed how it dissipates your anger.

That's it, just talking and listening without interrupting?

There's one other thing. Avoid using the word "you," since that usually ends up being an accusation or a criticism. "You always do this. You never do that."

How can you have a disagreement without using the word "you"?

You start by not accusing your mate of having ulterior motives or doing something with the intent of hurting you. You can say something like, "I've been feeling pretty discouraged lately and I really need to be held." Or, "I've been under a lot of pressure at work and now that I'm home I need to be left alone for a while." Statements such as those reveal your own feelings and needs without criticizing your mate or accusing him or her of doing something wrong.

What's wrong with just having a normal conversation? Do we have to pretend we're at a burger joint?

In most cases, a normal conversation is great. But make sure you're not using it to try to gloss over the anger you're feeling. Anger is such an unsettling emotion that we're tempted to shove it aside and not deal with it. But it won't just go away. If we don't take responsibility for our own anger, it will come back later to haunt us.

Walter and Thanne Wangerin

Starting Over

Walter Wangerin admits that he really messed things up early in his marriage. How did he prove himself trustworthy again, and how did his wife find the grace to forgive him?

Interviewed by Annette LaPlaca

So far, this chapter has analyzed the problem and the pain of failure. But the redemptive aspect of failure is that, when handled biblically, it can lead to a new beginning. That's what happened in the marriage of Walter and Thanne Wangerin.

Years ago, Walter was consumed by the responsibilities of a demanding parish ministry; and Thanne wondered whether her husband even remembered he had a wife. One night Walter woke up in an empty bed. He went looking for Thanne, who was curled up on the sofa with tears streaming down her face. When he found her, all she said was "Don't touch me."

Thanne had been quietly withering, feeling abandoned by Walter as she cared for their four young children. She also was struggling to address the needs of their extended family. Meanwhile, Walter devoted longer hours to his work—failing to notice the burdens weighing down his wife. Until he found her that night on the sofa, so distraught she refused to be touched.

Thanne's anger and pain were deeply rooted, and Walter feared he had doomed their marriage to years of emptiness. But he began to set aside time and energy for his wife, and Thanne worked out a freeing balance in their life together. These efforts, along with the giving and receiving of forgiveness, made it possible for them to start over.

Today, after twenty-nine years of marriage, the Wangerins find their life has been far from empty. A few years ago they moved to northern Indiana, where Walter is a professor and writer-in-residence at Valparaiso University. Now that their children are grown, Thanne plans to return to graduate school.

In this interview, they share the lessons they have learned about starting over.

The concept of two flawed people living in the same house for fifty years or more seems to necessitate a lot of forgiveness.

Thanne: A marriage can't exist without it.

Walter: Without forgiveness, sin will destroy a marriage. Forgiveness is daily renewal. It's like your blood—it keeps pumping through your body, picking up fresh oxygen and renewing every cell. If that renewal stops, death begins. Forgiveness is a marriage's lifeblood.

What do you mean, exactly, when you say "marriage's lifeblood"?

Walter: A long-lasting marriage does not have a flat-line of growth. Trust and hope grow in spurts. It's like your relationship with God. Certain events—like the moment you become aware of your need for God and accepted His salvation—are so significant that they illuminate everything that follows. From then on, you understand your status as a person forgiven by God.

Likewise, the one "big" marital crisis Thanne and I faced created a lasting atmosphere of forgiveness in our marriage. She had so much to forgive me for and so much change to trust me for, her forgiveness was an obvious work of God's grace. That crisis shines on the rest of our marriage. It showed us God could do something even in that terrible moment of terrible emotion, so we never have to feel that hopeless again.

Thanne, how did you manage to forgive Walter when the hurt went so deep?

Thanne: Well, I didn't do it myself. I couldn't forgive Walt; I didn't even choose to forgive him. It was God's miracle that moved us both. I forgave him. But it's important to note that he forgave me too, for my anger, for my part in the misunderstandings, and everything else. It worked both ways.

Walter: Once Thanne woke me up to how I had hurt her, I crashed. We were both in despair. It didn't look like a beginning, but it was. The subtle, beautiful beginning of God's forgiveness comes when the sinner realizes his sin.

Thanne: I didn't forgive Walt because he had changed or because our problems had been solved. Forgiveness had to come before the change. People get it backward, thinking "I'll forgive as I see that the person is really sorry and is really changing." But the forgiveness is the beginning of healing.

Walter: That's a crucial truth. Also, Thanne wasn't forgiving me just to save our marriage or because it would be the best thing for our family. It wasn't a pragmatic decision. Grace offers forgiveness as a pure gift. That's when forgiveness becomes marriage's lifeblood. Forgiving doesn't remove all the hurt feelings. It's not a love potion. Fears and anger can remain, but something new—God's intrusion of grace—comes in to energize your relationship.

The conventional wisdom is that it's important to "forgive and forget." Are you able to "forget" something that has been forgiven between you?

Walter: Often it can be important *not to* forget. I shouldn't forget how I hurt Thanne early in our marriage because "forgetting" would mean I could easily go back to taking her for granted and breaking her spirit. Change was necessary. And I don't want Thanne to forget either, because she's the one who sends up the red flag when she sees me slipping back into neglect.

Thanne: It's good for a husband and wife to become sensitive to a particular sin and help each other avoid it. Walt does the same for me.

Walter: But the fact that we both occasionally confess sins to each other doesn't mean we're "even"—with an unsteady balance of "you forgave me, so I forgive you." That's not grace. Grace extends the forgiveness and doesn't keep score.

How does not forgetting past sin and forgiveness work to improve your marriage?

Thanne: For one thing, it means when things go wrong, neither of us finds the situation hopeless. When we were first married, Walt was quick to think, "This is the end." He didn't think we would divorce, just that our marriage from that point on would be grim. But when he learned that forgiveness would eventually come, it actually gave me a lot more freedom. Before that time, I thought if I expressed completely how I felt Walt would sink into hopelessness and I'd have to "fix" that too.

Walter: Now when tension arises, I retain a trust that God will enable us to forgive each other. We don't underplay problems or sweep them under the rug. We now know that God will bring our marriage along another step beyond them.

With this understanding of the power of forgiveness, do you find yourselves frequently asking each other for forgiveness?

Thanne: No! Walt knows it would drive me nuts. I mean, we sin against each other every day. If I felt I had to say "I'm sorry" every time, I'd just be creating a set of little laws for myself. Walt and I assume we're living in grace with each other, that part of our marriage covenant is forgiveness. We trust each other that we are forgiven, in the same way that we're vulnerable with God, trusting that His forgiveness is a reality.

I wouldn't want Walt to have to analyze his every action—what an awful lot of work! Both of us have a responsibility to confess to God the sins we are aware of. But think of all the sins I must be committing that I don't even realize are sin! Do I really want my life, or Walt's, to consist of rooting around for all that? It seems healthier to assume the forgiveness is there. I don't need to know every private sin Walt deals with, but I do expect him to take care of those things before God.

When do you feel it's necessary to apologize and ask each other for forgiveness?

Walter: You should usually confess to your spouse only things that affect your relationship. For years now I've met with a friend once a week, and he is my confessor. Talking with him helps me objectify a sin or struggle enough to know whether it's something I'd better talk with Thanne about.

Thanne: Formal "apologies" or asking forgiveness aren't always necessary. I'd rather come to the end of a hard day and have one of us say, "I'm sorry I was such a crab today," or something general like that. Of course, in a very troubled marriage, the "little things" are often "big" problems that need to be confronted.

Walter: If the little things are like small weeds growing in a garden, a good raking will take them out. But sometimes the "little things" add up to evidence of one big, deep trouble root in the soil of the marriage. Usually, in those instances, one person is involved in a persistent sin—something like profound self-centeredness or habitual sexual sin. That calls for confession and forgiveness.

But how often do people who are mired in their own sin realize their obligation to seek forgiveness?

Walter: Sadly, it's almost always the "sinned against" spouse who has to say, "You're hurting me, and it's more than just all these small hurts. Something deeper is going on." It's a painful task, a sad task. But this is the irony of Christianity: What begins in pain may end in healing and life again.

Few people really feel comfortable talking about their own sin. How do you do that?

Walter: Individuals who are already dealing with their sins with God have a good start. For Thanne and me, the confession to God that is a regular part of our worship setting is crucial. Thanne, especially, finds communion to be a significant time of self-examination. Knowing that the genuine forgiveness of Jesus is just moments away gives Christians an ability to look with cold eyes at their sin. That's important.

In marriage, though you might find it difficult to tell your spouse there is some persistent sin between you, you usually find that he or she already knows things are not right. Changes in behavior patterns have been providing clues all along. Your tone of voice has changed, or you're suddenly more guarded in conversation. Your spouse may already be asking you, "What's the matter?" A spouse's awareness that something is "different" can persuade you to approach a moment of confession or to ask for forgiveness.

You have mentioned that we are able to forgive one another because we have experienced God's mercy firsthand. Does that mean

Christians can forgive, while nonbelievers really can't?

Thanne: As people made in God's image, we all have the capacity to love, and love includes a capacity to forgive. Whether a person is a Christian or not, that capacity to forgive in love comes from God.

Walter: But being exhaustible humans, our capacity to forgive is limited. People who have never connected with the infinite source of forgiveness—God—will find their capacity strained to the limit and sometimes broken. But the presence of Jesus in a marriage can become power to forgive, especially in crunch periods. When you're too angry or too exhausted to deal with things, God can be the source of a divine ability to forgive.

Have you had many "crunch periods" where you really needed that divine ability?

Walter: Not too many really, because we've tried to live with grace in a daily way. One time that comes to mind is when we moved here to northern Indiana. We left behind a beautiful home, and I was responsible for buying the new house. And we bought a house that really was not good.

Thanne: It should have been bulldozed! Everything was wrong with it, right down to the frame. But Walt wanted acreage and the land is beautiful, so we ended up with this old farmhouse. And I was responsible for getting the house in shape, on top of working full-time. I finally fell apart.

Walter: Thanne had been getting more and more defeated. Not only was she facing the challenges of the ugly house and a new job, but we were living in a new area where she didn't have friends. When her pressure and exhaustion reached a crisis point, she was very articulate and forceful in expressing her emotions.

Thanne needed my attention and support, and she needed me to acknowledge the burden I had thrown on her by choosing this house. Over the years we've lived here, we've never stopped working on the place.

Thanne: Now, after all that work, it's a good house.

Walter: But back at the beginning, when Thanne's negative feelings seemed so strong that they would last forever, my blessing was that I knew there would be forgiveness. This is what I mean when I say trust and hope grow in a marriage: Every instance of significant forgiveness and grace in your marriage makes trust and hope grow—trust and hope in your spouse, and trust and hope in God.

SOMETHING TO TALK ABOUT

1. Lewis Smedes draws a distinction between sins, which call for forgiveness, and annoyances, which don't. Are the things that bug us most about each other merely annoyances, or are they moral failures that call for forgiveness? For which things should we hold each other responsible?

2. How has our culture's emphasis on self-fulfillment interfered with our efforts to establish a biblical marriage?

3. Based on Donald Harvey's definition of betrayal, in what ways have we betrayed our marriage vows, either by action or by inaction?

4. Were those betrayals isolated incidents, or have any of them become a pattern of behavior? If the latter, how can we break the damaging pattern?

5. Gary Smalley says anger is often buried, but it's always "buried alive." In what areas do we see buried anger surfacing in our marriage?

6. Could our problems with anger be rooted in a failure to forgive others? If so, what circumstances prevent us from offering forgiveness, and how can we overcome those circumstances?

7. How can we apply the "drive-through" communication technique to help us resolve a current conflict?

8. At the end of this chapter, Walter Wangerin tells about failing his wife, Thanne, and the process of forgiveness and reconciliation that followed. Can we see forgiveness as the "beginning of healing" in our marriage, coming even before changed behavior is evident?

9. In what ways has "keeping score" interfered with real forgiveness in our relationship? How can we change that tendency?

Chapter Ten

L E S S O N S   O F   L O S S

Grief
H. Norman and Joyce Wright

Doubts
Larry Crabb

H. Norman Wright and Joyce Wright

Grief

What it was like for the Wrights to lose their son—and to try to help their wayward daughter. How they reacted differently to these crises. How they supported one another in times of loss.

Interviewed by Annette LaPlaca

No parent expects to outlive his or her child, but it happens more frequently than we like to admit. And losing a child is only one of the many causes of grief that couples have to deal with.

Just ask marriage and family counselor H. Norman Wright. Several years ago, Norm and his wife, Joyce, lost their twenty-two-year-old son, Matthew, who was profoundly mentally retarded and required regular medical care. Before Matthew's death, their daughter, Sheryl, went through a long period of rebellion. Norm and Joyce described these struggles in their book *I'll Love You Forever* (Focus on the Family).

In this interview, the Wrights share the lessons they learned about how a couple can survive difficult times.

Joyce, because of Matthew's disabilities, his day-to-day care meant a heavy workload and a heavy emotional load for you. Where did you go for encouragement during those years?

Joyce: The eleven years that Matthew lived at home, before he moved to a group home, were hard. I was often exhausted and discouraged from caring for him through his episodes of illness and his seizures. But the Lord encouraged me, and I learned to be thankful for God's many answers to prayer and for His faithfulness in bringing us through these challenges.

Norm also gave me a lot of support. From the very beginning, he loved Matthew and was committed to caring for him. I handled the majority of the childcare, but Norm affirmed and reassured me, and his objectivity was very helpful. I had the scary responsibility of making decisions about adjusting Matthew's medication, and Norm always expressed his confidence in my decisions.

After a serious medical problem, Matthew died in the hospital. How did the two of you handle that loss?

Norm: We grieved together—and we grieved separately. Men and women don't typically grieve the same way. Joyce and I did a lot of crying and talking. And we received incredible support from friends and family.

Having Matthew in my life helped me learn to feel deeply and talk about those feelings. But generally, when men grieve it's difficult for them to face their fears and share their feelings. They have an urge to *do* something; they want to try to make things right again.

For example, when we placed Matthew in the hospital to undergo surgery on his stomach and esophagus, I started painting the house. My mind was focused on Matthew and my desire for him to get through the surgery and to get well, but I still felt the need to accomplish something.

Joyce: After the surgery, infections set in that weakened Matthew's lungs and heart. We knew the end of his life was near.

Norm and I grieved differently because our personalities are different. Norm is an extrovert, and I'm an introvert. When Matthew died, Norm immediately called his secretary. She called other people, and a friend who had loved Matthew mentioned his death over the radio. Soon our phone was ringing and ringing. So Norm's grief over Matthew became very public, which was normal for him. He had always been public about his relationship with Matthew.

Less than a week after Matthew's memorial service, Norm was scheduled to do a seminar on grieving and loss. I was concerned it would be too much for him, but he said, "No, this is the way I grieve. This works out my grieving process."

But your own grieving process was different.

Joyce: The way I responded was more internal. Initially, I got along beautifully. Matthew's memorial service lifted me—and I wasn't broken-hearted. I was thrilled for him, knowing the excitement and blessings he was experiencing with God. It was later that I started dealing with my loss.

That first weekend we went to Norm's seminar, but I would have liked to have gone home and had time to process the grief in my own way. After the seminar, it was time for my private grieving.

Although my grieving was more internal, Norm was able to help me. He was so tenderhearted, and tears would come suddenly, even when other people were around. When I saw Norm's tears, my reservations broke down and I cried with him. My feelings were strong, but they didn't always find their way out. Norm helped me get those tears to the surface.

Norm: One of the things we've learned is to accept our individuality and be glad for our differences. We encourage each other to be who we are because this is how we complement one another and blend our strengths.

From your years of counseling, Norm, what problems do you see couples struggling with when they're in the middle of a time of serious loss or grief?

Norm: During the first emotional stages of intense feelings, one spouse sometimes blames the other. A grieving person often needs to express anger or relieve his or her own sense of guilt. A spouse is the closest target for those expressions, so one spouse might say to the other, "If you hadn't allowed him to get that motorcycle, he'd still be alive!" Or "If you had been at home that day, this tragedy wouldn't have happened!"

A child can be a bonding agent that holds a couple together. But if the husband and wife haven't built a close intimacy in their relationship apart from their child, and the child becomes chronically ill or dies, it's easy for the marriage to crumble. The marriages of people with disabled children and of people who lose a child have a failure rate of 75 to 80 percent. The stresses that come with the crisis intensify any existing problems in a marriage.

What advice would you give couples who are grieving?

Norm: I'd remind them that it takes time to work through their grief. And they have to accept the fact that, at the moment, there might be very little that is holding them together. But it is possible to come together again. The vast majority of troubled marriages I see could be turned around if the two partners would commit themselves to the time and hard work required to solve their problems.

It's essential to remain patient during the time of recovery. When one spouse seems to be recovering quickly from loss, he shouldn't say to his spouse, "Snap out of it! You should be over it by now!" God created us as unique individuals—with a different sense of timing, perspective, and intensity. We need to respect the differences we see in each other.

Joyce: It's also important to realize that the grief tends to come back. Little things bring Matthew to mind. When he was young and we were home together, I used to call out to him and say, "Hey, you!" He would use that same phrase himself, so it became very special to me. Recently I said "Hey, you!" to our dog—and suddenly I missed Matthew very much. Couples shouldn't be surprised when grief comes back in a rush, just when they think they're over it.

Norm: Most people work through grief in about two years, but sometimes it can stretch into five. The loss of a child is especially difficult since parents never expect to outlive their children. And, as Joyce mentioned, there is residual grief—grief that hangs on. For example, every year on the date of Matthew's birthday, we can't help but wonder what he would be like at twenty-seven, at twenty-eight. When little things trigger that residual grief, a couple needs to realize that it's normal.

You experienced another type of grief when your daughter, Sheryl, got involved with alcohol and drugs, and then later told you she was living with her boyfriend. How did you handle it when she decided to reject the values you had taught her when she was growing up?

Joyce: I realized she was searching, in a desperate way, for happiness, and her choices as an adult were taking her in dangerous directions. God gave Norm and me great commitment to fight for Sheryl in prayer. Our daughter is a precious, beautiful girl. Her emotions are strong and when she's hurting, she reaches out to us. Even during that painful period, the communication between us never broke down. It hurt more as we'd hear how she was suffering, but we wanted it that way. We hurt with her.

Norm: I remember riding our exercycle and listening to a song about a wayward daughter who wanted to "go home, be daddy's girl." I listened to that tape almost every day for several weeks, and I would weep as I thought about Sheryl and longed for her to "come home."

How did you show your acceptance of Sheryl at a time when you couldn't condone her choices?

Norm: We just kept talking to her. Now and then, we'd ask a question or offer a suggestion. But telling her what to do never did work with Sheryl.

Joyce: As parents, we'd wonder, "Doesn't she care about the way we raised her? Doesn't she care about all the warnings in God's Word about these behaviors?" But Sheryl was willful, and she was consciously making these choices. We could either close the door on her, or we could offer unconditional love and let her know we were praying for her and that we loved her no matter what she was doing. We made a commitment to keep loving her.

How do you advise parents to show that kind of unconditional love?

Norm: Parents in that type of situation should talk about their own hurts, fears, and frustrations and try to deal with them together so they won't take it out on the wayward son or daughter. Often, when a parent confronts his child, the backlash of the parent's frustration comes out and pushes the son or daughter even farther away. But if the parents express all the anger and frustration to each other ahead of time, they can come up with better ways to respond to their child.

Joyce: During those years, it helped me that Norm was very honest with his feelings—both with me and with Sheryl. He could say, "I'm very disappointed" yet still communicate "I love you."

Talking about the situation helps, but there came a point when Norm and I could have talked about nothing but Sheryl's problems. That wasn't helpful; it just intensified the pain and the stress. We learned to talk about it and then get on with an assurance that God was with us.

I also prayed for Sheryl with another friend. We'd pray that God would protect her. And we'd even pray, "God, bring her back to You no matter what it takes." That's a scary kind of prayer, since we didn't know what extreme measures it might take for Sheryl to come back to the Lord. And during those years, she encountered some terrible times of turmoil. When she'd call, sobbing, about some awful thing that had happened to her, it was horrible to watch her suffer. But I grew in my prayer life as I realized God was working in Sheryl's life even when she was making poor choices.

Norm: Our prayers were answered. Sheryl is now married to a

Christian man and is following the Lord again. She operates her own business—a nail salon. That fits her; she always was independent and artistic.

Sheryl has a real heart for people and is a gifted listener. It's ironic that she spends long hours listening to women talk about their problems. As a counselor, I spend my week working with people and their problems, too. Sheryl especially seems able to connect with these women—precisely because she has once been where they are. She has developed her own unique ministry.

In your writing, Norm, you emphasize the qualities of families who survive despite serious problems. What are some of those qualities?

Norm: Families who see problems as a normal part of life and an opportunity to learn and grow are the best prepared to handle the challenge of difficult times. To some degree, each crisis that comes and goes helps prepare a family to tackle the next one, even though what they experience the next time may be very different. We have the element of hope, since we have God's care and the assurance of his salvation and provision. But we expect that there will be detours along the way.

Second, encouragement is always important, but even more so during a time of trouble. The word encouragement literally means "to give courage." It's good for spouses to pray together and to tell each other, "I'm praying for you."

People outside your family can also help. Our ability to be frank with other people about our stresses over Matthew and with Sheryl was critical. We heard from others how they had handled similar crises, and it helped us to know that other families had suffered in this same way—and had gotten through it. Families that survive a crisis tend to be the ones who reach out and let others help them.

Joyce: Blame is another problem that comes up. During the years of Sheryl's trouble, I had a tendency to blame myself: "How did I fail as a mother?" But Norm would reassure me that these were choices Sheryl was making as an adult, and that though we weren't perfect parents, we had done what we could do.

Norm: Another characteristic of couples who survive is that they don't get stuck in the past. They say, "Life is going to go on. We have a life together, regardless of what happens."

A large part of getting on with life is being able to resolve conflict. It's important to develop good conflict-solving skills early in marriage, long before a serious crisis strikes. You can work through a crisis if you have learned how to resolve conflict.

Joyce: It also helps to realize that God has eternal purposes that we don't necessarily see when we're in the middle of troubled circumstances. We can look back now and see God's hand at work, preparing us, caring for us, and teaching us. We can see God's great mercy and grace in taking Matthew to be with Him.

Norm: God either prepares you in advnce to handle these detours in life—sometimes when you're not even aware of it—or He gives you the strength you need when the problems come. The number-one characteristic of families that make it is that they have a foundation in the Lord. Scripture becomes a grid through which they see everything that occurs in life, and they rely on the strength that God's Word can give.

Larry Crabb

Doubts

What to do when the unfairness of life forces you to question God's goodness.

Interviewed by Ron R. Lee

*I*n the preceding interview, Norm and Joyce Wright described the tremendous grief they felt over their children. Loss and grief go hand in hand—and both circumstances can cause us to doubt God. If He really does love us, and if He really is holy and just, why does He allow these tragedies?

Larry Crabb is familiar with these questions since he has spent a great deal of time wrestling with them himself. As he explains in this interview, the tragic circumstances of life demand honest answers. And those answers often bring strange comfort that doesn't end the pain.

Crabb is a clinical psychologist, a Bible teacher, and the author of fifteen books, including *Inside Out* (NavPress), *Understanding People* (Zondervan), and, with his father, Lawrence Crabb, Sr., *God of My Father* (Zondervan). Here's what he recommends for couples who feel that God has fallen strangely silent.

Your books have been very well-received, but you'll never be accused of offering three easy steps to spiritual happiness. Is it your nature to see the glass as half empty, or is it more a matter of seeking honest answers to hard questions, wherever that might lead?

It really goes back to my childhood, and the example set by my dad. His life has been marked by lots of good things, but also by seasons of deep pain. Yet he never allowed the hard times to turn him against God. Instead, he chose to search out answers to the things that made no sense.

Most people in his circumstances would have stopped pursuing God long ago. But no matter how dark things get, Dad never quits. He always keeps moving ahead, and in that way his life reflects an aspect of God's character—that God is a mover.

The Scriptures say that in the days of Noah it grieved God that He had created mankind. Evil had multiplied, but God didn't stop His work. He took appropriate action and He kept moving. And He's still at work in the world and in our lives.

Most people assume mothers are the most influential adults in the lives of their children. But you've said your father was the greatest influence in your life. Why are dads so important?

A father's influence is unique, but it's no more important than a mother's influence. My dad taught me about God's movement—His ongoing work in the world. And my mother taught me about God's beauty—the fact that there is beauty in everything God does.

Several years ago, my dad had open-heart surgery. And for ten days my mom left his side for only one night. And that was because I insisted she go to a hotel to get some rest.

I looked at her devotion to my dad and thought, "I've never seen such beauty." Her care for my father was a rich picture of God, who hovers over His children. He's always watching over us and caring for us. That's the beauty we see in God's work, and that's what I learned from Mother.

Why do we fail to recognize much of what God is doing in our lives?

Part of it is that we expect God to act according to our wishes. But when He allows things to happen that we fear might destroy us, it throws us into confusion. Why would a loving God do that?

You alluded earlier to the tragedy in your father's life. How did he handle his own questions about God allowing good people to suffer?

He started dealing with those questions at a very young age. When he was five years old, he stood at the foot of his father's bed and watched him die. Dad couldn't understand why a loving God would take his father away from him.

Through other circumstances in his life, that same question came up again and again: If God is good, why does He allow all this suffering? Dad eventually learned to accept the hard truth that God doesn't always act according to our wishes.

Have you found yourself questioning God's goodness when life doesn't make sense?

Sure, time and again. Rachael and I have been married thirty years, and she has seen me get really discouraged. But she knows I'm committed to never getting so discouraged that I'll just chuck it all. In the middle of all the despair, I won't stop pursuing God. I might be limping a bit, but I'm still moving ahead.

Do you think God allows suffering to force us to seek out his strength?

The Bible is full of examples of human weakness being a good thing in God's eyes. The hard truth of the Christian life is that the path to knowing God well is never very pleasant. But it's not that way because God wants it that way. It's because we're proud and arrogant. Sin has made it that way.

I believe a central theme of the Christian life is that we shouldn't use God to solve our problems. Instead, we should see our problems as an opportunity to find God. Doing everything you can to relieve the hurt doesn't address the source of the pain. Reality is much more like a dentist who says, "In order to relieve your toothache, I'll have to stick a needle in your gum and then do some drilling. When I finish, your face will be puffy and uncomfortable and you won't be able to eat anything for a few days. But it will get better eventually."

That's much closer to how God works. Life on earth is basically our opportunity to trust God in the absence of blessing.

You have endured your own share of tragedy, losing your brother, Bill, in a plane crash. How did that affect your understanding of God's love?

Bill's death made absolutely no sense. After drifting in his spiritual life, he had recommitted himself to God more than twenty years before he died. And he still had so much more to give to his wife and children.

Losing Bill shook us all. My dad was seventy-eight at the time. When he got word of the crash, he went outside and screamed at God for ten minutes. And then, he told me later, "When God wouldn't repent, I had to trust him."

Hearing my dad say he trusted God even when he wouldn't "repent" helped me think through one of the core issues of my faith. Of course God didn't repent. What does He have to repent of? He never makes a mistake.

In the midst of my questioning and my bouts of despair, I still believe in God. I believe He made Himself known in His Son. And I believe that when I look at the cross I get the clearest picture of the character and the heart of God. His character is He hates sin, and His nature is He loves sinners. Those are the bottom-line issues.

Even when a person believes those "bottom-line issues," how does that help when God seems to be silent in the midst of unwarranted suffering?

It's difficult for any of us to accept the fact that God doesn't always conform His behavior to our agendas. And He never will.

I'm troubled by a lot of things, such as why my brother and twenty-four other people lost their lives in a plane crash. I don't pretend to understand why they were taken, but I'm actually grateful for the troubling questions. I believe it's in the middle of asking questions that can't be answered that our faith has a chance to mature.

You have written about a time when God refused to follow your agenda after your dad's open-heart surgery. What did you learn from that experience?

Dad was in the hospital for ten days, and during that entire time he didn't sleep well. I was worried about his ability to recover from such major surgery, and I knew getting some rest would help. So I fasted and then I got down on my knees and prayed for an hour. I did everything I could to get God to cooperate with my agenda.

The next morning I went to the hospital and asked how things had gone. My mom said, "It was the worst night yet." I just wanted to scream.

Later that day medical personnel stormed into Dad's room when his heart threatened to stop beating. He survived that emergency, and afterward one nurse commented, "He'd do so much better if he could get a good night's rest." I was so angry I didn't know what to do.

That night I went back to the hotel and began to plead with God: "Let him sleep tonight. Please!" But I stopped after one sentence. I didn't want to pray, but I didn't know what else to do.

Even when God allows us to suffer and gives us no explanation for it, He still asks us to call Him "good." As we're screaming in pain after open-heart surgery or the death of a loved one, we still need to find the faith to call God "good." When you do all these things, not because they feel right but because you believe in God, that's when you're growing as a Christian.

Are you saying God is more interested in sending trials our way than He is in sending us blessings?

Not at all, because He sends both. We don't live in the middle of suffering all the time. The seasons come when you're having a great time in your marriage and your kids are a continual source of joy. Rachael and I have had our rough times, and as our sons grew up there were problems I never imagined would come about. But right now we're doing great, and I'm all for it.

But I can't count on the good times as a definition of life. For the most part while we're on earth, God asks us to trust Him no matter what—when things are going well, and when things are going against us. It's still worthwhile to love my wife, even when I'd just as soon walk out.

It's still worthwhile to be involved in my kids' lives even when they're breaking my heart. It's still worthwhile to go to work every day even though my boss is driving me crazy.

Oswald Chambers' statement comes to mind: "The root of all sin is the suspicion that God isn't good." Amid all the pain and the questioning and the anger, we need to say to God, "I'm not going to give up on believing in Your goodness, but I've got to know You better. I'm not demanding a better job, or that You get my wife to love me, or that You get my kids off drugs. I'm not going to come to You requiring anything. I'm coming to You just for You."

That's when an appetite for God begins to develop. That's when you begin to understand what it means to seek Him with all your heart.

SOMETHING TO TALK ABOUT

1. Earlier in this chapter, Norm and Joyce Wright describe the differences in the way they each reacted to the death of their son. When we have faced grief or times of extreme distress, how have we reacted differently? Did those differences draw us together or create distance between us?
2. Have we faced major disappointments in the way any of our children were living? If so, did we communicate love to him or her? Did we hang together as parents, or did we allow ourselves to be pulled apart during that time?
3. In dealing with past losses and disappointments, have we moved on in our relationship or are we stuck in the past? If the latter, what do we need to do to get on with life?
4. Larry Crabb refuses to settle for pat answers; he insists on digging deep to find the truth about God's character and His dealings with humankind. What do we really believe about God's love, His holiness, and His justice? How do those beliefs shape our understanding of how God feels about the suffering we endure?
5. When, in the past, have we felt confused about God's love or

doubted His goodness? How did we resolve those doubts?
6. When we face major difficulties, do we approach them with the expectation that God will solve the problems for us; or with the desire to know God better through them?

Chapter Eleven

T E A M I N G   U P

Opposites Together
Bill and Gloria Gaither

Blessing Others
Howard and Jeanne Hendricks

Cross-Training
Jack and Anna Hayford

Bill and Gloria Gaither

Opposites Together

How to maintain your individuality in the midst of a close, lifelong relationship. How to maximize your individual gifts. How to utilize each mate's giftedness to complement one another's strengths and weaknesses.

Interviewed by Harold B. Smith
and Elizabeth Cody Newenhuyse

*M*arriage brings together two different people—usually two *very* different people. And while individual differences add challenges to the relationship, they also give it greater strength. Just ask Bill and Gloria Gaither.

After thirty-six years of marriage, the Gaithers say it has been their differences that have kept them together through three kids (now grown), more than sixty Gospel albums, and countless concert tours. In describing their marriage, they are almost painfully honest—which is encouraging. You listen to them and think: "Hmmm. Maybe it's okay that my spouse and I haven't solved everything in *our* marriage."

The Gaithers have won more than twenty Dove Awards and three Grammy Awards, and their music has changed the way churches across the country approach worship. They have written hundreds of praise songs, including "He Touched Me," "Because He Lives," "Something

Beautiful," and "The King Is Coming." But with all these accomplishments, they're still growing and still challenging each other to live up to God's best. For starters, we asked them how they define a Christian marriage.

What do you believe a marriage that is committed to Christ should look like?

Gloria: A true Christian marriage seeks what is eternal, and it shares a commitment to a larger purpose. I see a lot of marriages where one partner is so security-oriented that when one spouse says, "I don't feel that we're doing anything that matters;" the other responds, "Well, you better keep doing it because we've got a house payment to make." I think a lot of mid-life crises happen over that type of mindset.

Bill and I have always been going in the same direction, and that has kept us together over the years. Of course, we haven't always agreed on how to get there. If we hadn't both had a sense that we wanted to be open to where God was taking us, we would have had real conflict. But we've always been able to sit down somewhere along the way and say, "What is it we're doing here? What is life about?"

Bill: We're both driven by the principle of being in the world but not of the world. We grew up seeing people attending church, dressing the right way, and saying all the right things, but never really affecting the world much.

But we've had a real passion to communicate the truth of Christ to all kinds of people—to infiltrate the culture through simple, yet profound, music that people can understand. When you're driven by that passion, you take a lot of risks and you spend time with people that some Christians would criticize you for associating with. I don't think we're of any earthly value if we don't risk getting our hands and feet dirty to try to go to where the people are.

Gloria: You can also define a Christian marriage by saying what it is *not*: It is not censorship and rules and legalities. The same holds true for Christian parenthood. When our kids were younger, our attitude wasn't, "Don't look at that. Don't read that. Don't ask that. Don't go there. Don't think." Rather, it was, "Let's consider it together and see how it stacks up against the Word of God."

How do you think the principle of mutual submission, found in Ephesians 5:21, fits into Christian marriage?

Bill: There are some things I do better, and other things Gloria does better. And we both have a genuine respect for each other's gifts. For example, Gloria is gifted with words. So when we perform and it comes time to make a statement, I stand back and say, "Tell 'em what we're all about." But I also feel the freedom to do that myself. Sometimes I say, "Let me handle this."

Gloria: Bill's gift to the church and to the world has been to be a "master programmer," to bring together people's gifts to create a whole thing that has impact—to put the gem in the setting, if you will.

Bill: My role has been to help other people look good, and I love doing that.

It sounds as if the submission issue hasn't been an ongoing tension in your marriage.

Bill: It hasn't been a tension as far as how we work out our art. The tension we feel, related to submission in marriage, comes in other areas: How we're handling the kids and how we're running our home. In those areas, we come at it from two different perspectives. I have accused Gloria of being an overly protective mother. She has accused me of reflecting an overly hard German work ethic.

Gloria: It's not the work ethic that we disagree on. It's more that we disagree when I feel the kids are getting the message that nothing—no matter what they do—is good enough. We also have tension over our priority list, what project should be done next. Bill is more practical and pragmatic, and I tend to be more philosophical and aesthetic.

Bill: After you get past the business decisions and the kids, the question becomes, "How do Gloria and I relate, just the two of us?" Actually, one of the things that attracted me to Gloria was her independence. I don't do well around weak people, people who cling, people who have no opinions. When I got to know Gloria, I thought, "Here is a wholistic person, someone who could easily make it in life without me." That quality has always appealed to me.

But the challenge of being married to such a strong, independent woman is that somewhere along the line, you need to feel like she really *does* need you.

Are you saying you want Gloria to actually say to you, "I need you, Bill"?

Bill: No, it's more that I'd like to feel that way.

Gloria: This is a real hard line to walk. First of all, Bill would know it if the "I need you" statement wasn't real, and he'd think he was being conned. But then, the times in our marriage when I haven't had something of my own going—when I have needed him more—have been the times when he would lose respect for me.

Gloria, you've said in the past that getting into music was a big stretch for you. Was that part of the submission issue?

Gloria: It was more a question of submission to God than to Bill. My opinion of my singing ability was something I had to deal with in terms of the lordship of Christ in my life. It was a matter of God's authority over both of us.

I used to become physically sick when I would think about leaving on the weekends to do concerts. I like to do things well, and I felt like I was going out to do something I couldn't do well. But that wasn't in conflict with Bill, it was with myself. The way I dealt with this struggle was to finally say, "What is God asking of me here?" And the answer was: My gift was being a communicator, even if that communication was delivered through what I sometimes felt was failure.

Bill, you must have had a sense of the spiritual struggle Gloria was experiencing at that point. How did you feel about it?

Bill: I don't know how many teary-eyed recording sessions we've had over the years. Gloria would sometimes say, "I'm not qualified to do this. Somebody else ought to be doing it." And to be honest, I probably haven't shown as much sympathy as I should, because there have been a lot of great communicators, especially in the pop and country music fields, who have not been great singers.

The point is to communicate a song's lyrics. So at times I've probably even been a little unkind to Gloria in helping her use her gifts to the fullest. That hurts sometimes, and it works both ways. There have been times when Gloria has said: "Bill, you're better than that, and I'm not going to allow you that kind of thinking."

Gloria, you've been challenged to do something you felt uncomfortable about. And Bill has said that perhaps he hasn't stretched as much as you have. Does that bother you?

Gloria: Sometimes. For instance, I wish he would stretch more intellectually. I wish he would read more, people like Frederick Buechner or the late Henri Nouwen. I think he would be enriched by it.

Bill: She's right.

Gloria: I make Bill listen to me. I read him these little kernels I think he can't live without. And he isn't always thrilled by that.

But he really is a wonderful internalizer once he's exposed to something, and his practical mind says, "How can I serve this up so regular people can understand it?" In contrast, I just enjoy the ideas—I don't care if I'm never going to "use" them. I don't feel like it's a lost day if I get seven great ideas that nobody's going to know but me. I wish Bill would get excited about these things, and sometimes it hurts me that he doesn't. But we're just different.

Bill: When you talk about growth, the question of commitment comes in. When we think of commitment to marriage, we think of a lifelong pledge, faithfulness to the marriage vows. For Christians that should be a given.

But there's another very important commitment. In the record business and the book business we often say, "It was a lot more fun being courted by the company than being contracted." The same thing is true in marriage. Let's say you're a young woman who sees this real bright guy and you think, "Man, is he going to become something!" Then you marry him and he becomes a couch potato—lets his mind and his body go to pot. And vice versa: A gal works hard to attract a guy, and then after she marries the guy she turns into another kind of person.

Gloria: Like a soap-opera freak.

Bill: Yeah. So in some ways the commitment to continue to become the person that we all agreed we were going to become is just as important as pledging never to be unfaithful to each other.

Gloria: I think most affairs happen because fidelity breaks down, because one spouse doesn't keep the commitment to grow. And you can always be sure there's somebody else out there who is growing. And you can almost be sure they're going to meet each other.

This brings me to something else I've been thinking about. It has been incredibly liberating to me—as a person, as a partner, and as a mother—to discover that my gift is also my fault, and my faults are my gifts out of whack. I get discouraged with waking up and saying, "Why am I dealing with this same dumb thing again? I thought I had it licked." It's been helpful to learn that our faults are our gifts, going out of whack again.

Can you give an example?

Gloria: I am intuitive, and I have enormous sympathies for everybody's predicament in the wide world. That's one of my gifts: I can adjust to almost anything; I can get excited about almost anything. The fault comes when I overextend myself, when I think I can fix everything for everybody, write everything for everybody, help everybody. I've had to learn to let some things go and realize that I can't get involved in everything.

It's the same with Bill. He is driven, impassioned, very singleminded. He can make our entire organization focus on one project. But on the other hand, sometimes you have to get on the two-way radio and say, "Earth to Bill. Earth to Bill. Where are you? There are some other things going on here. You might want to check in."

One of the results of all this drivenness, of course, is your shared life in the public eye. How do all the demands on your time, and all the people around you, affect your personal relationship?

Bill: We have worked hard from the very beginning to learn how to say no. If you think God's will is for you to drop everything every time the phone rings, you're going to become a basket case. You have to learn how to focus in on what you're supposed to be all about—and then say no to other opportunities.

Howard G. Hendricks and Jeanne Hendricks

Blessing Others

How to merge two very different personalities and combinations of gifts into a partnership that makes a difference in the lives of others.

Interviewed by Ruth Senter

Howard and Jeanne Hendricks work well together. They have coauthored books, hosted "The Art of Family Living" radio broadcast, served as chaplains to the Dallas Cowboys and their wives, and conducted training conferences in more than seventy countries. Howard has been instrumental in developing leadership for the church into the next century through his work at the Center for Christian Leadership at Dallas Theological Seminary.

Few couples have a résumé that is so crowded with joint ministry and shared accomplishments. But getting to that point wasn't easy. In this interview, the Hendrickses talk freely about their fifty-year journey—highlighting both their pain and their tremendous shared joys.

You have written books and led seminars together. How do two people who have different gifts, talents, and personalities work together without competing against each other?

Jeanne: I am Jeanne Hendricks, wife, mother, and grandmother. There is no way Howie is going to compete with me in those areas. And because I am a woman, even when Howie and I speak to the same person or group of people on the same topic, we come at it from different viewpoints.

Howard: One of the things I learned from working with the Dallas Cowboys is the importance of the team. When you are on a team, you play off the strengths of your teammates. You don't tackle the guys who wear the same color uniforms.

Jeanne and I are the team. We are, in a sense, fighting the opposition—Satan, who would have our ministry diffused. But our approach is to constantly ask each other, "What can we each invest in this work, this marriage, that will strengthen it and keep it a united front against our enemy?"

Jeanne, at times yours has been a behind-the-scenes role. Have you ever had trouble accepting a lower profile?

Jeanne: Yes, the tension has been there, especially when our children were small. There is always the temptation to think it's more glamorous out there under the bright lights. I had my moments when it was difficult to see Howie get on a plane and fly away from it all. But those years when I was often home alone with the children, I never once doubted that I was of value. I have a husband who never lets me forget how special I am. When you live with praise and appreciation, it isn't hard to serve on the home scene because you aren't depending on the bright lights or the book covers for your sense of self-worth.

Howard: It has been interesting to see the effects that Jeanne's positive attitude has had on our children. One day I invited all four kids to visit a class I was teaching on the Christian home. I told the students they could ask my children any questions they wanted.

One of the questions was, "How do you explain the positive attitude all four of you seem to have toward ministry when it took your father from you so much of the time?" Bev's answer was, "It was my mother. I remember the times that we'd drop Dad off at the airport and Mother would turn around at the wheel of our station wagon and say, `Just think. God has given us another opportunity to share our daddy with other people. Isn't that great?'"

Jeanne: One of the things that helped was that the direction of Howard's ministry has always been a joint decision. I remember him coming to me once during the early years and saying, "Honey, there are more and more speaking invitations coming in. You will be the one stuck at home with the kids on the weekends. What do you think we should do about these invitations?"

It was an agonizing question. We prayed and talked about it for a long time. I admit, weekend single parenting was not a prospect I looked forward to. But in the end, I knew God had some important lessons to teach me.

What kinds of things did you do that helped you keep a positive perspective when your husband was gone?

Jeanne: One of our children once said, "When Daddy goes away, Mommie becomes a little girl again." The children and I became informal, relaxed our schedules. We had impromptu picnics. Casual drives in the country. Visits with neighbors and friends. One Saturday when Howie was gone our picnic got rained out. It took some thinking to redeem the occasion, but I turned things around when I turned the picnic into a treasure hunt. I took everything out of the picnic basket and hid it around the house. Everyone had a great time trying to find the hot dogs and rolls and mustard. If I ever felt sorry for myself, we all ended up feeling miserable. So I decided, why not have fun instead?

Like everyone else, you must have hit some turbulence in your marriage. What have been the biggest tension points?

Jeanne: Howie is a ninety-mile-an-hour person, and I operate at about one-third that speed. I spent the first ten years of our marriage trying to keep up with him. Howie had been in ministry before we were married. I came as a new bride, green to the ministry, a native Easterner trying to adjust to Texas. On top of it all, here was this man who moved at an incredible speed, was out accomplishing great things for God.

I was overwhelmed, and for ten years I was the quiet, meek one who just tried to survive the pace. I suppose I assumed that I had to be like Howie. But the real tension came because we never talked about our differences. I kept my discomfort inside.

I remember taking a weekend away from the kids to celebrate our tenth anniversary. As we were leaving Austin to return home, we had some difference of opinion about the luggage. We drove all the way home in silence. We simply didn't want to argue, and we didn't know how to lovingly tackle our differences of opinion.

Howard: I spent the first ten years of our marriage trying to change *Jeanne*. I thought if she would just get organized, everything would be okay. Then it dawned on me that if I ever got her organized, I'd probably hate her. The thing that had attracted me to her was her warmth, her graciousness, the time she always took for people.

I finally got off this organization kick when I realized Jeanne had what I desperately needed—the ability to relax and take life as it comes. When

I learned to take Jeanne's strengths and weld them with my strengths, then we were building our marriage out of each other's strengths rather than our weaknesses. We began to realize we had a stronger unit as a couple than we could ever have as individuals.

She's still a thirty-mile-an-hour person, and the Lord knows that's exactly what I need. Jeanne has a calming effect on me.

Jeanne: God doesn't lead two people into marriage to pull them in two opposite directions. He leads them into marriage to blend and maximize their usefulness. Much of the tension that I see today in marriages comes from grasping and holding onto what we consider our individuality. No matter what our gifts, talents, or personalities, when they are given to God, He will blend them with those of our spouse.

Howard, how did you come to the place where you could accept Jeanne as she was without trying to change her?

Howard: I began to change when I realized Jeanne knew me totally and yet she accepted me and loved me! It was a revolutionary thought. I came from a broken home. My father was a military man who brought me up with military discipline. I was painfully aware of the times I didn't measure up.

When I came to marriage, I was afraid that if Jeanne really found out what I was like, she wouldn't love me anymore. Rejection was one thing I knew I couldn't handle. It was at about the ten-year point in our marriage that I began to realize I didn't have to prove myself to Jeanne. Knowing of her unconditional acceptance, I was free to make the drastic changes in myself that I needed to make in terms of being a partner in marriage. That's when I stopped trying to change Jeanne.

What kinds of changes needed to be made?

Howard: I had a serious problem with depression during the early years of our ministry. I was out speaking, winning souls to Christ, and encouraging and strengthening the believers. I hardly ever said no to an opportunity to speak.

One week I spoke thirty-four times. But it seemed that the greater God's blessing on the road, the more severe my depression when I got home. I could feel it coming the minute the plane landed. I would come home and fall apart. I didn't want to talk. I didn't want to eat. Then on top of my depression, I'd feel tremendous guilt. I was a perfectionist, and when I couldn't be the perfect husband and father, the only thing I knew to do was to withdraw.

Our children would come to me and want me to play a game with them. I didn't want to play a game. Jeanne would hand me the Bible to read to the children. I didn't want to read the Bible, much less pray. But they kept loving me anyway. Jeanne and the children were the instruments that God used to bring me around.

What kinds of things did Jeanne do for you that helped pull you out of depression?

Howard: The greatest thing Jeanne did was to give me permission to be human. She didn't try to pull me out of it. When she saw that I didn't want to enter into family activities, she'd just say, "That's okay, Honey. I love you. You have every reason to be tired. Go ahead, relax."

She also used questions very skillfully. She'd ask me things like, "Howie, why do you think people get depressed?" Now, I was egotistical enough to think she was looking for answers. I'd have a five-point outline all ready for her. But the truth of the matter was I was beginning to articulate answers for myself in the process. Jeanne was smart enough to know that's what would happen.

How can a woman develop the kind of self-control that makes it possible not to interfere when she feels her husband isn't contributing to the marriage in ways she considers healthy?

Jeanne: I can't say that I didn't get angry with Howie. It's hard not to be upset when you are trying to support and help, and in return you get a husband who comes home and tightens up the happy, relaxed atmosphere of the home.

One of the things that helped me when Howie was going through depression was to realize he wasn't lashing out against me personally. There were other reasons he was responding the way he was. I remember lying awake one night, praying for some kind of insight. I happened to remember a course in child psychology I had taken in college. The one thing I learned from that course was how to ask questions in a nonthreatening way.

I began asking Howie questions about his childhood, and I realized how much fear had been a part of his background. Slowly I began to piece together some valid reasons for his depression. As our relationship clarified, I was able to help the children understand that there is a reason why Daddy is this way and it has nothing to do with us.

Howie needed my help, but not in a condescending way. So instead of telling the children to tiptoe around Daddy, we just went about life as usual. We ate our meals, played our games, read our books, and hoped that soon Daddy would join us. And eventually he did. Slowly depression became a thing of the past and God's grace enabled us to move beyond.

Howard, what does Jeanne do for you these days that you appreciate?

Howard: I still tend to operate on high speed, but Jeanne has learned how to calm me down. She gets me on her turf—we walk and talk. Jeanne still asks me questions, but not in a threatening way. She provides a calm, secure environment for me, and before I know it, I've opened up and relaxed.

Jeanne: One of the secrets to a healthy marriage is for both partners to be good observers. I've learned how important it is for me to listen to Howie. To hear what kinds of things he says when he's not even aware I'm listening. To observe his moods. To find the activities that relax and slow him down.

On the other side of the coin, Howie has been very sensitive over the years to my need for self-esteem. I don't get depressed, I just get sleepy. Give me enough sleep and I'm on top of things. But I have struggled with confidence. Howie observed that about me and has encouraged me to develop my writing and my speaking skills. When we were first married and pastoring a church in Ft. Worth, if someone called on me to pray I would be on the verge of a coronary. But Howie saw gifts in me before I could see them in myself. He is a born teacher and he wanted to help me develop my potential strengths.

Being in ministry together, how do the two of you keep each other true to what you're teaching others?

Jeanne: We are accountable to each other. If I've been teaching one thing and living another, I know I'll have to face Howie. On the other hand, if one of his sermons reminds me of something we used to do effectively, but have allowed to slip, I'll usually bring it up in conversation later on. By waiting a while, I have time to pray about what I need to say, or not say, as the case may be.

Howard: I don't know why, but it seems that prayer is the one area in my life where I'm always shot down in flames. But I can wax eloquent on the subject when I'm preaching. I remember one day Jeanne came to me with the challenge: "What do you think about the idea of our increasing the prayer time in our schedule? We are both committed to that idea. Now, how can we get around to doing it?"

There was no, "Why aren't you praying more?" tone to our conversation. She was just saying, "We are two people struggling to practice holiness. Now, how can we do it?" I can't think of one time that I've resisted that kind of gentle prodding. And if ever I am critical of Jeanne, I just stop and ask myself, "How long has it taken the Lord to get me where I am? A long time, right? So why can't I give Jeanne the same kind of room to grow?"

Jeanne: I suppose it's these daily dilemmas that have kept us depending on each other and on God for all these years. One thing we are learning is that as testings grow more intense, our God is always completely adequate and available.

Jack and Anna Hayford

Cross-Training

How to forge divergent interests and areas of strength into an unbreakable bond. How to make things right after failing your mate. How to hear the feelings behind your spouse's words.

Interviewed by Ruth Senter

Most of us marry someone who, in many ways, is our opposite. And few marriages demonstrate that better than Jack and Anna Hayford's.

Jack is a popular author and the senior pastor of The Church on the Way in Van Nuys, California, where he and Anna minister to some of Hollywood's more recognizable faces. He loves being in front of people; he enjoys talking theology; and he's an accomplished composer. He has written more than 500 songs, including "Majesty," a worship chorus used in churches across the country.

In contrast, Anna feels more comfortable as a behind-the-scenes person. She loves helping people, but she's not in love with theological debates. And while Jack gets excited about the precise meaning of words, Anna is more concerned about reading the message of a person's heart.

In this interview, the Hayfords look back to the ways their opposite personalities have shaped their marriage.

Which of your many differences has been the biggest challenge for you?

Anna: Early in our marriage, it was our opposite backgrounds. Jack grew up in a solid, middle-class family. His parents didn't have to struggle with finances, so they were able to concentrate on other things. And Jack grew into adulthood as a very confident man.

My background was just the opposite. I was the seventh of nine children from a poor farming family in Nebraska. The house I was born in had straw for a floor. The house I grew up in would have rattled around in this living room we're sitting in today. My family was on welfare until I was seventeen.

How did your family's poverty affect you?

Anna: It showed up primarily in my lack of confidence. When I was growing up, our clothes came from welfare. So I never had the opportunity to develop style and taste on my own—I had no choice in what I wore. Through the years, I have struggled with self-confidence. My favorite line in the early years of our marriage was, "I'm not any good at that."

But gradually, I began to hear the praise others gave me. Women in our congregation would say to me, "Anna, you really have something to give to others." At first I didn't hear it. But when your husband and friends say it long enough, after a while it begins to get through.

Jack has been a help over the years. But I had to learn to be open to his help, and Jack had to learn how to help. It took a long time.

Jack, why do you think it took so long to figure out what Anna needed from you?

Jack: One of the most painful things in my life is to look back and see how miserably I failed in my responsibility to help Anna be all that she could be. I always saw her as an amazingly strong woman with great gifts. The fact that she couldn't see them in herself was frustrating.

Some of the worst arguments we had in the early years of our marriage had to do with her inability to see herself as she really was. She would be down on herself, and I would try to convince her of her worth, which only seemed to make things worse. Those discussions always ended in arguments.

Looking back on it, what do you think you were doing wrong?

Jack: I didn't realize the difference between trying to help Anna for my sake and just loving Anna for Anna's sake. I was amazed to learn that I could do or say almost the same thing, but it was my motivation—whether I was doing it for my sake or for Anna's sake—that made the difference in how my message came across.

I was good at trying to talk her into changing. I remember making statements like, "Why did you say that?" or "Have you ever thought of wearing this?" I think I was really functioning out of my own fear of rejection or my desire that we look good as a couple. I guess I thought that if Anna didn't perform up to standard, it would reflect poorly on me. And that was no way to establish healthy communication.

Do you remember when it dawned on you that there might be a better way?

Jack: There were several "moments of truth." The first one came not long after we had arrived to pastor a struggling little group of people in Van Nuys, California. In my youthful enthusiasm, I looked at that pastorate as a stepping-stone to something more significant. When it became clear to Anna and me that we were to commit ourselves to the people of Van Nuys indefinitely, I thought of it as career suicide. I had to recognize my own ego-centeredness.

One day as I read the Word and prayed, I seemed to see a large trophy with the word "position" written on it. I realized that was a picture of me. I was dominated by my concern over what other people thought—their expectations of me. When I handed God that trophy, I opened myself to His dealing with me concerning my relationship with Anna as well.

The second moment of truth came one day as Anna and I were driving through Colorado. We had spent the previous night talking with college friends who were having serious marital problems. As we headed out across the plains the next morning, I took Anna's hand and said, "Let's pray for them."

Suddenly, I saw myself as the one in need of prayer. My mind flashed to that passage in Genesis where God tells Adam to "subdue the earth and replenish it." Actually, God was telling Adam that he was responsible to bring the earth to its fullest potential—no manipulation, no exploitation. Adam was responsible to maximize the earth's potential.

"Anna is my 'earth,'" I thought to myself. "And I have failed to encourage her to be all that she can be."

Recognizing that you have failed your wife could be a pretty devastating revelation. How did you handle it?

Jack: I didn't feel that God was telling me I was a failure. Our marriage was not on the rocks. We were solidly committed to each other. My oversight was not intentional. I wasn't out to wound Anna. I was simply ignorant and needed to be stopped in my tracks.

In what specific ways had you failed Anna?

Jack: The one area I thought of immediately was the area of music. That morning as we drove through Colorado, it dawned on me that I didn't hear Anna singing around the house anymore. She used to sing all the time. Being musically oriented myself, I had always assumed that anyone could hear harmony or write music. Anna's musical tastes and abilities were different from mine.

When I was growing up, music was always a big part of the church programs I was involved in. Anna's small-church background didn't include such elaborate music programs. Her musical tastes were much simpler. But I assumed that her approach to music should be the same as mine.

Sometimes we'd try to work on music together. I remember getting angry with her because I thought she wasn't trying or wasn't listening when she couldn't get a certain chord. And driving across Colorado, I realized Anna hadn't been singing anymore. She didn't play her favorite hymns on the piano the way she used to. I had silenced the music in my wife by demanding that she be something that she wasn't.

So that morning in the car, I didn't pray for my friends' marriage. Instead, I prayed, "Lord, I don't know how to bring my world—my wife—to fruition, but I'm willing to learn. I want to help her be all that she is capable of being."

I didn't know anything I could do except nurture Anna the way you nurture anything to life—just love it and cultivate it with time. It was a life-changing experience.

Did anything change for you, Anna?

Anna: Yes, because as soon as Jack started to change, I began to change too. For example, he had always been a great one with words. He could talk circles around me. It came to a point where it was hard for us to have discussions because I felt so intimidated by his command of the language. I've always felt that I talk very simply, so it was hard for me to think that my words would mean anything to anybody. I felt that Jack was critiquing every word I said, so I learned to say nothing and be quiet.

Jack: Actually, I *was* critiquing her words. I'd pick apart everything she said. I tried to force her to be precise, to explain exactly what she meant, and sometimes she didn't even know what she meant.

For example, on numerous occasions she told me, "You haven't been home at all this week." So I would start dabbling with her sentence. "What do you mean when you say 'at all this week'? I was home Monday night, Tuesday at noon" and so forth. I was requiring a definition from Anna when all she wanted was to make a point.

Anna: One day I was so frustrated by trying to explain what I meant that I said, "Honey, listen to my heart instead of my words." It was my cry for understanding. I wanted Jack to know me for who I was, not for what I was saying.

And did you understand what she meant, Jack, when she said, "Listen to my heart"?

Jack: It has taken a long time. There is something inside me that has to have some kind of an intellectual point of response. The interesting thing is that I can empathize with others, but somehow it's difficult for me to epathize with my own wife.

Why do you think that has been true?

Jack: When you're a pastor, your parishioners come to you for counseling out of need. They are depending on your strength, your insights, and your wisdom from God. You relate to them primarily with words rather than feelings.

But the person you live with doesn't approach you out of dependency. She doesn't need your words as much as she needs your ability to feel with her. As a pastor, I'm a person of words. But words often get in the way when it comes to loving your wife.

Anna: Another thing that made it difficult for us to communicate was that Jack's mother, when he was growing up, would go to great lengths to talk through problems with her children. In my family, things were different. My dad would say, "Anna, do this." I was never allowed to ask why. My dad had serious heart problems, and we all felt that if we asked too many questions, we'd disturb him—and maybe end up losing him.

So when I married Jack, we were at opposite ends of the spectrum. I would get upset about something, and he would start to talk. He would talk and talk until I got worn out listening, and I would look at him through my tears and say, "Honey, I'm so sorry." It was all I could say.

What is different about your conversations today?

Jack: A verse from Scripture that has been a tremendous help to me is the verse that says, "Jesus is touched with the feelings of our weaknesses." He is touched with feelings. I knew that was what was missing in my relationship with Anna. I was trying to relate to Anna analytically, on the basis of her words. She needed for me to try to feel what she was feeling. So I do a lot less talking today.

Anna: And I am more willing to enter into a conversation because I know Jack isn't going to critique my every word or force me to be precise. I feel now that he is relating to me out of trust and respect for who I am rather than trying to change me.

Can you describe an incident that showed you Jack was accepting you rather than trying to change you?

Anna: Some years ago, Jack took a trip to Israel. In his three-week absence from the congregation, he wanted his presence to be felt each Sunday in the worship service. So he asked me if I would be willing to give a short report on his progress in Israel. He was asking me to be his representative before the people of our church.

There was a time when I would have said, "You are the person they want to see." But through God's grace, I had come to the place where I was willing to be Jack's representative before our congregation. I felt great apprehension at first, but I also sensed Jack's trust in me.

Amazingly, he also suggested that since I was up front giving the Israel report, I should go ahead and lead the congregation in the hymn of the morning. So every Sunday morning while he was gone, I'd give a brief report on his travels and then lead the congregation in a hymn. I'll never be the musician Jack is, but he knew my heart. He didn't ask me to compose my own tune or write the lyrics like he does. He asked me to lead a hymn. Music, the thing that used to be a major point of contention between us, has come to be one strong point of my identification with Jack.

We've talked about Jack accommodating to your needs. But doesn't a wife also have a responsibility to consider the needs of her husband—even if he's an analytical person?

Anna: I have a responsibility to listen to the things that Jack is interested in, but I don't think that means we have to be fluent in the same things. He doesn't try to force me to be theological. Sometimes we talk theology or discuss the meaning of a particular Scripture. But, for the most part, we realize our interests are different.

Jack, do you ever wish Anna would talk more theology or philosophy with you?

Jack: There were times when I wished Anna were more interested in theological issues. But over the years, I've come to realize she doesn't have to be interested in everything I'm interested in. There are some things she and I don't spend hours discussing just because I know she's not interested in them. And that's okay. It's not a matter of intellect; its a matter of interest. Plus, I can talk theology and philosophy with other people.

Anna: I don't feel that it's a deficiency on my part. It's just that Jack gets greater input on certain issues when he talks with someone who is on the same track he is. I love to cook, and I'm interested in recipes. But

Jack and I don't talk recipes at great length. He likes what I cook, and that's enough.

Although, the other day I was starting to plan ahead for our Christmas dinner that we serve to the church board and their spouses. I was pulling out some new recipes and reading the ingredients to Jack. There was a time when he would have said, "Honey, you go ahead and decide." But this time he listened to me read recipe cards and offered his opinions. That shows how far we've come.

Jack: As she was reading, I thought to myself, "Maybe the more you do anything that is right and loving, the more natural it will seem." I tried to visualize how the dish would look, how it would taste. Anna does the same thing with my music. I hear some pretty intricate things going on in an arrangement. I will get all excited and say to Anna, "Honey, listen to this." She doesn't hear all the overtones I hear, but she tries to appreciate the fact that I hear harmonics and am excited about it.

Anna: Jack isn't trying to make me into someone I'm not. His spirit is one of acceptance, that's where the change has come.

You've had to walk each other through some difficult times. What was one of your hardest challenges?

Jack: One very trying time happened years ago when I was serving at our denominational headquarters. I became emotionally involved with a woman I was working with. When I realized the depth of my feelings for her, I went home, lay down on the floor, and groaned before the Lord.

Obviously, it didn't take Anna long to realize things were not right. It can be very devastating to find out that your lifetime partner has been attracted to another woman—even though there was no physical involvement. Anna's trust in me through those difficult six months or so was probably the greatest factor in the deliverance that eventually came. She had her moments, but the overall message she communicated to me was "I am committed to you and I trust you."

Anna, what was happening inside of you during this time?

Anna: I had little clues along the way about Jack's growing admiration for this woman. He came home one time and commented on something she was wearing. It made me angry. I was thinking, "Yes, she can look nice because she's not home changing your baby's diapers!"

When Jack finally admitted to me what was happening, I was hurt and angry. But I've always been a practical person, so I handled it from a very practical standpoint, thinking, "The kids still need to be cared for. Dinner needs to be fixed. The house needs to be cleaned." I probably survived by keeping to my regular schedule, doing what I always did, and then trusting God to see us through.

Jack and I had an older friend, a father figure to us both. One night when I was feeling discouraged, I called this friend and poured my heart out to him. I didn't know it, but Jack had also gone to him for counsel and prayer. He was a great support. I also called my parents and said, "I can't tell you the details, but Jack and I are going through a very difficult time. Please pray even harder for us." They never asked for details, but I knew they were praying constantly.

Every couple needs people who will pray consistently for them. Jack and I can look back on our lives and see the grace of God in so many instances. We know it's because we've been surrounded by the faithful prayers of a few of God's people, even during the times when we may have been too weak to pray for ourselves.

SOMETHING TO TALK ABOUT

1. Bill and Gloria Gaither, at the beginning of this chapter, explain how they have challenged each other to attempt new things. In what ways do our individual differences—both strengths and weaknesses—lead to personal growth?

2. In what aspects of our marriage are we living out the principle of "mutual submission" found in Ephesians 5:21?

3. In many ways, Howard and Jeanne Hendricks are opposites. However, they have used their differences to form a strong and effective ministry team. On a scale of one to ten, how would we rate ourselves as a team? Why?

4. In what area of marriage do our differences seem to push us apart? In what ways do our individual strengths meet specific needs in the other? What is one clear example of complementary

strengths and weaknesses in our relationship?

5. Jack and Anna Hayford tell about going through some rough times before they found a way to truly understand and appreciate each other. What opposite traits do we possess? What were the "opposites" that first attracted us to each other?

6. What is one area in which our differences continue to clash? How can we begin to handle those conflicts more constructively?

7. When have we had to do some "interpretation" in order to really understand the feelings behind each other's words?

RECOMMENDED MARRIAGE RESOURCES

The introductions to the interviews refer to many of the books written by the experts featured in this book. Those books are well worth investigating. Listed below are additional marriage resources, including books, Bibles, a magazine, seminars, and videos.

BOOKS, BIBLES, AND A MAGAZINE

Communication

Communication: Key to Your Marriage, by H. Norman Wright (Regal)
There's a good reason this book remains popular more than twenty years after its release: It teaches skills that are basic to successful marriage. Included are how to work through problems, manage your anger, and become an effective listener—communication skills you'll use throughout your marriage.

The Five Love Languages, by Gary Chapman (Northfield)
People express love—and receive it—differently. So differently, in fact, that the things you do to show your love might say absolutely nothing to your mate. Chapman has identified five primary ways people express love: acts of service, quality time, words of affirmation, physical touch, and giving gifts. His book shows how marriages change when a spouse is willing to learn a new language—the one that communicates love to his or her mate.

Men Are from Mars, Women Are from Venus, by John Gray (HarperCollins)
Husbands and wives butt heads, in part, because their needs and approaches to life differ so greatly. John Gray says it's as if spouses come from two different planets. But he handles gender differences in a down-to-earth way—helping couples gain perspective and mutual understanding so they can work with, or around, their differences.

Conflict

Fighting for Your Marriage: Positive Steps for Preventing Divorce and Preserving a Lasting Love, by Howard Markman, Scott Stanley, and Susan L. Blumberg (Jossey-Bass)
Love isn't the glue that holds a marriage together. Instead, it's a matter of how you fight. This book examines the different ways wives and husbands tend to work through conflict. It also shows how couples can lay down ground rules that provide the safety and structure they need to handle conflicts without damaging their relationship.

I Love You—Talk to Me! by Donald R. Harvey (Baker)
Many of us assume marriages are wrecked by one of the "biggies," such as infidelity or substance abuse. But Harvey says it's actually the little steps—such as avoiding conflict and intimacy—that are the true marriage breakers. His book reveals the reasons behind our inclination to protect our innermost self, even when doing so results in a less stable marriage.

Making Love Last Forever, by Gary Smalley (Word)
Are you suffering from the effects of anger without even knowing it? Smalley's book will help you uncover your buried anger, unload it, and then begin to balance your expectations with reality so anger will no longer block intimacy in your marriage.

Finances

Master Your Money, by Ron Blue (Thomas Nelson)
The Master Your Money Workbook (Thomas Nelson)
Financial adviser Ron Blue removes the mystery from good money management. His advice is biblically based and practical, making these books the perfect primers for getting your marriage on a sound financial footing. Included is a candid discussion about the dangers of debt, ways to control your cash flow, and how to make budgeting a natural, virtually painless part of your life.

Gender

The Battle of the Sexes, by James D. Mallory (Crossway)
God didn't create males and females to fight each other, but to complement one another. Mallory presents a convincing argument that we are to

call a cease fire not just to make peace with the opposite sex, but because we are to love one another as God loves us. He shows that in the process of loving one another, you'll no longer consider your spouse an adversary, but instead a person created to balance and bring forth the best in you.

His Needs, Her Needs, by Willard F. Harley, Jr. (Revell)l
Harley's formula is rather simple: men and women each have five basic needs that must be met for a marriage to stay on track and out of trouble. For instance, most husbands' top need is sexual fulfillment, whereas a woman's primary need tends to be affection. Harley shows how you can fulfill one another's needs to build a mutually satisfying, loving, and most importantly, lasting relationship.

In-laws
Boundaries: When to Say Yes, When to Say No to Take Control of Your Life, by Henry Cloud and John Townsend (Zondervan)
Part of developing a sense of "couplehood" comes from knowing when and where to set boundaries. While this book covers much more than in-law issues, it will help you set healthy boundaries for yourself as a person, and for the two of you as a couple, without feeling guilty. A companion workbook is especially helpful for applying the advice to your marriage.

High-Maintenance Relationships, by Les Parrott III (Tyndale)
We all know some really annoying people, and we prefer to avoid them. But if the annoying person is an in-law, you're going to have to learn to live with him or her. Parrott cleverly describes the top fifteen annoying personalities, helping the reader understand why people behave as they do. He also explains how you can work around or through a person's idio-syncracies.

Marriage Enrichment
The Marriage Track, by Dave and Claudia Arp (Thomas Nelson)
The Ultimate Marriage Builder, by Dave and Claudia Arp (Thomas Nelson)
Many couples get so busy that they push their relationship aside—believing the myth that their marriage will "take care of itself." But no marriage can remain healthy without regular care and attention—which is where these books are helpful. The Arps provide simple, step-by-step exercises,

checklists, and discussion guides that you can work through together. Your marriage deserves—and needs—your best efforts. These books will help.

Marriage Ministry

The Marriage Mentor Manual, by Les Parrott III and Leslie Parrott (Zondervan)
Young couples benefit greatly from the support and guidance of concerned older couples. To help veteran couples use their marriages to minister to others, the Parrotts created this manual, covering a year's worth of material to discuss with newly married couples. The added benefit is that ministering to a younger couple enriches the mentor couple's relationship.

Questions Couples Ask, by Les Parrott III and Leslie Parrott (Zondervan)
Couples sometimes hesitate to offer help because they don't feel qualified to address another couple's problems. This book helps solve that dilemma by providing authoritative answers to the 100 most-asked marital questions—ranging from conflict, careers, and money to sex, spiritual issues, and personality differences.

Parenting

The Gift of the Blessing, by Gary Smalley and John Trent (Thomas Nelson)
Kids need to be assured of their parents' love, but it's not always easy for parents to know if that message is getting through. Drawing on the Old Testament practice of fathers conferring a formal blessing on their children, Smalley and Trent apply the same principle to modern-day parenting skills. Far more than a one-time event, blessing your children can become a key, ongoing ingredient in demonstrating your love.

Please Don't Tell My Parents, by Dawson McAllister (Word)
In the past twenty-eight years, McAllister has spoken to millions of teenagers, and they tell him about their biggest problems. In this book, he describes eight of the most common, and most troubling, adolescent struggles. If you're wondering how you can help your teens deal with the pressures they are facing, this book will help.

Personality Differences and Individual Needs

The Birth Order Book, by Kevin Leman (Dell)
Do you go out of your way to please others, or do you feel that others

exist to serve you? Do you feel responsible to solve the world's problems, or would you rather just kick back and enjoy life? Your birth order might help explain why you approach life the way you do. Since you're probably married to someone who sees things differently, this book will help you gain some much-needed perspective.

Please Understand Me, by David Keirsey and Marilyn Bates (Prometheus Nemesis)
The key to understanding your mate involves understanding his or her personality and how it differs from your own. This book divides personalities into sixteen different types, easily definable after readers fill out the authors' questionnaire. You'll then see how your different temperaments complement one another, as well as how they can lead to marital conflict.

Traits of a Lasting Marriage, by Jim and Sally Conway (InterVarsity)
Every marriage goes through stages, and one of the most challenging comes at mid-life. Counselors Jim and Sally Conway explain what it takes to protect your marriage during the period of intense inner turmoil many men (and women) feel in their forties. Even if you're not experiencing a mid-life crisis, this book will help you build your marriage to last.

True Colors, by Roger Birkman (Thomas Nelson)
If you're intrigued by personality types and want the inside track on why your spouse would rather take a bike ride when you'd prefer reading a book, the Birkman Method will help solve the puzzle. Using colors to describe the various temperaments, Birkman takes into consideration your entire personality—including your thoughts, interests, needs, actions, and reactions. The result is a clearer understanding of yourself and others, and a solid foundation for strengthening your character.

Sex
A Celebration of Sex, by Douglas E. Rosenau (Thomas Nelson)
This frank and heavily illustrated volume explores how to increase communication, build a close companionship, and enjoy God's gift of sexual pleasure—no matter how long you've been married. Topics include developing a sense of playfulness, growing in your knowledge of your mate, building a sense of trust and honesty, and tips on creative romance.

The Gift of Sex, by Clifford and Joyce Penner (Word)
The classic sex manual for Christians, this book underscores the biblical standards for a spiritually, emotionally, and physically satisfying love life. The Penners address what is and isn't acceptable, ways to keep your love life from becoming boring, and solutions to common sexual problems. If you are engaged or newly married, check out the Penners' book *Getting Your Sex Life Off to a Great Start* (Word).

Great Sexpectations, by Robert and Rosemary Barnes (Zondervan)
Harmful myths and unrealistic expectations can sidetrack your sexual relationship. But after debunking the myths, you can take the leap from merely having sex to truly making love. In this book, the Barneses explore eight common myths, from "couples are born compatible" to "good sex is when you fill my wish list." Their frankness about their own struggles shifts this book away from an impersonal, clinical approach.

Men & Sex, by Clifford and Joyce Penner (Thomas Nelson)
While this book was written with male readers in mind, women will benefit from the candid insights on male sexuality. The Penners explain that improving your sex life begins not by mastering a new technique, but rather by changing your attitude. The shift they recommend isn't new—put your mate's needs first—but their advice and forthright discussion makes it seem new.

Spiritual Growth

The Art of Forgiving, by Lewis B. Smedes (Ballantine/Random House)
Smedes' remarkable understanding of human nature, combined with his sensitive writing, makes you feel as if this book were written exclusively for you. He probes all aspects of the difficult but necessary act of forgiveness—from what it is and isn't to how and when to offer it.

Marriage Spirituality, by R. Paul Stevens (InterVarsity)
Chores, kids, errands, jobs, and home repair all make marriage fertile soil for growing a down-to-earth and realistic faith. Stevens provides a blueprint for making the spiritual dimension of your marriage something that can be embraced rather than avoided. He presents ten spiritual disciplines for couples to practice together—from prayer and service to conversation and confession. The ultimate outcome is a stronger family and a more vital faith.

Quiet Times for Couples, by H. Norman Wright (Harvest House)
This daily devotional guide offers Wright's timeless principles for a growing marriage and encourages simple sharing between yourself, your spouse, and God. Each reading is brief and to-the-point, ending with questions that encourage further thought.

Spiritual Intimacy for Couples, by Charles and Virginia Sell (Crossway)
The Sells' warmth and wisdom go a long way toward taking the mystery and fear out of sharing your spiritual life with your mate. They cover topics such as why we're hesitant to share the spiritual dimension of our lives; different ways couples define worship; and how to feel comfortable praying together. Of particular note are the exercises that help you apply the concepts to your own marriage.

Starting Out Together, by H. Norman Wright (Regal)
A collection of sixty short devotionals, covering topics of concern to couples who are newly married, engaged, or involved in a serious dating relationship. Wright helps couples get their relationship grounded in biblical truth by exploring such issues as breaking free from the past, controlling anger, resolving conflict, and learning to forgive each other.

Work

The Dual-Earner Marriage, by Jack and Judith Balswick (Revell)
Both spouses working outside the home doesn't have to be a recipe for disaster. If you approach a dual-earner marriage carefully and thoughtfully, it can become an ideal opportunity for mutual empowerment and intimacy. Based on their thirty-plus years in a dual-earner marriage, the Balswicks help you strengthen your communication, manage your stress, and work out conflict so you can make the best of both your home life and your careers.

General

The Life Application Bible: New Living Translation (Tyndale)
This study Bible offers a ready reference for understanding the relevance of God's Word in today's world. Included are more than 10,000 notes, application-oriented book introductions, cross-references, maps, and charts. Of note is the topical Living Index—an excellent resource for clearly interpreting God's teaching on marriage and a devotional reading plan that you can easily adapt to your needs.

The NIV Couples' Devotional Bible (Zondervan)
Designed to strengthen communication and encourage spiritual growth, this Bible includes daily devotions by well-known Christian leaders such as Jill and Stuart Briscoe, Ruth Bell Graham, Lewis Smedes, Charles Swindoll, H. Norman Wright, Bill and Gloria Gaither, and Larry Crabb. Also included are weekend marriage-building exercises that help you work together on specific relational needs.

Marriage Partnership magazine
The interviews in this book originally appeared in *Marriage Partnership*, a quarterly Christian magazine devoted to strengthening and enriching your marriage. You can save $5.00 off the regular one-year subscription price of $19.95—getting four issues for just $14.95—by calling 800.627.4942 and mentioning offer #C7GBK8. When you call, ask for your risk-free trial issue.

SEMINARS AND VIDEOS

Dave and Claudia Arp, interviewed in Chapter 7, lead Marriage Alive Seminars around the country. For information, contact:
Alive Communications
1465 Kelly Johnson Boulevard
Suite 320
Colorado Springs, CO 80920
719.260.7080

Gary Chapman, interviewed in Chapter 2, conducts a weekend marriage-enrichment seminar called Toward a Growing Marriage. For information about his seminar schedule, contact:
Chapman Seminar
127 Ninth Avenue, North
Nashville, TN 37234
615.251.2277

For information regarding the two-session video version of Gary Chapman's *The Five Love Languages*, contact:
LifeWay Press
127 Ninth Avenue, North
Nashville, TN 37234
800.458.2772

Kevin Leman, interviewed in Chapter 1, presents seminars on relationships and a variety of other topics. For information, contact:

Kevin Leman
7355 North Oracle Road
Suite 205
Tucson, AZ 85704
Phone: 520.797.3830
FAX: 520.797.3809

Gary Smalley, interviewed in Chapters 8 and 9, presents his Love Is a Decision seminar across the United States. For information about his seminar schedule, videos, and other marriage and family resources, contact:

Today's Family
1482 Lakeshore Drive
Branson, MO 65616
800.848.6329

The Association for Couples in Marriage Enrichment (ACME) is a nonsectarian organization that teaches couples how to use practical relational skills to strengthen their marriages. ACME sponsors regional conferences, marriage-enrichment weekends, and local marriage-support groups. For more information, contact:

ACME
502 North Broad Street
Winston-Salem, NC 27108
800.634.8325

BIOGRAPHICAL INDEX OF CONTRIBUTORS

Charette Barta is a writer and publishing consultant who formerly served on the editorial staff of *Decision* magazine and as director of the Decision School of Christian Writing. She interviewed Jerry and Mary White on friendship, which first appeared in *Partnership* magazine (January/February 1987).

James D. Berkley is associate pastor of First Presbyterian Church in Bellevue, Washington. He formerly was editor of *Your Church* magazine. He interviewed Lewis Smedes on forgiveness, which first appeared in *Marriage Partnership* magazine (Winter 1991).

Scott W. Bolinder is vice president and publisher in charge of the Book and New Media Group of Zondervan Publishing House in Grand Rapids, Michigan. He formerly taught a marriage class at Wheaton (Ill.) College and has led marriage workshops. Bolinder interviewed Dennis and Lucy Guernsey on setting boundaries, which first appeared in *Marriage Partnership* (Spring 1988).

Lorraine Mulligan Davis, a former magazine editor, is the author of hundreds of articles and stories. She and her husband, Scott, live in the Chicago area with their two children. She interviewed Jay Kesler on recreation, which first appeared in *Marriage Partnership* (Summer 1989).

Louise A. Ferrebee is associate editor of *Marriage Partnership* magazine. She served as general editor of the *Questions Women Ask* book series, published by Bethany House and Questar/Multnomah. She interviewed Lee Ezell on gender differences, which first appeared in *Marriage Partnership* (Fall 1995); and Judy and Jack Balswick on dual-earner marriages, which appeared in *Marriage Partnership* (Winter 1997).

Janis Long Harris is a freelance writer and consultant who has written a number of books, including *What If I Married the Wrong Person?* (Bethany House) She and her husband, Paul, live in Illinois with their two children. She interviewed Mary Ann Mayo on Inhibited Sexual Desire, which first appeared in *Marriage Partnership* (Fall 1990).

Dave and Neta Jackson are a husband/wife writing team whose work includes more than seventy-five books. Their most recent projects include the *Trailblazer* series of historical fiction for young readers; and the two-volume *Hero Tales*. They interviewed Merton and Irene Strommen on becoming parents, which first appeared in *Partnership* magazine (May/June 1986).

Annette LaPlaca is associate editor of *Marriage Partnership* magazine. She is coauthor of *Making Summer Count* (Shaw) and the author of several other fun and worship activity books for children. She interviewed Stuart and Jill Briscoe on shared ministry, which first appeared in *Marriage Partnership* (Fall 1993); Dave and Claudia Arp on having more fun, which first appeared in *Marriage Partnership* (Spring 1994); Walter and Thanne Wangerin on starting over, which first appeared in *Marriage Partnership* (Fall 1996); and H. Norman Wright and Joyce Wright on grief, which first appeared in *Marriage Partnership* (Summer 1994).

Ron R. Lee is editor of *Marriage Partnership* magazine. He served as general editor of the devotional material in *The NIV Couples' Devotional Bible* (Zondervan) and was editor of *A Scruffy Husband Is a Happy Husband* (Focus on the Family). *For The Marriage You've Always Wanted*, he interviewed Gary Chapman on love's languages, which appeared in *Marriage Partnership* (Fall 1997); Jim and Sally Conway on being heard, which first appeared in *Marriage Partnership* (Winter 1993); Charles Swindoll on making friends, which first appeared in *Marriage Partnership* (Winter 1992); Stan Jones on appropriate sex, which first appeared in *Marriage Partnership* (Winter 1995); Bill Hybels on career dangers, which first appeared in *Marriage Partnership* (Fall 1991); Ben and Lauretta Patterson on rest, which first appeared in *Marriage Partnership* (Fall 1994); Dawson McAllister on raising teenagers, which first appeared in *Marriage Partnership* (Summer 1993); Donald R. Harvey on betrayal, which first appeared in *Marriage Partnership* (Winter 1994); Gary Smalley on anger, which first appeared in *Marriage Partnership* (Spring 1997); and Larry Crabb on doubts, which first appeared in *Marriage Partnership* (Spring 1995).

Gregg Lewis, former senior writer for *Marriage Partnership* and former senior editor of *Campus Life* magazine, is a widely published author of books and magazine articles. He interviewed Larry Crabb on the purpose of marriage, which first appeared in *Marriage Partnership* (Spring 1991); and Clifford and Joyce Penner on unfulfilling sex, which first appeared in *Marriage Partnership* (Spring 1991).

Marian V. Liautaud is a free-lance writer who served as general editor of *Swatting the Mosquitoes of Marriage* (Zondervan). She is also part-owner, with her husband, Dan, of Big Mike's Super Subs in Minneapolis, where she builds a mean sandwich. She interviewed Evelyn and Harold "Chris" Christenson on prayer, which first appeared in *Marriage Partnership* (Spring 1996).

Mark Moring is senior associate editor of *Campus Life* magazine. He is a former sportswriter who lives in Illinois with his wife, Nina, and their two sons. He interviewed Jim Burns on teaching by example, which first appeared in *Marriage Partnership* (Winter 1996).

LaVonne Neff was founding editor of *Partnership* magazine. She writes regularly for *Publishers Weekly* and *Books & Culture*. She and her husband, David, have two grown daughters and two grandchildren. She interviewed Kevin Leman on family influences, which first appeared in *Partnership* (July/August 1987).

Elizabeth Cody Newenhuyse is former senior editor of *Marriage Partnership*. She is a speaker, an editor with Harold Shaw Publishers, and the author of several books, including *God, I Know You're Here Somewhere* and *Sometimes I Feel Like Running Away from Home* (both published by Bethany House). She interviewed Bill and Gloria Gaither on individual differences, which first appeared in *Marriage Partnership* (Spring 1992); and Louis and Melissa McBurney on achieving balance, which first appeared in *Marriage Partnership* (Winter 1989).

Ruth Senter, former editor of *Partnership* magazine, is a speaker and the author of ten books, including *Have We Really Come a Long Way, Baby?* (Bethany House) and *Seasons of Friendship* (Zondervan). She interviewed Jack and Anna Hayford on teamwork, which first appeared in *Partnership* (November/December 1985); Howard and Jeanne Hendricks on blessing others, which first appeared in *Partnership* (May/June 1985); and Ruth Bell Graham on spiritual growth, which first appeared in *Partnership* (July/August 1984).

Ken Sidey is publisher and editor of the Adair County Free Press in Greenfield, Iowa. He formerly worked on the editorial staffs of *Christianity Today* and *Moody* magazines. He and his wife, Vicki, have three children. Sidey interviewed Ronald Blue on family finances, which first appeared in *Marriage Partnership* (Summer 1991); and Gary Smalley on demonstrating love, which first appeared in *Marriage Partnership* (Spring 1991).

Harold B. Smith is corporate vice president in charge of editorial operations for Christianity Today, Inc. He is author of the humor book *Hey Dad, Are We There Yet?* (NavPress). He and his wife, Judy, lead marriage retreats and teach Sunday School classes on marriage. He interviewed Bill and Gloria Gaither on individual differences, which first appeared in *Marriage Partnership* (Spring 1992).

Lynda Rutledge Stephenson is a professional writer whose work has appeared in the

Chicago Tribune Magazine and the *Chicago Sun-Times,* among other publications. She interviewed H. Norman Wright on expectations, which first appeared in *Marriage Partnership* (Summer 1988); and Stan Jones on self-esteem, which first appeared in *Marriage Partnership* (Summer 1988).

SUBJECT INDEX

If you enjoyed this book from *ChariotVictor Publishing,* check out these other books about marriage, relationships, and family.

When Prince Charming Falls Off His Horse
by Jerry & Judy Schreur
ISBN: 1-56476-628-4
Retail: $10.99

Take a realistic look at marriage with all its love, joy, boredom, and disappointment. Using the fairy tale analogy and experiences from their own marriage, the authors help couples deal with tough marriage issues in a context of softness and laughter.

Inspiration for Couples
ISBN: 1-56476-626-8
Retail: $5.99

This book features nearly 120 Scriptures compiled specifically for couples, making them perfect when you need quick, helpful inspiration. References are taken from a number of leading translations and paraphrases.

Also from
ChariotVictor Publishing,
a special book about passing on a godly heritage to your children.

The Heritage
by J. Otis Ledbetter
& Kurt Bruner
ISBN: 1-56476-694-2
Retail: $10.99

ChariotVictor Publishing is honored to partner with Heritage Builders to help parents assume their role as the spiritual leaders of their families. Heritage Builders is a growing network of families who want to pass on a spiritual heritage to their children. They use methods that are both fun and effective to make a lasting impression on their children.

Deuteronomy 6:7 outlines the responsibility of parents to impress their Christian values and beliefs upon the next generation. What an awesome responsibility! ChariotVictor Publishing and Heritage Builders seek to help parents create and capture opportunities to impress Christian values on their children. *The Heritage* is an overview book that describes how to pass on a godly spiritual, social and emotional heritage.